Museum Branding

Museum Branding

How to Create and Maintain Image, Loyalty, and Support

Second Edition

Margot Wallace

ROWMAN & LITTLEFIELD
Lanham • Boulder • New York • London

Published by Rowman & Littlefield
A wholly owned subsidiary of The Rowman & Littlefield Publishing Group, Inc.
4501 Forbes Boulevard, Suite 200, Lanham, Maryland 20706
www.rowman.com

Unit A, Whitacre Mews, 26-34 Stannary Street, London SE11 4AB

British Library Cataloguing in Publication Information Available

Library of Congress Cataloging-in-Publication Data

Names: Wallace, Margot A, 1941-
Title: Museum branding : how to create and maintain image, loyalty, and support / Margot Wallace.
Description: Lanham, MD : Rowman & Littlefield [2016] | Includes bibliographical references and index.
Identifiers: LCCN 2015046133 (print) | LCCN 2015048352 (ebook) | ISBN 9781442263444 (cloth : alk. paper) | ISBN 9781442263451 (pbk. : alk. paper) | ISBN 9781442263468 (Electronic)
Subjects: LCSH: Museums—United States—Management. | Museums—Public relations—United States. | Business names—United States. | Branding (Marketing)—United States. | Museum attendance—United States.
Classification: LCC AM11 .W35 2016 (print) | LCC AM11 (ebook) | DDC 069.068—dc23
LC record available at http://lccn.loc.gov/2015046133

♾™ The paper used in this publication meets the minimum requirements of American National Standard for Information Sciences—Permanence of Paper for Printed Library Materials, ANSI/NISO Z39.48-1992.

Printed in the United States of America

Contents

Preface

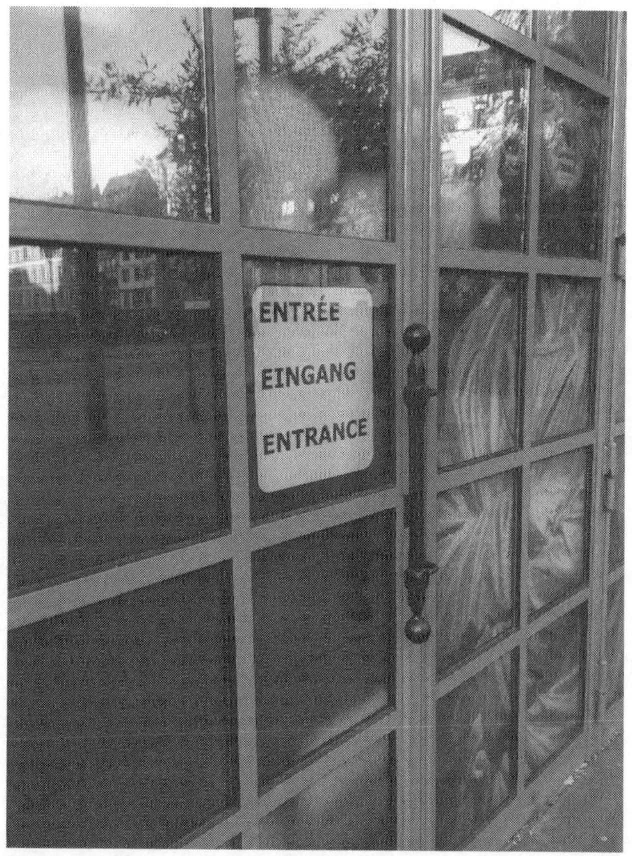

Figure P.1 Entrée, Eingang, Entrance. Musée de la Ville de Strasbourg, Strasbourg, France.
Source: © 2014 Margot Wallace.

At the threshold of a nineteenth-century log cabin in a Midwest suburb, two costumed interpreters from the Historical Society chat in a neighborly way as visitors approach. A twenty-first-century visitor nearby says, "My grandkids used to love their school field trips here."

Across the country, in upstate New York, a museum dedicated to a local celebrity holds a guest book filled to bursting with fond visitor comments.

Down in Florida, a bold new building has emerged among the surrounding palm trees as if to say, "Be aware, art lovers, one of your favorite artists is about to mystify you again."

And farther away, in a small French city, a red medallion identifies a grey stone house as one of the "Maisons des Illustres"—Homes of the Illustrious—of once local artists, now scientists and statesmen recognized for their cultural contribution to the national pride of France.

What do these interpreters, guest books, grand architecture, small labels, and visitors have in common? They speak to a museum's community, and they speak with the details that add up to great brands. Details are worth some scrutiny. Details are the evidence that prove the claims of your mission. Details demonstrate what you stand for. A museum can say it's distinctive because of this or that; details *are* the "this and that." Details are the stuff of life, and of brands. It's hard to express all the things you are in one mission paragraph or logo tagline. The accumulation of details embodies what you stand for.

Among and around all those details is an ongoing compact with a museum's community. Museums with strong, living brands engage with their stakeholders and remain part of their lives.

In taking a fresh look at museum branding, *Museum Branding*, Second Edition, uses eyes that now explore digitally, as well as actually. Although the physical museum stands firmly embedded in our cultural experience, the experience now happily embraces the aid and comfort of the Internet. They're a good combo, because of the shared goals of museums and the digisphere: discovery, engagement, and respect for limitless types of communities. They sound familiar-to-hackneyed, but tectonic changes brought them to the surface. Technology in general and social media specifically have made the fun of discovery universal and democratic. Multiple voices have revealed the joy of details. Instant communication makes community and connection viable. People—your visitors, prospects, and supporters—crave being in touch. Their lives are based on a variety of cultural affinities, many beyond the usual borders. They listen to each other and trust each other's judgment. They have a bold acquaintance with difference and are amenable to innovative thinking.

The objective of museum branding—the discipline, and the books—has not wavered: identifying the many touchpoints at which the museum comes in touch with its stakeholders, and reinforcing the brand at every point.

The stakeholders who interact with the brand include visitors, of course, and also members and donors, employees and volunteers, scholars and board members, sponsors and community partners, and educators. Touchpoints are not so quickly itemized.

Touchpoints are limitless, and this book culls the list to about one hundred in nineteen chapters. Expect your museum to touch stakeholders—and therefore reinforce its brand—at these points:

- Collection, displayed and in storage
- Exhibits and exhibitions, including panels and labels
- Website and social media
- Educational programs, for adults and schoolchildren
- Tours, docent-guided and audio
- Public relations, with all your publics
- Events
- Publications, including magazine and annual report
- Building and lobby
- Marketing materials
- Fundraising and membership initiatives
- Core values, from original founders to today's interpreters
- Store, online and bricks and mortar
- Restaurant
- Campus
- E-mail, including newsletters
- Partnerships, corporate and community
- Database of stakeholders
- Board and volunteer recruitment

Each of the above chapters contains examples of practices from museums of all types, small and large, all over the country (and some of the world). The examples will not necessarily still be in place when you read this, but they remain exemplary; they've been selected for their instructional excellence. Museum professionals across the spectrum were part of the author's research and writing process, and informal talks yielded facts and clues to the needs of museums in the teens of the twenty-first century. Museum conferences provided a wealth of information and literature. Webinars, many of them free, delivered professional advice from both real-time presenters and participants. My near-weekly visits to museums—close to home and afar – were rich beyond imagining in the insights they provided .

Branding was a new concept to many museums in the early 2000s, when *Museum Branding* pioneered the discipline. Now, it's accepted by not-for-profit organizations as plain good business. Museums are operated and managed—you don't need an author to tell you this—very smartly. Leveraging assets, increasing revenue, and growing the visitor and member base now join the conversation, along with creating ever better exhibiting and learning scenarios.

There's a lot of new information in this book, and it's written for all who labor with love in a museum environment. Branding isn't ordered by the director, or executed by the marketing department. It is the result of constant strategizing by all parts of the museum, and it occurs every time content is proposed and developed by the many constituents who now develop it. Branding occurs when curators research, educators interpret, and tweeters tweet. Museum branding is a virtuous cycle: It can start with one activity and activator, and then grows by the additions and responses of many others. A brand is never made; it's earned and shared and made successful by the people involved.

Branding is everyone's responsibility. You're part of the brand.

Chapter 1

Exhibitions

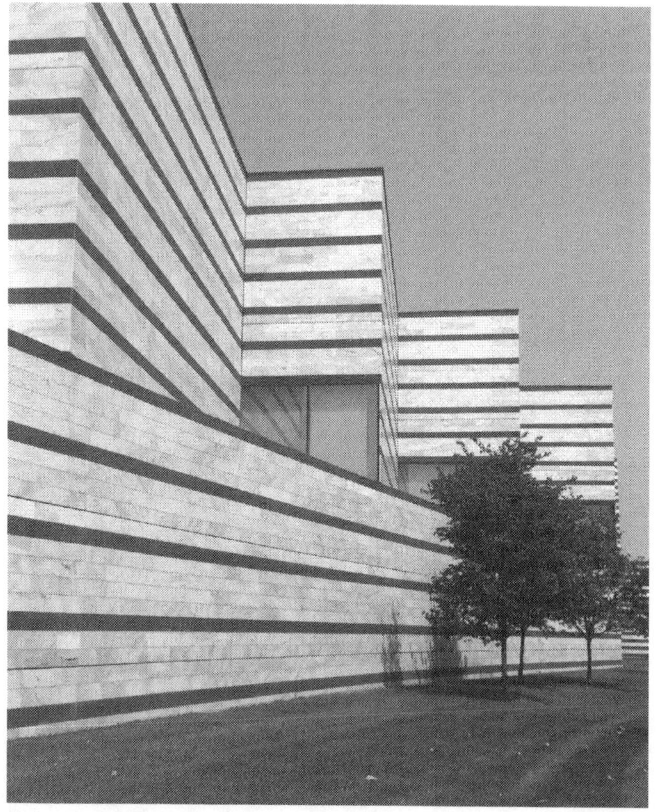

Figure 1.1 The Cleveland Museum of Art has expanded its exhibition space, and its brand promise, with a large space devoted to exhibiting conservation techniques. *Source*: © 2013 Margot Wallace.

The woman in the museum was admittedly cranky. She'd had a tough day tending to the family store by herself, her husband having gone to war. The teenaged boy was fed up; he was never going back to fight those gruesome battles, yet he was just as lost at home. These lifelike mannequins were talking to museum visitors as they walked by, talking about the impact of the Civil War on the home front, about the experiences of those back home in the Upper Middle West. As part of a well-branded exhibition, they made their point.

The Civil War Museum in Kenosha, Wisconsin, positions itself as "the Civil War Museum [that] is like no other Civil War museum in the country . . . [focusing] on the Civil War from the perspective of the people . . . [in] Illinois, Indiana, Iowa, Michigan, Minnesota, and Wisconsin." Its exhibits portray storekeepers and farm wives, their newspapers and their lives in places like Stillwater, Minnesota, and West Salem, Wisconsin. It's not easy to stay on brand when there's so much one could say about the Upper Middle West and the Civil War, but this museum does.

Crystal Bridges, Bentonville, Arkansas, is another museum whose exhibitions hew closely to its brand mission to "explore the unfolding story of America." Exhibitions such as "*Fish Stories: Early Images of American Game Fish*" (April 4 through October 4, 2015) and "Changing Perspectives of Native Americans" (January 17 through August 3, 2015) cover a wide swath of American life, yet always refer back to the museum's main self-identity.

Exhibits, exhibitions, and gallery design all combine to depict and bolster a museum's core values. In a blog that documents how curators arrange a gallery, Crystal Bridges Curator Chad Allgood explains that "works should be grouped or arranged to . . . tell a story about the history of art in America." But you know that.

This chapter doesn't tell you how to conceive and design an exhibition. Rather, it starts before one enters the museum and continues afterward, following the path a visitor takes from online search to website to actual visit, to socially mediated commentary.

BRANDING THE EXHIBITION PATH

Consider just how long the path through a museum exhibition is: visitors read labels and panels, see objects, listen to docents, press buttons on audio guides, take and send photos, post opinions, peruse gallery handouts, explore further at computer work stations, refresh memories with store souvenirs, reflect in the café, and review the experience again when they leave comments in the guest book. At all these touchpoints, your exhibitions are reflected upon and reviewed. The well-conceived exhibition is a multifaceted immersion in your mission; it exemplifies and enhances your brand at many different touchpoints. This chapter reviews eleven of them.

TOUCHPOINTS

Visitors stop at the following chronological touchpoints, each one of which connects an exhibition to the museum and its core identity. The museum's name and brand identity should appear on each one.

1. Brand the exhibition visual
2. Establish brand authority on labels and panels
3. Talk the brand: audio guides and docent-guided tours
4. Identify brand-appropriate sites for photographs
5. Put your brand on generic-seeming hashtags
6. Author gallery guides
7. Reinforce your brand in study rooms and rest area tables
8. Curate store merchandise to align with your exhibits
9. Prompt brand awareness in guest books
10. Promote the institution in exhibition promotion materials
11. Remember the brand in exhibitions that entertain

Exhibitions pack a lot of power. They dazzle and intrigue; they also inform and persuade. They have clout in many circles. They have a wide ripple effect. So there are also informal exhibition interpretations taking place all the time. This chapter also discusses the importance of talking points, the informal conversations that proclaim the brand message among friends.

Brand the Exhibition Visual

Exhibition visuals appear on all the marketing materials for an exhibition; they are everywhere and for the duration of the show, they *are* the museum. The iconic pattern of a Norwegian sweater in the Vesterheim Museum's "From Underwear to Everywhere: Norwegian Sweaters" is one of many examples of how this museum consistently reinforces its brand. When you see the Dutch-reminiscent vase of cut flowers publicizing "In the Garden," for the George Eastman House, you realize the importance of the garden to this historic house.

These exhibition visuals capture two aspects of your museum: the exhibition itself and the brand. Vesterheim is a master marketer in its thoroughly consistent and intelligent adherence to its Norwegian heritage in America.

Its visuals, seen regularly in web and e-mail marketing, never stray from the brand message. The flower visual for a photograph exhibition is appropriate for the same two reasons: It announces the subject of the exhibition and reinforces a major aspect of the Eastman House brand—its gardens. The floral visual appears on brochures and posters displayed throughout the museum. In a museum as large and complex as Eastman House, which comprises new galleries, a large garden, and a palatial turn of the twentieth-century house, the visual publicity inspires visitors to return.

The branding importance of an exhibition visual goes to the heart of our culture—national and global—which inhales information on multiple screens at a dizzying pace. We browse headlines, skim stories, and only pause longer when we *look* at pictures and *compose* snapshots to send. The advent of selfie sticks underscores how much we care about the look of our graphic depictions. These visual descriptions are made for branding—they last and last. Even the gasping magazine industry still sells issues if they have cover photos that announce stories that consumers want to read. As for currently successful visual communications, consider graphic novels and Pinterest.

Select the visual that symbolizes your exhibition carefully. It should represent and reinforce an aspect of the object of the exhibition that:

- Epitomizes the curator's plan
- Provides talking points for the staff
- Polls well in research sessions with visitors, educators, or volunteers
- Reads legibly when reduced in size
- Reproduces well in black and white
- Communicates at a distance
- Looks different from other exhibition visuals
- Conveys the museum's brand

Your choice is important because your exhibition visual appears everywhere, including in:

Website
E-mail
Social media
Apps
Posters
Banners
Brochures
Media coverage—traditional and digital
Books
Souvenirs

Ephemera
Archives

Each of these appearances communicates to different audiences in different ways. E-mail reaches people who have already expressed interest in you. Banners are seen by strangers walking down the street. Social media disseminates your exhibition free and worldwide. Books are purchased at a relatively high cost only in the store. Ephemera such as event invitations and handouts are seen by members or other supporters. Websites are seen by people still shopping for where to spend leisure-culture hours. Scholars, sponsors, and donors also visit your website. Young women planning weddings check out your facilities' rentals on Pinterest. Chapter 8, "Marketing," strategizes your many options for communicating with the public. And much of this communication hinges on the powerful exhibition visual.

Establish Brand Authority on Labels and Panels

Labels and panels help the visitor learn what you are communicating, and you're communicating more than the exhibition. In the competitive cultural climate that envelops all museums, one of the things you must communicate is the institution that's making an exhibition possible. The excellence of the final curated offering is diminished if the visitor doesn't realize who brought it all together. Exhibitions have strong branding tools at their disposal. Each object has been selected to reinforce a theme, which itself has been selected to reinforce a distinctive vision. And that vision has been approved and funded because it reinforces the museum's mission and brand.

The Chicago Botanic Garden, in suburban Cook County, offers several examples of how to connect your labels and panels to the mission of the museum. The Garden has a statement that appears throughout its marketing efforts:

> "We cultivate the power of plants to sustain and enrich life."

It also deploys this headline on two of its major print pieces:

> "Keep Growing"

The concept of community involvement in sustaining nature is repeated in its labels.

At the Plant Science Center at the Chicago Botanic Garden, interactive displays show visitors how to get personally involved in the green way of life, and how to involve their community.

The Center's long, rectangular gallery, lined by glass walls, lets visitors look in on a series of labs at work. And even this science-first gallery lets in some brand-appropriate nurturing with its interactive labels. At one lab, an interactive panel titled "Adventure Task" asks:

What you can do?
What your community can do?

And then it provides some activities:

Change your own actions.
Support science and tech literacy at schools.
Collect seeds for your local botanic garden.
Bank your own seeds.
Garden with [different color] plants that attract pollinators.
Encourage local officials to protect natural areas.

Talk the Brand: Audio Guides and Docent-Guided Tours

It is expected that exhibitions reflect the mission of the museum, yet it's easy to stray off track. This is one instance where a well-branded docent-guided tour—or audio tour—can keep you on track and on brand.

Although discussed more thoroughly in chapter 2, "Tours," the brand importance of audio-guided and docent-guided tours, as part of the exhibition path, bears repeating. Here is where the exhibition gets related to the museum's brand and mission. And it's so easy. Here are four phrases your docents can use:

"Here at the Smith-Jones museums, we believe that . . . [paraphrase mission statement] and you can see that concept throughout this gallery."
"We've just covered a lot of ideas in a 45-minute tour. There's more information on the subject in the Smith-Jones Museum store."
"Welcome to this wonderful [name of exhibition] exhibition here at the Smith-Jones Museum."
"Thank you for joining me in this wonderful exhibition here at the Smith-Jones Museum."

Archiving the Audio Tour

If your tour is recorded, it's part of the digital record, and this branding tool can reside on your website forever in the "Past Exhibitions" pages. You may not use audio elsewhere on your website, but when scholars and other in-depth visitors look for information, audio guides augment not only the information, but also the museum itself. An example is that of the

Whitney Museum of American Art, whose audio-guided tours might include announcer narration, comments by experts in related fields, sound effects, and music. An audible label I remember from fifteen years ago told the backstory of George Bellows' "*Dempsey and Firpo*, 1924," and it lives on in the website's section "Watch," where it breathes new life into a brand's old files.

Identify Brand-Appropriate Sites for Photographs

If your museum allows photography, take a proactive approach and highlight the stops along an exhibition path that are photogenic for the museum's brand.

An example was the Monet chair, at the Museum of Fine Art, St. Petersburg, Florida. The children's "Explore More" gallery always relates its exhibits with current exhibitions, and during "Monet to Matisse—On the French Coast," February 7 to May 31, 2015, a prop red chair was placed by a prop window that gave a prop view of a seaport village street and the Mediterranean—a detail of "Girl by a Window," Henri Matisse (1921), where children could pose for photos. This is a strong memory-building device, a photo that gets sent to grandparents and exported to screensavers, and stays in digital albums forever. In reinforcing the exhibition, it reinforced the museum visit as a whole; and in this exhibition, making the photo op a waterfront painting was perfect for the host museum, which is located on a St. Petersburg waterfront.

Put Your Brand on Generic-Seeming Hashtags

Anyone can start a conversation on your exhibitions, and that steals your brand. Suddenly, someone else is the authority. Worse, with each retweet, repin, and re-anything, another author's name gets affixed to your exhibition. For example, there are a lot of tweets about Van Gogh. And just as many on the Metropolitan Museum of Art. But when the hashtag reads "#MetVanGogh," the reader gets directly to the Van Gogh exhibition at the big building on Fifth Avenue and 80th. The Museum of Modern Art, New York, tweeted the Yoko Ono Exhibition with "#YokoOnoMoMA."

The best way to own tweets, pins, and posts is to designate brand-appropriate sites for picture-taking. We live in a pictorial world, and that's how the socially networked visitors will communicate about your museum.

Author Gallery Guides

Museums, large and small, can provide photocopied descriptions of the objects in greater detail than a fifty-word label can. Inexpensive to produce, these gallery guides can also delve into the theme of the gallery more meaningfully than a panel on the wall outside. These ordinary, 8 1/2 × 11 white sheets of paper are effective, but they must be branded. They're the touchiest-feeliest of all the touchpoints on the exhibition path. They're handheld, portable, perused at leisure, and user-friendly. Type the text on letterhead stationery at the very least. Better yet, design a sheet that contains both the museum logo and the exhibition visual. If you have a museum tagline, write it here. If your budget allows a large printing, let the visitor take it home so that the visit can be reconstructed and remembered for a long time. Congratulations! You've just created a lasting brand message that's valuable and cost-efficient.

Reinforce Your Brand in Study Rooms and Rest Area Tables

Never let visitors rest without something to rest their eyes on. When visitors stop in study rooms or computer work stations, they're deeply involved in an exhibition, and it's the ideal time to strengthen your museum's role in the learning. When visitors simply sit and relax, you add another dimension to the branded visit: comfort. Museum visitors translate much of what they experience through their feet, and a chance to sit and absorb information is appealing. It's a homey, hospitable way to provide more information on your exhibits. Add a pad of notepaper with your name and logo on it, and you've gone a long way toward attaching your museum's identity to the visitor's visit.

Maybe you've published works that explain the exhibits and fill in background information; they supplement the branding that the exhibition offers. Not only do they verbally reinforce the museum's role, but their very existence enhances the museum's image. Make sure your name and logo are prominent, along with your mission statement.

If your museum sprawls over several buildings or a campus, you'll need some reminders of your name. If, say, visitors start at a garden, wander to a historic building, then encounter a pop-up art exhibition, they could lose sight of the overarching brand. Refresh their memories and their bodies with branded signs at the far-flung rest stations.

Technology comes to the rescue of wandering visitors in the form of GPS-enabled apps that let them find places and each other, not to mention events and in-depth information on exhibits. It's branding that rests on the visitor's hand. The description for the Miami Zoo app says:

> "Take your zoo experience to the next level today!"

In fact, the app takes museum branding to a new level of exploration, familiarity, trust, and relevance.

Curate Store Merchandise to Align with Your Exhibits

You already stock books and souvenirs that double down on the theme of an exhibition, and this is more than smart merchandising; it's using the power of an exhibition to help brand the entire institution. Your exhibitions make these purchases happen; visitors remember the museum visit because they remember the specific exhibits they've seen. Chapter 15, the museum's "Store" describes the branding process from the store's perspective. Curators' perspectives also belong in the conversation of what items to stock, and how to merchandise them. During the Magritte exhibition at the Art Institute of Chicago in 2014, a pop-up store charmingly constructed a Magritte bowler hat springing out of the wall above a display case. It was witty and memorable. It demonstrated a human side to a great museum's personality; it built Magritte into the very structure of the building and was very good branding.

Use Books as Visual Displays

Whether it's a $50 coffee table tome or a paperback quick read, a book about a current exhibition reinforces your mission visually. Show the cover, not the spine. This was done with wonderful effect at the Loyola University Museum of Art, where a beautiful book on Shaker life, "Gather Up the Fragments," helped reinforce the positioning of a museum dedicated to spiritual life.

Prompt Brand Awareness in Guest Books

The big guest book at the end of the exhibition at the Lucille Ball Museum is a primer in branding: first-hand testimonials on why people love Lucy, how they remember her, how their children/parents/grandparents responded to the cultural phenomenon of the beloved redhead. One entry from an 8th grade teacher tells how she uses two vintage shows—"Chocolate Factory" (job switching) and "Aunt Martha's Salad Dressing" (start-up company)—to demonstrate entrepreneurship. The sixties star is still relevant and, hence, a great brand. The book at the end of the exhibit demonstrates that for all to see, and to maintain.

Promote the Institution in Exhibition Promotion Materials

People read a lot about a museum when they read about its exhibitions. So your brochures and posters, website and e-mails, magazines and social media posts, all are taken at their word. When you write about an exhibition, tie it inextricably to the brand of the museum.

Anchorage Museum clearly linked its 2015 exhibition "Polar Night: Life and Light in the Dead of Night" to its brand uniqueness, which is stated on its Polar Lab page:

> The Museum resides in a North that is pivotal to the world—not a frontier, but a horizon . . . [that] . . . connects Anchorage with the globe.

On the sprawling web, where a visitor can wander far from your exhibition and even farther from your brand, it's important to say how an exhibition reinforces your brand.

Your promotional print materials actually sprawl from pocket to countertop to all over the lives of your many constituents. The Chicago Botanic Garden puts its message on materials ranging from the member magazine to the volunteer information sheet:

> "We cultivate the power of plants to sustain and enrich life."

Certainly, your logo should appear on all materials, but it's doubly important for it to give the seal of proprietorship to exhibition materials. Brand the institution that makes the exhibition possible. Here's a quick test to take. Collect all the exhibition pieces you've produced in the last year and see if there's one consistent logo, tagline, or statement of purpose on all of them. Most museums, including the very biggest, fail this test, but even the smallest should find consistency among at least three of the pieces that appear everywhere, from lamp posts to chamber of commerce packets all over town and beyond.

Promotional Material for Traveling Exhibitions

For print materials that are included with exhibitions you don't create yourself, you'll have to have an identification sticker that can be added to brochures for use in local hotel racks and Chamber of Commerce packets or to any other print materials that are used in promoting your museum. Whatever shows visitors see, they'll see it in your museum and associate it with your brand. In materials that you prepare, such as newsletters and magazines, add a line that conveys the traveling exhibition's aptness for your museum. Here are some suggested lines:

"This special exhibition offers a new way of telling the Smith-Jones Museum story."

"We're proud to host this exhibition and its perspective on our mission."

The Spencer Museum of Art at the University of Kansas took a scholarly approach in branding a temporary exhibition that also visited major museums throughout the country: "James Turrell: Gard Blue," May 19, 2014, to April 12, 2015.

On its invitation to members, the Spencer provided informed commentary that showed authority on the exhibition, if not actual authoring of it. The artist is described as "the pre-eminent light artist of our time," a statement that reflects the pre-eminence of the museum. The time of the event is given as "after sundown," not just 7:30 p.m., thereby exhibiting some of the museum's personality. The back of the invitation provides a brief description of the artist's work and a website address for anyone who wants to better understand him. In this way, the museum appears as a teacher, not just the renter of the classroom.

Chapter 8, "Marketing," goes into detail on branding promotional materials, for both traveling exhibitions and your own.

Remember the Brand in Exhibitions That Entertain

Attention, living museums everywhere: If any of your exhibits are entertaining, they are memorable, and might be remembered for themselves, not as part of a museum. Here are some words to use to tie the entertainment to the museum:

"Welcome to the blacksmith's shop here at Jonesfield Village."
"If you want to learn more about smithies and the craft of blacksmithing, you'll find books in the Jonesfield Village store."
"Every time you see a key or hook that looks like this, remember the blacksmiths in Jonesfield Village."

If your museum offers photogenic activities where children learn how to pump water, spin wool, or track animals, be aware that grandparents won't open their smartphones to these photos of, and think about, your curating genius. This is another occasion to designate photography stops and place branded signage nearby.

With field trips, schoolchildren will remember the fun excursion, but not necessarily that it was to a museum. In your materials to teachers and parents, make sure the museum's name and logo are on the same page as the field trip details.

Homeschoolers will adapt your exhibitions for their curricula and be grateful. Make sure your name and logo are on materials you send them. And, of course, select exhibits that unambiguously reinforce your core brand values. The Mariners Museum offers a long list of exhibits for homeschooled children of different grade levels. Their names evoke both appropriate learning and the mission of the museum:

"The Life of a Ship's Boy"
"Abandon Ship: Stories of Survival"

Educational diversions for parent and child alike, museums' homeschool initiatives are appreciated but getting so universal that they could be taken for granted. They make for high-quality community engagement, but make sure the parents and children remember your name.

The authorial narrative belongs to curators, but exhibitions have to be housed in a structure where visitors can see them. Objects can be stored in a warehouse, but when they are brought out for the public to see, that very action suggests that communication is meant to occur. Awareness of the museum's brand underlies every aspect of an exhibition. It heightens the goal of the exhibition for everyone's benefit.

TALKING POINTS

Talking points are informal branding; they pop up in casual conversations with family, friends, and supporters, as well as the general public. They deliver all the information that museum administrators, staff, volunteers, and board members provide in their professional capacity—when they're off duty.

Talking points about an exhibition are important because exhibitions are talked about so often. Timely, one-of-a-kind, and highly promoted, exhibitions naturally are chatted about. Nobody says to a friend, "Hey, how's the facility rental going these days?" Lots of people will say, "I hear the new exhibition is wonderful" or, better, "I saw your new exhibition and I thought . . ." Every member of the museum family could be in this situation and should be prepared with talking points. Points that people talk about are not written as a script, or a PR release, nor are they meant to be read word for word. They're a guide to keep everyone in your big museum family in the loop.

Before starting to write the talking points, understand how much they'll be used in informal conversation.

Here's a partial list of the people who might hear the message:

- Prospective visitors
- Donors and prospective donors
- Sponsors and business partners

- Educators
- Community leaders
- Media
- Vendors and suppliers
- Meeting planners
- Scholars
- Museum community

You want these people to understand the relevance of the exhibition to the museum's mission.

Here's a partial list of the people who must be prepared to talk the talking points:

- Members of the administration
- Staff
- Part-time staff
- Volunteers
- Board of trustees
- Visiting curators, exhibition designers
- Store personnel
- Restaurant personnel
- Guards
- Suppliers such as designers, bloggers, caterers, and electricians

All of the above are advocates for your exhibitions. However casual the conversation, they should adhere to the museum's brand values and mission, and anything else is (best case) sloppy or (worst case) misrepresenting.

Thirteen Suggested Talking Points

Here are some categories of talking points to emphasize. Each must be individualized to your brand and the concept of the exhibition. Give your staff an actual sheet of paper with the numbered talking points that should guide their conversations:

1. Background of the artist or maker
2. Theme of the exhibition, why it is timely or expository of your brand
3. Museum's special expertise—authority—in the exhibition subject
4. Distinctiveness of the exhibition; comparison with the way the theme was handled by other museums or institutions
5. Role of citizen input or curating, if any

6. Interesting facts and findings that enhance your museum's brand in a competitive environment
   For example, in 2015, the seventieth anniversary of the end of World War II, there were a lot of Churchill exhibitions, from London (the Science Museum) to Hobart, Tasmania (Tasmanian Art Museum and Gallery), to Savannah, Georgia, United States. The website description of the Telfair Museum's "The Art of Diplomacy," an exhibition of Winston Churchill's oils says: "He . . . saw painting as a testing ground for such leadership strengths as audacity, humility, foresight, and strength of memory. The exhibition includes . . . a landscape called *The Tower of the Katoubia Mosque* (1943) . . . the only piece that Churchill painted during World War II . . . a gift to President Roosevelt after the summit at which the initial plans for D-Day were decided." Don't confuse this kind of brand-appropriate fact with this one, which is not brand-appropriate: "In 2011 Brad Pitt and Angelina Jolie bought the painting. Never before has the couple loaned the painting for display."
7. Comments from visitors
   Incorporate visitor comments as they occur; talking points can be amended throughout the run of an exhibition. A docent at the Museum of Contemporary Art was told by a visitor that the young woman in a Gerhard Richter photo was the future Queen of Sweden. That tidbit was later folded into other museum commentary, with full credit given to the visitor.
8. Brand appropriateness of donated collections
   In many museums, donated objects are the foundation of an exhibition. Remember to connect the collecting philosophy of the donor to your brand identity in all materials. These include, but are not limited to, labels, panels, websites, brochures, fundraising packets, media announcements, and collateral programming. It will be more meaningful for the donors to have their collection thus aligned with the museum, and it's essential for the museum's brand and mission integrity.
9. Label talk
   For exhibitions that display a lot of smaller objects such as personal items, letters, and artifacts, be prepared to condense the text of dozens of labels into short verbal narratives. This talking point probably should be a "talking paragraph."
10. Story consistency
    For museums that are story-reliant, like the Tenement Museum in New York, make sure everyone at the museum tells the same tale. The Tenement Museum's brand is immigrant stories. The stories are told by trained docents and the museum's website, and they are consistent.

If your stories are integral to your brand, write them carefully so everyone stays on message.

11. Brand role of auxiliary buildings
    As museums extend their scholarship and exhibition philosophy, their physical, tangible, highly visible buildings beg to be explained; they so perfectly explain the relevance and core values of your brand. These noteworthy additions tend to come up in informal conversation, so everyone should be prepared to connect them verbally to the brand. Some examples:
    Why does the large campus of the Ringling Museum contain an art museum, a Venetian-style palazzo, a reconstructed eighteenth-century Italian theater, and a circus building? Because each represents John and Mable Ringling's dedication to art—fine and popular.
    Why should visitors take the tour of the George Eastman House Garden, in addition to a tour of the eminent businessman's house? Because the inventor of marketable cameras and film was also a plant scientist.
    And why would a botanic garden promote an indoor library? In the case of the Chicago Botanic Garden, because it holds "*Historia Plantarum* by Theophrastus (d. 287 B.C.E.) published in 1483 . . . the first known classifications of plants in the Western world."
12. Branding a generic-sounding museum
    Take for example, a museum devoted to Abraham Lincoln, maritime culture, or a culture group. People are bound to ask how your Lincoln, maritime, or ethnic group museum is different from the others. This is your brand positioning, and it needs to be memorized by heart.
13. Current and/or controversial issues
    Controversial exhibitions attract a lot of talk and you should prepare and distribute their talking points early. With 24/7 social media coverage, even small local exhibitions can receive a lot of unexpected questions. Double check these talking points with several advisors so that the message is not only diplomatic but also assertive. These exhibitions excel in enhancing your brand.

Teaching the Talking Points

If your talking points are written as points, not paragraphs, they'll be easy to learn. So, write concisely and disseminate quickly:

- Distribute them at staff and board meetings.
- Add them to vendor and supplier contracts.

- Include them as a part of teacher lesson materials, homeschooling guides, and lectures.
- Instruct docents in how they relate to tours.
- Discuss them with store personnel so that souvenirs or books can be related to an exhibit or exhibition.
- Show them early to fundraisers, because so much cultivation of donors occurs informally. Incorporate them in packets sent to renters of facilities and meeting planners.

Consider a version of talking points—"Letter from the Director," "Behind the Scenes" column—shared with members in newsletters, Facebook posts, and the magazine.

It goes without saying that talking points should be given to any designer creating a logo, signature visual, or web page, and to any writer writing posts, tweets, or blogs for social media, a twitter feed, or other marketing vehicle.

Exhibitions are visuals worth 1,000 words and more. Example of the year goes to the Corpse Plant at the Chicago Botanic Garden, which in August 2015 was scheduled to bloom and emit its nominative smell in a matter of days. Video cams, YouTube videos, local TV news coverage, e-mail blasts, and signage throughout the garden pushed undreamed-of numbers of people to the small greenhouse where Titan Arum was spiking toward glory. Alas, the exotic plant ran out of "energy," and this last talking point was distributed to guides and administrators alike who worked extra-hour shifts to explain the rise and fall of the botanical star.

The rest of this book will discuss the near-limitless ways your museum brand is identified, maintained, and communicated to the audiences who care for it. Nothing highlights your brand as eminently as your exhibitions.

Chapter 2

Tours

Docent-Guided, Audio-Guided, Walking, and Video

Figure 2.1 A brand from the 50s and 60s endures and thrives. Its audio tour—at once sophisticated and heartwarming—expands the relevance of the brand to new generations. *Source*: © 2015 Margot Wallace.

"Welcome. We're so happy to see you at our museum. Let me show you around." Guided tours provide more than structure and knowledge; their hospitality puts visitors at ease. Many visitors won't know how they're supposed to act in your museum. Guided tours are the beginning of familiarity and trust, and so the branding begins.

The docent starts the branding process with a short definition of the museum, its place in the community, and its value in the social fabric. This friendly person reinforces the visitor's decision to visit and outlines what lies ahead. The tour is a serious commitment on the part of the visitor, and therefore an important opportunity for museums to build their brand. Tour takers are entrusting themselves to your guidance and investing time in your exhibits; they are prospective repeat visitors, potential members, and probable goodwill ambassadors. Take a new look at the tour. It's another engagement opportunity; it's not a lecture.

In small museums, some of this welcoming is handled by front desk personnel, store personnel, and guards, so consider some of the following information as useful to their training, as well.

Starting with the tours and tools you may already have, this chapter surveys how your museum can heighten your brand identity with:

1. Docent-guided tours
2. Audio-guided tours
3. Walking tours
4. Video tours

DOCENT-GUIDED TOURS

The costumed guide on the doorstep of the log house could have been a neighbor. In small communities, the historical society is an active participant in the town's cultural life. And when this long-skirted, bonneted woman began the tour of the 1840s home, her story of an early settlement was as real as if she had started spinning wool. Guided tours attempt to do more than just educate and interpret: They make other cultures relatable to our own. They elevate what could be just another historic site to Your Historic Site. Docents, in costume or civvies, polished speakers or plain talkers, give the museum a face and a unique brand personality.

Set the Stage

Tour guides are like an overture; they set the stage for the stories of your museum. They briefly introduce your brand history—the equivalent of the

"About" tab on your website. They expand the facts of each exhibit and relate them to the whole. For tours shorter than forty minutes, or small tours, they add robustness. They help visitors imagine a big picture for the coming experience.

Talk and Share

On a docent-guided tour, visitors can comment constantly and ask questions of the guides. Docents who have gone through your training will be able to parry just about any question. And if they can't, there's a brand-building solution: have your guides distribute Q & A cards with room for two things: the question and an e-mail where they can be answered. You will stand out as helpful; you'll earn trust; and you will have established a line to further communication.

Docent tours permit talking time; docents can pace a tour with a few stops for questions or comments, those valuable small-group interchanges that help connect visitors to your brand. Even if they don't talk to each other, visitors hear what each has to say, the give and take of information so necessary to a meaningful visit.

Personality really comes into play at the end of the tour, the wrap up. Summarizing what the visitors have seen helps etch the memory and reinforce the museum's brand. It could be as simple as a guide asking:

"What was the happiest room of the Smyth-Jones House?"
"What will you tell your mom or dad about your trip to the Smithville Science Museum?"
"Which one of the Spring Grove gardens was an inspiration for your own home?"

This will start a conversation, and a lively discussion on your museum is the best way to impress the brand on visitors' minds.

Personalization

Today's media is based on personalization. That's why there are hundreds of cable channels, movies available in varying formats, ranging from theaters to mobile devices, and social networks that allow every personal question to be answered by someone—quickly. If you think of museums as media—an intermediary between artists/makers and audiences—you must get personal, too. Have docents arrive early for their tours to informally chat with tourers. Ask them to start a tour with the basic question: "Where's everyone from?" Encourage them to briefly query the tour group about their own museum experiences. It's an agreeable way to make strangers feel at home and connect them to your brand.

24/7 Changes

With round-the-clock immersive news and culture coverage, external events assume more importance than they used to. In fact, you can rely on something external bearing on what a docent will be talking about somewhere in the world. Here are some of the topical issues hitting the author's Twitter feed on Saturday, July 18, 2015:

- Met Museum @metmuseum
  Cat Photos
- Time.com @TIME
  Retweeted by metmuseum
- Cuba reopening embassy in US
  Brookings @BrookingsInst
- Happy #World Emoji Day
  Vine @vine
- Bees
- Anniversary of Caravaggio death is 1610

Visitor Input

If your museum exhibits art, science, Latin American culture, popular culture, or American history, any of the above topics might be relevant to a tour group. You can't engage your visitors seriously if you aren't aware of what interests them.

For a docent to be aware of the world outside, the museum doesn't mean having all-round expertise but, rather, having sensitivity to what's on the minds of visitors. If an external reference comes up, the docent can simply say: "That's really interesting. Thank you." On a tour some years ago at the Museum of Contemporary Art Chicago, a member of the tour group pointed to a group shot in a Gerhard Richter work and said: "That's the current Queen of Sweden when she was a girl."

The docent replied, "That's really interesting. Did everyone hear that? I'll be sure to tell the curator." Score two branding advantages generated by that docent-guided tour:

Interchanges with visitors are memorable and reinforce your brand for them.

Input from visitors often provides useful information for the museum that makes its exhibition of an artist distinctive.

Outlining a Docent-Guided Tour

Start with the "So What" question—in other words, the purpose—of the tour. Just as you have to justify docent training costs to the budget people, so you have to justify the tour to the visitors. The reason is the same: The docent tour enhances the visitor's experience of the museum as a whole. You won't use the museum brand in talking to tourers, but you will talk about the museum's vision or mission that underscores the tour. Begin by telling tour members what the tour includes, such as background on the artists/makers, the works' impact on their era and culture, and the unique role your museum plays in putting this information together. This is your first chance to reinforce your brand.

Here are the guidelines to give your docents:

- Announce the big idea—the theme of the tour—right at the beginning.
- Select 5–10 stops that you're most comfortable relating to the theme.
- Address the different levels of learning in your group.
- Use "look," "stop," and "go."
- Ask for final impressions—what they'll post, tweet, or send. It helps reinforce the impression of the whole museum.

You can't tell a docent what to say. You can provide a template from which the docent will organize his or her talk. The goal of an outline is to put the guide at ease, so he or she can talk from the heart, not from the provided labels, and make your tour distinctive.

The Big Idea and Theme

If your museum has a powerful brand, let's say George Eastman, you have many ideas to explore and themes to follow as you construct a forty-five-minute tour: photography, garden architecture, the camera business, Hollywood films, the medical advances he funded. Dare to focus; it is good branding. Generalization is always boring and runs counter to a brand.

Stops the Guide Can Talk About

Be selective with the artworks or objects you choose. Select the ones the docent can conversationally discuss. Their personality is important to making the tour memorable, and the brand distinctive.

Address Different Learning Levels

Throughout the tour, it's thoughtful to pause and say, "Who here remembers . . .?" or "Maybe you're studying something like this in school . . ." A docent at an Andy Warhol exhibition once stopped mid-sentence to verify ages; she asked if everyone recognized the woman in one picture, the Jackie Kennedy assassination photo. Most of the group said they knew who it was, although one woman thought it was Monica Lewinsky. And some people reading this won't know who *she* is. Good brands embrace relevance, which includes knowing what your audiences have never heard of.

Look, Stop, Go

Use your hands and point your finger. Call visitors' attention to an object in a gallery and a detail of the object. If you want to vary the pace, tell them to stop for a moment. Direct them to the next stop with a hospitable gesture. Use body language to indicate the entire museum. It's all too easy for touring visitors to take the lesson and leave, feeling they've learned a little. You want them to learn a lot, to feel enriched by the entire museum experience.

Final Impressions

This is what counts: the brand message the visitor takes away. Docents have the incomparable opportunity to start a sociable little discussion, the kind of sharing that social media has demonstrated to be so effective.

Practical advice to the docent:

- Decide well in advance what you can cover in the allotted time. Walk the itinerary you've chosen to see if your selected stops communicate the message you want to convey. Modify the tour as needed.
- Before the tour starts, break the ice by asking your group where everyone's from.
- During the tour, mentally note which exhibits get photographed. It may help you edit the itinerary for future tours.
- Repeat the museum's name as often as reasonably possible.

In Support of Real People

People, in their limitless individuality, make connections and memories. And that's good branding. They are the face of your museum, some of the few museum people visitors come in contact with. And docents spread the brand message far and wide; they are good connectors everywhere they go.

Audio-Guided Tours

Audio-guided tours solve many problems inherent in museum tours. Technology, fortunately, is no longer the domain of techies alone, and its creative, friendly applications are ready to tackle traditional jobs, such as guided tours. The purpose of this section is to show how to get human connectivity out of digital connectedness.

Navigating Physical Limitations

Audio-guided tours solve a space problem. Whereas a docent can walk a group only so far, a voice can guide visitors over more territory. If the museum is crowded—good news!—an audio tape can make the visitor feel he or she is in his or her own space. In both instances, the visitor will be able to connect individual exhibits to the whole museum. The narrator can say: "To see how this object connects to others at the Smith-Jones Museum, please continue to Exhibit 9." The visitor has time to stop and reflect before moving on. And an audio tour can provide additional context to reinforce the brand mission.

Note to Museums with Docent Tours: Remember to tell each tour about other galleries in the museum and other exhibitions, current and future, that aren't covered in the tour.

Avoiding Personality Discrepancies

An appropriate voice with a message scripted perfectly conveys the personality of the museum. Scripting guarantees consistency of message, the *sine qua non* of branding. You have more control of your message with an audio guide narrator who:

Comes with a credential: curator or historian or art collector
Holds a script you have written, and who has time to practice his tour talk
Can be diplomatically replaced by a different voice-over announcer

Although a docent adds genuine personality to tours, it can overwhelm the institutional personality. You can't control whether a tour group perceives the docent as a spokesperson or as just a nice person, but you can control how an audio guide narrator represents the museum.

Note to Museums with Docent Tours: Take advantage of docents' people-to-people skills to engage visitors in brief discussions at several points in the tour and at the end. In conversational sharing, visitors will discover your brand authority and distinctiveness.

Competing with Entertainment

It's hard for museums to compete with all the entertainment available at a visitor's fingertips. However, audio-guided tours—with their vivid scripting, multiple voices, music, sound effects, and fingertip technology—utilize entertainment meaningfully. They're platforms the young and progressive understand. Many years ago, the Whitney Museum of American Art in New York produced a vivid, interactive audio tour that included sound effects. In the George Bellows work *Dempsey and Firpo*, which was narrated by popular sports journalist George Plimpton, cheers and ambient sound of a boxing match filled the visitor's ears with sound. It added memorability to the painting and to the Whitney's brand as a museum unafraid of exhibiting daring new American artists.

Note to Museums with Docent Tours: At the end of a tour, ask visitors what was fun about the exhibition (not the docent), or if there was anything that made them laugh, or surprised them. Your museum has a personality, so leave your visitors with that thought.

Respecting Curator Intent

Pre-scripted audio-guided tours are the surest way to present objects and exhibition concepts the way the curators envisioned. Curated exhibitions represent the museum's mission and are preeminent branding vehicles (see chapter 1, "Exhibitions"), and a well-written audio script can manifest that.

Note to Museums with Docent Tours: Organize a curator tour for the docents. Remember that curators are the experts; docents are the people who translate that expertise to learning.

Adhering to Educator Goals

Dramatic stories amplify learning. Schoolteachers already use multiple media platforms in the classroom to stimulate discussion and to target different student levels. Just as museum educators take a fresh look at content, structure, and delivery for different audience segments, audio tours can be scripted and programmed to reach different interests, as well. How would a forty-five-minute tour sound if it were specifically designed for ESL students or home-schoolers? That's a challenge audio-guided tours can address.

Note to Museums with Docent Tours: Utilize the flexibility of docent tours to determine, at the time of the tour, what particular interests the tour group has. A guide of the grounds at Chautauqua Institution, Chautauqua, New York, told the author that his best tours are those where the visitors prompt him with questions. And, with just a little encouragement, they always do. I saw it happen.

Increasing Gallery Time

Count the minutes: Audio-guided tours, with their structure, keep visitors in the galleries longer. Studies show that the average time visitors spend in any one gallery is 2 minutes and 56 seconds, with an average of 20–30 seconds in front of any one work; they don't indulge in much reflection. But the audio technology forces visitors to pause, to find the next exhibit they want to hear about. The more time visitors spend with you, the better your opportunity to build a relationship with the brand.

Note to Museums with Docent Tours: Before a tour moves to the next gallery, the docent can slow it down a little, stop, pause, look around, and say, "Now we'll go through that door to see . . ."

Corralling Youth

When it comes to school tours, what all young people have in common is their youth. They grow up with technology in the classroom, multiple screens, and instant answers. And if their school districts don't provide those basics, you can. These people have quick intelligence and their energy doesn't suffer a slow pace. Audio guides allow for the unstructured pacing that help agile minds explore. Handheld devices are familiar and may even add reassurance in strange surroundings. And since many bring their own mobile devices, you won't need to invest in hardware.

Note to Museums with Docent Tours: Young people, in their limitless individuality, make connections, bridge divides, and discover new answers. They're good at following their curiosity, even if they don't realize it as such. You can help them follow their curiosity, and appreciate the museum a little bit more, by asking: "Which part of the Smith-Jones Museum would you like to know more about?"

Utilizing Emotion

A good audio tour is emotional. It makes visitors feel happiness, outrage, awe, or surprise; and feelings help them not only hear the facts, but also grasp the overall concept. The old building in downtown Jamestown, New York, that houses the Lucille Ball Museum could easily be just a collection of memorabilia. The entrance—which looks like a storefront—does not indicate a visit full of information and enrichment. However, the visitor gets tons of fascinating facts, thanks to the loving audio narration of Lucie Arnaz, the daughter of "I Love Lucy." Under her firm narrative, the journey through the museum is an informative and memorable survey of early American television, its place in American culture, and the breakthroughs wrought by Lucille Ball and Desi Arnaz. To be sure, this narrator is a good actress and reader, but it's the emotional connection that delivers such impact. Visitors relate to a daughter's knowledge and pride, and trust the museum that delivers it.

Note to Museums with Docent Tours: If your docent has a personal connection to the subject of the tour, encourage him or her to state—briefly—the nature of his or her relationship. All docents have, for starters, an emotional interest in the museum. Visitors can ask insider questions at the end of the tour.

Pronouncing Foreign Names and Scientific Terms

Where precise use of language matters, pre-recorded tours guarantee that foreign, scientific, and multi-syllabic terms will be pronounced correctly. As museums integrate STEM learning (discussed more thoroughly in chapter 6, "Education"), scientific terms will crop up more often. Digital scripts can go a step further by offering the option of a full explanation of a term.

Note to Museums with Docent Tours: Record foreign names and scientific terms for your docents to hear.

Accommodating Hearing- and Vision-Impaired Visitors

Americans with Disabilities Act (ADA), requirements for the hearing impaired state that museums should provide hearing devices or interpreters, and that need becomes more pressing as America ages. Audio tours fulfill a legal and moral requirement and spread their brand image to another audience.

The script meant for the hearing or vision impaired differs greatly from those you're accustomed to hearing. Seattle Art Museum provided audio tours for people with low sight—in its 2014 exhibition "Peru: Kingdoms of the Sun and the Moon"—that described the layout of the room, position of the object, and whether the display was in a case or on a stand. The script gave words to the minutest details of the artwork, from the pattern of a woven basket to the skin color of the people in a wedding party portrait.

Note to Museums with Docent Tours: Tour leaders must speak clearly, slowly, and full-throatily. This is not a job for the faint of voice.

Taking the Offensive with Q & A

An audio-guided tour can forestall many questions by programming handsets with frequently asked questions. It can program questions and answers for different learning levels. At thc Salvador Dali Museum in St. Petersburg, Florida, a curled mustache symbol marks the paintings with child-appropriate audio tour description. A good brand should speak meaningfully to its audiences, and technology allows this niche segmentation.

Note to Museums with Docent Tours: Don't be afraid of sounding too knowledgeable; that's expected of docents. Do encourage questions at any time. Sometimes it pays to ascertain just how old someone is.

Mobile Phone Tours at George Eastman Museum

The three advantages of using the visitors' own devices are cost, familiarity, and spontaneity. The museum doesn't invest in handsets or check-out desks; visitors use the platform they're familiar with; the museum can add audio content at any time and the visitor can come and go between galleries without returning the device. The George Eastman House in Rochester, New York, provided a cell phone tour for its 2015 exhibition, "In the Garden." In three-minute narratives, accessed with an 800 number, the highlighted works were narrated by the individual artists who talked about their concept and creative process. The comments could have been scripted by a professional writer; each was rich in specific information, insightful and sincere without being wordy.

Two nice branding touches were woven into the mobile tour. At the end of each three-minute recording, the visitor was invited to leave a comment. And when a visitor who had hung up returned to complete the tour, an announcer said, "Welcome back to the George Eastman House." These are excellent uses of technology; the visitor is engaged by being asked privately to voice his or her thoughts. And the museum has a record of telephone numbers.

Script an Audio-Guided Tour

Producing an audio-guided tour costs money. To keep costs down, write the script yourself or provide a detailed outline. Either way, you save a lot of rewrite time as the words are fitted to the stops. The essential talent you provide is the brand theme—how the tour reinforces the mission of the museum.

The outline is similar to the outline you give your docents, but more explicit:

- Determine the length
- Assess the audience
- Find the big idea—the theme of the tour
- Select one or two takeaway thoughts
- Plan five to ten stops along the tour that reinforce the theme and takeaway thoughts
- Plot the itinerary, taking into consideration the space around the selected stop
- Interweave attention-getter statements
- Summarize, evaluate and sign-off with the museum's full brand name.

Length

The length of the script should be the same as the length of a tour. About three minutes per stop is the limit; for comparison, the standard television commercial is thirty seconds. Depending on the complexity of the technology, expand the levels of information at each stop. Depending on the size of your museum, allow enough time for all walkers to move from exhibit to exhibit. Even though visitors can end the tour whenever they want, don't leave them hungry. Each stop represents the whole museum in microcosm, and gives the visitor time to absorb the brand environment.

Assessment of Audience

Who's listening to you? Be honest and try to imagine why a visitor wants to invest in the immersive experience of an audio-guided tour. After all, these tours require a set schedule, preclude free-range exploration, and may cost money. Will your museum's visitors appreciate facts? Do they love local color? Are they amateur historians, future scientists, avant-garde connoisseurs, or some version thereof? You won't ever satisfy everyone, but a rule of good communications—think TV commercials again—is to say one thing and say it well. Anyone curious enough to visit a museum has the ability to adapt your message to his or her interests.

The Big Idea

This is as simple and daunting as knowing your brand mission, and as daunting as putting it into non-Missionese. Happily, when you start wording your mission in real-people words, you'll arrive at your brand. The audio-guided tour of the George Eastman House in Rochester, New York, revolves around the lifestyle of a very wealthy, entrepreneurial, well-connected man. When a visitor walks into the mansion part of the museum (as distinct from the art galleries), the first impression is, "Wow, this guy did well for himself!" The tour corroborates this at every stop.

Takeaway Thoughts

What do you want visitors to leave with? What do you want them to remember when they're commenting on Facebook or TripAdvisor? If you're a historic home with a garden, do you want tourers to click and send photos of a rose's stamen, or of the statuary, or of the entire layout? Do you want them to remember the famous person's dining room furniture or the dinner guests? Small details explain the brand.

Stops Along the Way

The first step is to take actual steps. Remember that you want to cover enough territory to get a sense of the whole museum—the brand—as well as the specific tour agenda. Time how long it takes to move from exhibit to exhibit. Look around and see what's included in this itinerary: a long haul, an important painting off to the side, a sculpture that should be viewed from all angles, and an object that's right in the line of vision. A case in point: I once observed visitors to the circular Hirshhorn Museum and Sculpture Garden in Washington, D.C., as they stood before two doorways and tried to decide whether to go clockwise or counterclockwise through the galleries. A large sculpture, five feet from the left-hand doorway, lured the majority to turn left. It was unavoidable.

Select your stops like a curator to best depict your narrative in a limited time frame.

Levels of Learning

If the technology permits, offer additional information at some of the stops. It enhances the understanding of the museum's knowledge and insights,

Not all stops require the same kind of learning. You could play music and simply identify it as a song of the era. You could suggest a quiet moment to enjoy an exhibit. Think about a sound effect and a brief statement describing it. In the 2013 *Scenes from the Stone Age: The Cave Paintings of*

Lascaux at the Field Museum in Chicago, a video at one exhibit showed a pair of hands scraping stone on stone to form a utensil. The video was interesting; the sound mesmerizing. Rasp. Rasp. Rasp. We can't imagine what the caveman went through to shape a culture, but sound helps.

Attention!

Intersperse a few exclamation marks along the way to change the pace. A docent would say, "Look at this!" So can an audio tour. Not every thought requires a complete sentence. Vary the sentences. Add a visual sentence. At the George Eastman House garden tour, after a list of plantings and the famous guests at the opening party, the narrator mentioned the thousands of lights, strung in the trees, which started to glow as night fell. One could see the glitter that surrounded the man. Visual cues bring a brand to life.

Summation, Evaluation, and Signature Line

Help visitors formulate a memory of your brand by explaining what they've seen and how it invigorates the brand message. You can't ask for the visitors to stick around and share their thoughts with each other, but you can stop at a representative object or space and say: here's what we showed you and here's why it's of value.

Just as you sign a letter or e-mail, sign off at the end of the tour with your name or location. Of course, they're read as the equivalent of the letterhead or the "From" line, but good museum branding demands that you remind visitors of the actual place that hosted their visit.

At the end of Lucie Arnaz's audio guide narration of the Lucille Ball Museum, she briefly recaps the promise of the museum brand: Lucy and Desi, the narrator's beloved parents, were two great talents who left an enduring legacy—the wonder of comedy:

> "And it all started in Jamestown."

Walking Tours

As museums embrace their communities, real as well as virtual, they'll find new reasons to fling open their doors and take to the streets. These reasons break away from the traditional garden tour or house walk; the choice of theme is up to you, and it is a big, inclusive way to redefine your brand. There are three examples John Veverka gives in his article on walking tours for AAM:

> The early architecture of our homes and buildings reflects our strong Swedish heritage.

Our community buildings reflect three different architectural or cultural styles or influences.

The Ohio River was responsible for our community's early growth and history.

While solid marketing—reaching new audiences—lies behind these tours, in planning them you'll discover new interpretations for exhibits you already possess and new themes for exhibitions you hope to mount. As you tell the story of your streets, architecture, businesses and natural environment, you become "The Storyteller." It enhances your role in the community and your brand.

The Lucy Black Chaney Museum in Augusta, Georgia, offers two neighborhood walking tours; its Civil Rights and Trolley Tours were developed by the museum as part of August Community Walks. The museum's brand is present on its website, where the sites, a map, and the story of the tours are clearly described. It reads as a seamless integration of the museum and its city, and that's a partnership all museums can hope for. You don't have to create your own neighborhood tour; being part of a larger picture is very brand-effective. Neighborhood tours position your museums in the sea of choices; they enhance familiarity and trust by being part of a bigger community.

If your museum is already part of a neighborhood walk, its brand automatically loses some of its identity; there are other interesting sites along the way. Place a sign outside which, in effect, is a wall panel that describes your place in the community's culture. The neighborhood walk already has a brand, and now you will be a sub-brand. Additionally, ask to write your own text for the neighborhood walk web page, social media posts, brochure, and other promotional material; they can be the same brief sentences that you write for the sign/panel at the door.

VIDEO TOURS

Video that promotes the scope of your museum—that walks the viewer through some of your spaces—is a tour. It's a preview of what guides would show if they could cover more territory. It's effective as branding because it familiarizes visitors with the totality of your presence. And when parts or all of a museum close, online video tours keep the brand alive.

Familiarization

If you want to expand visitorship, everyone who walks through the door is a stranger to whom you must become familiar. And the bigger your museum, the farther the distance to get there, the more unfamiliar these strangers will feel. Then look at the demographics you target: schoolchildren, minority groups, low income, high income (new donors and sponsors); talk about bewildering! Start introducing yourself early through videos.

One example is the 35-second walk through the nighttime paths of Longwood Gardens, a wonderful video that choreographs sound and illumination to presage the museum's light-and-sound event after the sun sets. The pre-welcome reassures visitors not familiar with the extent of the museum; not everyone can read a map, and some may be wary of garden paths, not to mention navigating them in the dark.

Filling Gaps in Your Map

Sometimes, galleries are walled up or taped off; these areas under construction that disappoint so many visitors can now be finessed by a video tour. When exhibitions are being installed, or taken down, they can still be seen, heard, and described in vivid detail. In fact, video tours are a good medium for promoting any upcoming attractions, and summarizing departing ones. Off-limit galleries are holes in a museum's story, and online video tours can keep the learning and the image whole.

Another example is the expansion of an already extensive space, occupying many acres and several years at the Chicago Botanic Garden in suburban Cook County. Time-lapse photography is used to show the Garden's new paths and structures. Although the video has high production values—it's part of the annual report to stakeholders—the technique is adaptable to a museum of any size.

Crystal Bridges Museum of American Art in Bentonville, Arkansas, is a sprawling destination in a remote, though beautiful, Ozark setting. Nearby airports are small. Highway drives could be long. Crystal Bridges doesn't downplay its size in the video, but just seeing its extent gives a trip-planner some idea of the goal. Utilizing a lot of birds-eye views and zooming out shots, the video gives a sense of distance; there will be no surprises for the traveler.

The biggest gap looms when a museum closes down entirely for reconstruction. San Francisco Museum of Modern Art did just that for several years before its 2016 reopening. In a five-minute video, which positions the rebuilding as expansion for more openness to the community, the shuttered museum comes to life: new galleries and sustainability initiatives, a diverse and engaging staff, comments by celebrated artists and new artists, realistic architectural renderings, and an interwoven stream of works from its wonderful collection. It's a tour de force that can be replicated on a small scale by museums with much smaller budgets. Similar descriptions of goals and intermediary steps can be accomplished with drawings and photographs and time-lapse photography. Any Ken Burns film demonstrates the charm and effectiveness of that approach.

THE BOTTOM LINE

Is the cost of tours justified? Just what is the return on investment in docent training or audio production? The answers are in branding. Tours tell the story of your individual museum; they guarantee reinforcement of your name and mission. Labels describe the object; tours describe the whole museum. Tours help a time-limited visitor understand the value of your museum, over and above its component parts. They also send a brand message to everyone else: other visitors, educators, donors, sponsors, and the connected world beyond your walls. Authored tours give the museum authority.

Chapter 3

Architecture and Building

Figure 3.1 Melting clock bench is the first thing a visitor sees when entering the Dali Museum grounds. It's the brand one expects. Dali, the artist, carried the surrealist brand for a long time. *Source*: 2015—Salvador Dalí Museum, Inc., St. Petersburg, FL.

Enter the grounds of the Dali Museum in St. Petersburg, Florida, and one of the first things you see is a towering, elongated, solid building of glass in a criss-crossed steel framework. It looks more like Buckminster Fuller's geodesic dome than a surrealistic fantasy. It turns out that Dali, despite the surrealist tag, loved science and spurned surrealism after just ten years of casual association with other surrealists. Truth be told, if he admired any artist besides himself, it was da Vinci, he of the airplane and machine sketches. You can't say you weren't warned when you first walked through the garden gate. It is classic rebranding.

The new Dali Museum set itself the mission of putting the already famous Dali brand in a new place—with its collection, building, and exhibitions, right down to the merchandise in its store. The small garden does feature a melting bench, but more prominent is the path of paving stones in the shape of the Greek letter rho (Greek letters being also used as symbols in math and science). Towering over the approach is a very rationale glass and steel behemoth.

For any type of museum, of any size, the building is a brand statement. No other touchpoint of your museum has as high a profile. It's a beacon from afar, and a haven within. It's the first tangible manifestation of your brand that visitors see and the last impression they receive when they leave. In between your welcome and your goodbye, your building immerses visitors in its unique personality and plan.

For many years in my youth, I salivated over the gorgeous four-color ads of paintings in the Arts section of the *New York Times*. How wonderful these works are, I thought, never realizing that they were supposedly advertising

Figure 3.2 This is the Dali Museum building that's your actual destination—another perspective on the brand image. The building is an important touchpoint for a brand-name artist who identified with science as much as the surreal. *Source*: 2015—Salvador Dalí Museum, Inc., St. Petersburg, FL.

the museums that were presenting the exhibitions of which the individual work was just a part. However, the only thing they communicated was the art and the artist. Museums risk that same confusion today if they don't clearly identify the museum itself as the institution bringing together the objects on display. With the spotlight on displays and labels, the content sucks up most of the oxygen in every gallery. But, beware, because the room itself matters if you want your museums to get any credit for the museum experience.

This chapter will point out how your physical plant reinforces your brand, and how you can take advantage of every wall, floor, and staircase leading to and through it. Much architectural thought has sprung forth with the splurge of building and renovation in the last fifteen years. With hard-hat activity all around, even small museums will look at their buildings differently—not to rebuild but to refresh. Many of the following examples may spring from new construction because small insights come from grand projects:

Façade
Galleries
Exhibition walls
Navigation
Outdoor spaces
Architect of the architecture
Promotion
Three-dimensional verbal logo
Architecture and your staff
Creative destruction
Community

One can learn about building brands from all of them.

FAÇADE—THE WALL THAT SPEAKS FIRST

The renowned architect Louis Kahn wrote: "The sun never knew how great it was until it hit the side of a building." No wonder photographers stop outside to click.

Of all the walls in your building, the outer wall is the one that engages visitors first. All those walls with labels and panels talk a lot, but the façade is a true conversation partner. Even casual strollers notice it, if only from afar or in passing. But the real interaction comes from camera-wielding visitors, who pose next to the sculpture, mug side by side with the statue, or send an "I am here" shot to friends. The best brand connection occurs when a stranger stops to take a group's photo; now that person is drawn in, too. Of course, photo sharing is allowed throughout museums now, but visitors who pose in front of your façade are connecting with the institution itself and that kind of architectural branding can draw them in to the wider panorama of the artifacts and art inside.

One notable façade is that of the Museé des Auto, the Automobile Museum in Mulhouse, France. The front of this rather modern-looking building is seen from afar and across a bridge, and it's the elongated bumps jutting out from the glass wall that hurry you closer. Turns out, these are rounded, generalized front ends of cars, lots of them, promising a car experience unlike any other. Inside is a long entrance ramp along whose walls are dozens of video screens with scenes from vintage movies and old newsreels, featuring historic cars in action. These videos are charmers, warming you quickly to the cult of the motorcar. The message here is not the extravagant architecture, although it's Insta-photogenic. It's the meandering walk to the interior that delivers the introduction to the brand, and any museum budget can emulate that. Remember, always, the power of media, large screen or small, to talk for you. More about that as we continue from the outside to the inside of your museum.

GALLERIES

Inside the museum, walking through the galleries, visitors become aware of distinctive spaces and their walls, floors, and ceilings.

The Holocaust Museum, in Berlin, was designed to feel claustrophobic; many visitors say it worked. A sign tells visitors they can call for a guard to show them to an emergency exit if they start feeling claustrophobic. Daniel Libeskind, the architect, played a different kind of disorientation in his Denver Art Museum, where walls are set at angles decidedly not perpendicular. They ensure visitors wander through the galleries, instead of viewing the art pieces in a purposeful, ordered manner.

Other museums rebel against the tyranny of exhibits on the wall at eye level, and place objects in corners, or in the case of museums exhibiting the work of Richard Tuttle, at a three-year-old's eye level, or up near the ceiling.

Signature Space

The Cooper-Hewitt Museum of Design in New York has a third-floor gallery designed as a putting green. The museum calls it a signature element because Andrew Carnegie, the original owner of the grand mansion that houses the museum, used the third floor as a gym and, specifically, a place to polish his golf game. With a new interior layout, revised name, and rededicated focus on repeat visits, the Cooper-Hewitt exemplifies the merits of branding.

It behooves other museums, large and small, to identify and magnify an element of their museum, or of their discipline, that can be similarly made into a signature space.

If the signature space also surprises, that's just fine in an era where newness is expected. The similarity to a retail or entertainment cannot be overlooked, because museum customers also come inside the door to purchase an experience. Art, science, and history share space in our culture with sports and entertainment, and special spaces can help museums establish themselves as purveyors of many kinds of knowledge. Visible storage spaces, such as those at the Brooklyn Museum and The Broad in Los Angeles, add brand distinctiveness, but there are simpler ways to make your galleries talk your brand.

Unite the Works Within the Room

The labels for some works in one twentieth-century art room at The Art Institute of Chicago reference other individual paintings in the same room. You find yourself looking around, suddenly aware that you're in a museum room, not just passing by a row of paintings.

Connect the Galleries

The Allen Memorial Art Museum at Oberlin College, Oberlin, Ohio, placed their art in unexpected places, so they could be seen by visitors before leaving one gallery and entering another. One was displayed high above a doorway, and another could be seen through wall niches. Again, the visitor was forced to acknowledge that somebody at the museum had actually hung these pictures on a wall; the museum was accountable.

Memorably and emotionally, the story of the brief collaboration of Van Gogh and Gauguin in the south of France was told in chapters at the Art Institute of Chicago in 2001–2002. At the doorway of each gallery, a large panel above the door described the artists' fraught relationship as the days and the paintings plunged ahead. Visitors read it like a book as they moved from gallery to gallery—a book they couldn't put down. Building architecture matters. The same exhibition at the Van Gogh Museum in Amsterdam told the same story, but to less dramatic effect. The museum has fewer galleries, but each is quite large, and the story was told, in just two large sections as the visitor walked around the room.

Connect the Floors

The Snite Art Museum at Notre Dame University, South Bend, Indiana, exhibits artworks in the stairwells.

EXHIBITION WALLS

The Art Institute of Chicago broke down some theoretical walls in its 2014 exhibition "Magritte: The Mystery of the Ordinary, 1926–1938."

Visitors were forewarned in the first gallery's wall text, which talked about Magritte's interest in dreams and the subconscious. And, in fact, visitors were then plunged into a dreamlike darkness, as around each of many turns they found themselves in small rooms, sometimes with only one illuminated artwork to view. There were labels, but in the gloom, reading them was less interesting than just falling under the mesmerizing influence of the art itself. The strangeness of the interior architecture became even more overwhelming toward the end of the journey when cramped galleries gave way to one long tunnel of gloom, intersected only by dark walls, like road markers, with one painting each.

Logical-minded visitors might be forgiven for not figuring out that the layout simulated dream or subconscious experiences. It was a bold experiment, and in the pop-up store at the end of the exhibition, a young volunteer with an iPad was fielding a questionnaire. Were you satisfied with the exhibition? Did you learn anything? On a scale of one to ten, do you feel that you were given enough information? Asked the purpose of this research, the volunteer confirmed that this exhibition design was so different, the museum was requesting visitor reaction. One hopes the research validated the use of such idiosyncratic design because, although even the best museums must distinguish themselves from the renown of the artists hanging on their walls. In this case, the walls unmistakably belonged to the Art Institute of Chicago.

Shrieking in the Store

In a more conventional way of asserting its brand, the Art Institute pop-up store reflected both the Magritte exhibition and its own identity. Not content with merely hanging the framed exhibition poster ("The Mystery of the Ordinary") on the wall, right above it the store displayed one of Magritte's signature bowler hats bursting through the wall—much like the train in the poster bursts through the back wall of the fireplace. One of Magritte's written edicts, mentioned several times in exhibition communications, was "Make everyday objects shriek aloud." In ways both large and small, the Art Institute of Chicago made its everyday walls shout, too.

NAVIGATION

As the Selfie Syndrome shows (see chapter 12, "Digital and Social Media"), the way visitors move through your galleries is changing, and smart branding stays relevant with traffic patterns. If young people want to move faster and learn with a multiple-screen perspective, good museums will burnish their brands if they give the customers what they want. Millennials may stop to snap a photo, but they'll quickly move on. They're spontaneous. Their retail experience has been to swoop in, pick up what they came looking for, and leave. Expect a more thoughtful pace in your museum, but understand that wandering and lingering is not their style.

To find out what exhibits Millennials storm toward, conduct some observation research and watch where they stop and where they take photos. Check out Instagram posts. These stops might be a good point for longer labels or wall cards that relate the exhibit to the museum brand.

Museums that aren't purpose-built face unique traffic challenges. There may be no logical flow in a renovated bank, university-donated space, or idiosyncratic historic home. Small museums can solve these logistics with wall panels and exhibit placement:

- Place the introductory panel well within sight of the entrance.
- Number the exhibits or rooms.
- Walk through a house route as if you were the owner, or the housekeeper.
- Post a sign, on the main floor, of what lies upstairs and downstairs.
- Script an imaginary audio tour for the vision impaired.

In 2013, the Seattle Art Museum provided an excellent recorded tour for its exhibition *Peru: Kingdoms of the Sun and the Moon.* It was not just the artifact descriptions that were noteworthy; descriptions of the artifacts' place in the rooms, the size of the rooms, the placement of the objects, and the location of the doorways to other galleries were also excellent. This is not just logical thinking. Millennials don't need a linear path through a museum, but they're accustomed to taking in everything in view, and then knowing what goes with what. Amazon.com and Netflix.com, to name a few of their leisure activities, have taught them about making connections between things. An imagined example:

"This parlor lamp would have been fashionable and prestigious in the main parlor; you can see why when you compare it with the candle holder still in use at the writing desk."

OUTDOOR SPACES

If a garden, terrace, or balcony is part of your architecture, don't rely on its charm alone. Brand it. Even if it's just a viewing space, or part of the facilities rental, post a sign that explains its role in the architecture of the building. The Ca d'Zan mansion on the campus of the Ringling museums describes its sublime viewing point, the Belvedere Tower, this way: "The ideal venue for a small, elegant affair, the Belvedere Tower is filled with stunning architectural details . . ."

And not only brides want a space with a meaningful brand image. Visitors resting on a pleasant terrace or balcony are clean slates, open for new information. Be subtle, but be brand-sensitive.

ARCHITECT OF THE ARCHITECTURE

After all the entrances have been entered, all the walls observed, all the gardens and terraces paused in to reflect, the sixth dimension can rightfully be contemplated. The spirit of the architect hovers throughout, and that real person helps visitors relate in another way to the distinctive personality of the place, as well as the art inside. Even non-star architects raise the profile of your physical structure because it's easy to love an architect's building and fun to argue about the unloved ones. If the building project motivates discussion, all the better for your brand awareness; a debate validates your exploration into new ideas.

Architects, by the way, speak very well in verbal language, so you may want to quote them in press releases. Some of these artists are eloquent. In a retrospective of his work at Vitra Design Museum, Louis Kahn—again, the guy was a poet—is quoted as saying of rooms: "The room is a place in the mind. One talks differently in a small room than one does in a big room." He also says: "Rooms, like streets, are human agreements."

That's why your walls and ceilings, indoor and outdoor spaces, are so important. Visitors bond only briefly with the objects on them; they can connect forever to the rooms themselves.

PROMOTION

Though a structure is only one manifestation of a museum's brand, it is undeniably the biggest. If you're doing any kind of work to it, it can be newsworthy. Use the construction opportunity to shout your brand all over town. If you're not changing a paving stone, there's still news available.

The first job is to relate the purpose of the construction to the brand. If you're adding a school bus drop-off area, it's because so many students want to learn about your singular story. Maybe you are increasing the size of your building; well, that's because you're adding more media and visible conservation areas, and don't want to limit the space to exhibit your collection. And if you're only repairing the front steps, announce that you're restoring your building to the way it was when your mission was first embodied.

Promotional Materials

The building or addition might loom large in your current day-to-day life, but it's just one aspect of the museum, and it must never overwhelm the institution itself. Select the one photograph of the building that highlights a distinctive feature, and use this shot only. Don't monopolize a brochure with "The Building from Every Angle"; your marketing piece will look like a baby book. If you create brochures or postcards with images of the new building on the cover, put an artifact on the cover, too. Always remind stakeholders of the whole, not just the new. And by all means use your building, just as it is, as part of your marketing. It symbolizes your core values, not just your capital campaign.

For example, The General Lew Wallace Museum in Crawfordsville, Indiana, selected as its emblem the image of its study tower, where retired General Wallace did all his research and writing. It's a fitting way to symbolize the brand of the museum, which stands for so much more than battles and history.

Your museum may also have a signature visual that relates to the building, and it reinforces your presence. At one time, the Courtauld Museum in London used the grillwork from its main gate on many of its materials. The Dali Museum uses the maestro's signature mustache throughout the museum: the smallest example is the symbol on wall labels that indicate a special audio tour stop for children; the largest is the spiraling staircase that ends, up on the top level, with a familiar curl to its banister.

Use photos of your museum on postcards (yes, people still buy them). Encourage Instagram shots with easy access to architecturally distinctive elements in your building or on its grounds. (Yes, life-size cardboard figures with holes under their hats where visitors can put their heads still attract cameras.)

One way to put a big building into human size perspective is to display models of the building in the museum store and restaurant. These will be small models, visually reinforcing that the new addition is just a part of a long and larger tradition. By seeing the models in a familiar place, visitors will connect the new structure with their own experience, rather than as an expensive, perhaps disruptive, change. Humanize any building, new or existing, by displaying samples of the building materials with a "Please Touch" sign. Let visitors feel the museum and the craftsmanship that goes into it. This piece of the past feels contemporary, better branding than showing yellowed photographs of the way things were.

DESIGNING A THREE-DIMENSIONAL VERBAL LOGO

"Boxy." "Like a Depression-era post office." "It's a tenement." To hear people describe their museum buildings, you'd never guess how visual they are.

Whatever its size, shape, or design, you must think of your museum as a big logo, one that identifies your museum and sets it apart from all the other sights and options in town. You can't redesign it, but you can redescribe it. Verbalize your building in such a way that its look reinforces its brand core values.

Start by describing it to a stranger who wants to visit:

- It's the big building with the columns.
- It's the little building with a hitching post in front.
- It's the building with lions in front.
- It's the building with a totem pole in front.
- You'll see a plain red brick building with a huge banner of Abraham Lincoln . . .
- Look for the building with black stripes running all around it.
- It's the only 200-year-old house on the street.

Can't afford a star architect to design you a bigger, more glamorous building? Back here on earth, there are achievable solutions with simple wording:

Post a sign at each corner of your property with an arrow that says Main Entrance.

Use a photo of your main entrance, or any distinguishing feature, on your website.

Use your actual address and ZIP code on all websites and mobile applications so that taxis, limousines, and app-based transportation networks can find it with GPS.

You can talk about your building in brand-specific ways, too. When you open your facilities to events, remind clients of your heritage, as the New Bedford Whaling Museum does, that:

> The century old New Bedford Whaling Museum is . . . nestled in the middle of 18th and 19th century homes and shops, along cobblestone streets and a thriving seaport.

If your museum is undergoing new construction that temporarily closes an entrance or building, flaunt it. It may not be major architectural news, but it demonstrates growth and robustness for your brand. Two construction signs that linger in memory:

"Watch this hole in the ground as it fills with an exciting new museum." (Spertus Institute for Jewish Learning and Leadership)

"Like many on Fifth Avenue, I'm having a little work done." (Cooper-Hewitt Museum/Smithsonian)

ARCHITECTURE AND YOUR STAFF

For the brief time that they reside in your museum, for the staff and volunteers, it's a home. Knowing their way around includes knowing the message of the building design.

Docents at the Museum of Contemporary Art in Chicago pointed out how the shape of the *koi* pond mirrored the elliptical spiraling of the stairs. At the Tenement Museum in New York, they highlighted the plumbing on each floor's landing: one sink for every family on the floor. At the other extreme of country and culture, at the Hearst Mansion in California, the docent explained that the current tour was one of several totally different tours; the mansion was too enormous to cover in one visit.

New construction requires a different kind of orientation tour. Staffers, especially, will find their work home under siege. Describe the changes as goals, rather than detours. Remind everyone that this hole in the ground that used to be your parking lot will provide better office space. That unbearable noise is making room for larger exhibition spaces. Think about specific ways to thank curators, administration, volunteers, store and restaurant personnel, and guards. Morale boosting is essential for good internal branding. Remember that employees, like customers, need to be reminded of your brand's core values.

CREATIVE DESTRUCTION

New construction motivates new thinking about your brand. You're not changing your identity, but you might redefine it. That's hard to articulate, so first think about what you're losing. Creative destruction has many appeals.

Throwing out old furniture, or knocking down an ugly wall? Don't avoid the negative. One of the best negative sells was on the website of San Francisco Museum of Modern Art, which was closed down tight for many months. Its website announced:

"We've temporarily moved . . . everywhere."

And then it proceeded to tell in photos and words about its temporary sites all over the Bay area, partnering with museums like the Museum of the African Diaspora (MoAD), for an exhibition on portraiture across cultures.

COMMUNITY

Open wide the doors! Museum buildings are places big-hearted enough to serve beyond their immediate audiences. Architect Renzo Piano says museum buildings are the kind of places "where people share values and stay together." Their social impact on communities is distinct from their economic impact on communities. Your museum may already welcome affinity groups with spaces for:

- Classrooms—from homeschooling modules to academic curricula
- Meeting rooms—for the business community and other arts communities
- Touching galleries—for the vision or mobility impaired, as well as a different kind of teaching
- Polling places
- Performance space—any size gallery can convert to a chamber music venue

As you get to know your many unsung communities, you'll learn how you might be more inclusive in welcoming new audiences. Social media teaches all brands how to expand the virtual walls of a museum. Just look at the hashtags that mushroom along your own Twitter trail to discover some new uses for your building. There's every group from brides and grooms, for whom you already roll out the carpet, to wildlife gardeners and gorilla lovers, whom you might have overlooked! Chapter 12, "Digital and Social Media," delves into social communities, but within four walls and a roof, there is plenty of room for a broader group of friends.

If your building is in a new location, your new communities are partially selected for you. And if your museum remains in the same building, the same place, be assured that you'll always be acquiring new neighbors. You will respond to new communities as you always have, but also with:

- Exciting exhibitions
- Relevant programming
- Accessible hours
- Sensitively trained volunteers
- Targeted marketing materials
- Appropriate store merchandise

If Walls Could Talk Research

So, what are the walls saying, anyway? Your building is your promise; it prefigures what all that enter think about your brand. Question visitors, members, educators, donors, partners, volunteers, and other stakeholders to discover what they think about your building. Informal focus groups and brief one-on-one interviews are ways to get different insights into your brand as it exists right now. Ask members what the building means to them; scholars, what the architecture communicates; visitors, their first impression; vendors, how it compares with other institutions' facilities. Educators, businesspeople, meeting planners, all construe the building differently. Gather the impressions and prepare to be surprised and pleased. Your building already has an image, and it will help you embody the museum brand.

Chapter 4

Events

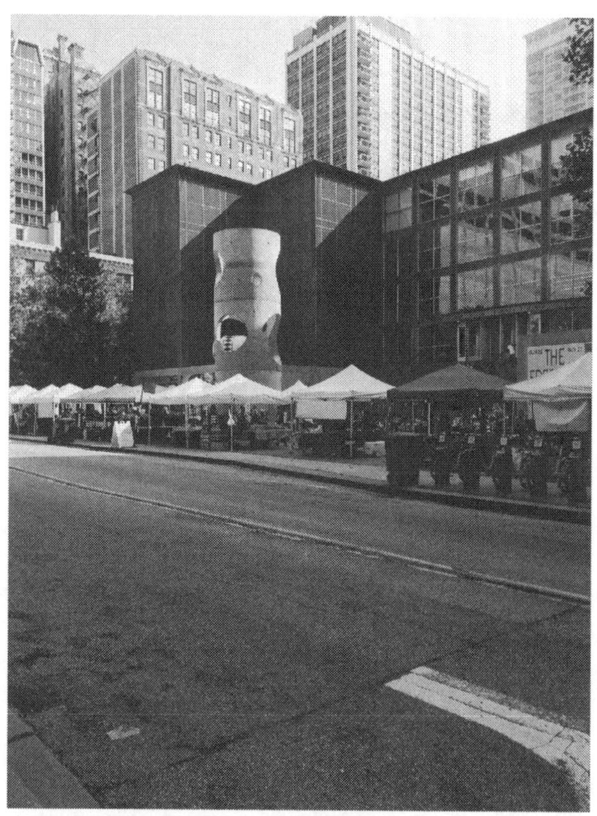

Figure 4.1 The Farmers Market at the Museum of Contemporary Art Chicago is a weekly event throughout summer and fall that brings farm to the tables of the museum's city neighborhood. *Source*: © 2015 Margot Wallace.

"Buck Day"
"Luminary Night"
"Tinker. Hack. Invent. Saturdays."
"Chant Macabre: Songs from the Crypt"

Events may be the most engaging of all your activities for one singular reason: their great names.

Events have singular personalities; they are memorable; their names betoken a focused purpose that connects emotionally with your consumer. Targeting a museum consumer is not a simple process. It's a complex matter of participation level, demographics, and psychographics—all the interests, habits, and social influences that every individual carries around. The thirty-five-year-old mom may be a realtor and also part of a tennis group. She has many calls on her time and energy and you would be missing your target if you tried to engage her with just one appeal. Events and special programs help you reach out to the many facets of an individual and make meaningful contact.

Once you entice these specially interested people to your special event, your brand becomes apparent to them. Your museum now embodies something they like—be it a serious lecture or a fun community get-together, a glam gala or a satisfying craft day.

Well-strategized events involve people with the personality and values of your brand. And look how engaging that can be! Here are the three major rules of engagement:

Rule 1: Show, Don't Tell

One event that visually showed the value of its brand was the gala auction at a contemporary photography museum. The committee accepted for auction donations only photographs that were surprising and thought-provocative, turning down so-called aesthetic photography. "Surprising and unexpected works that narrate a provocative theme" is the museum's collecting philosophy; it's what the museum promises. The event auction, highly visual and impressive, would actively demonstrate that distinctive brand.

Rule 2: Give the Consumer an Experience

An example: White Glove Wednesday at the Harry S. Truman Library and Museum where the archival white gloves are donned to show rare artifacts and how museum professionals handle such fragile objects. This is a museum of serious history, not just a paean to a famous man, and the event lets the visitor experience that history.

Rule 3: Share with a Friend

Brands are built by word of mouth and always have been. With book signings and fundraisers, "Night Safaris" and "Tastings at the Tenement," strong museum brands reach not only people with special interests, but, because events are by nature social, also the friends they bring along and the ones they tell later. What's more, events last at least 60 minutes, time to discuss and evaluate other essential features of engagement.

TWELVE PLANNING STEPS

There are twelve key steps to planning an engaging event or program, from a large fundraiser to a small gem of a program. At each stage, ask the question: Is this "On Brand" or "Off Brand?" It will make the process easier, and the engagement worth it:

1. Ask: Should we even consider doing this?
2. Choose a topic for the event and a name.
3. Identify the speaker or honoree.
4. Find sponsors.
5. Decide how you'll be profiting—awareness, new members, revenue, loyalty building.
6. Grow your database.
7. Schedule for optimum timing.
8. Consider alternatives such as trips and webinars.
9. Keep staff and vendors happy.
10. Emphasize networking.
11. Promote through social media.
12. Ask: Did we do this right?

Step 1: Ask: Should We Even Consider Doing This?

There are four reasons to have an event: acquire new members, thank existing members, raise money, and raise awareness. Any one of them is justification to have an event. Beyond this basic strategizing, there are four values of a specific event: strengthening your brand identity, reinforcing your brand values, delivering on your brand promise, and embodying your brand DNA. Any one of these achievements is worth the time and treasure spent.

Before a next step is taken, ask: "Will this be on brand?" For example, the opportunity to nab a celebrated writer on a book tour. Don't start budgeting the honorarium until you're sure that this person—a brand in his or her own right—will enhance your brand. Tweeted selfies with honored guests feel good, but don't necessarily do any good for your brand. Having said that, here's a seemingly misfit opportunity that did reflect the brand: author David McCullough's 2015 talk to the Harry S. Truman Library & Museum. Although McCullough was on the road promoting an airplane book—his new best-seller, *The Wright Brothers*—he also was the Pulitzer Prize-winning author of *Truman*, a 1992 biography of the thirty-third president. Many organizations in the country probably wanted David McCullough at the time; this museum had a good reason.

Step 2: Choose a Topic for the Event and a Name

There's no limit to the kind of event that you can offer; the problem is deciding its purpose: fundraising, increased visitation and membership building, member retention, branding, or raising your profile within your community. A science museum might reach out to the community of paleontologists; a botanic garden's niche could be members who are gathering forces for wetlands preservation; perhaps you're a historical society whose region is developing a wine industry. The topic and name reflect that audience's interest. Plimoth Plantation welcomes a very specialized community—historical reenactors—every year with a series of active weekends of "Lifeways," the way ordinary people lived in the seventeenth century—from historical costumes, food, tools, and militias, to actual labor around the farm and village. Plimoth Museum also presents a weekend conference on industries of "post-medieval life." If that shocker about how close we lived to the Middle Ages isn't enough to convince you of the uniqueness of an event, the 2015 event, "Trimmings: Adorning the Fashionable Figure in the 17th Century," should. This was an economics course in the clothing guilds of the 1600s. Credit a museum for the kind of American-historical insight you don't get in school these days, for the wondrous learning available so close at hand.

If you identify a distinct community within your membership or physical community—educators, history buffs, scholars—just one event would raise awareness, visitation, and membership. It might become a reliable source of revenue should it become a recurring, anticipated event.

How do you gauge whether an event might excite your audiences into new levels of engagement? According to an "ideas exchange" webinar hosted by an event management system:

"Event-goers crave an experience that takes them away from their day-to-day lives."

"They want to learn something they know nothing about . . . even the experts."

"They want to know that someone they know will be there, or they want to use the event to network."

Names should inspire the question, silent or verbalized: Where did that name come from? It's what people think when they meet a new person. We like to make connections and hearing the story behind a name is a start to understanding who that person is.

That's why the name of the monthly Saturday event at The Henry Ford, in Dearborn, Michigan, is so good: "Tinker. Hack. Invent." It identifies the audience it hopes to attract and simultaneously defines its brand. As the announcement says, "Americans are famous for their ingenuity and resourcefulness, for their eagerness to improve and explore new ideas . . . . Learn firsthand how that spirit is alive and well today."

The Henry Ford is more than a display of automobiles, more than its original recreated village. It's a museum that looks ahead, not back—its copyrighted logo is "Take it forward"—and in addition to honoring the maker whose vision inspired the museum, seeks to engage today's makers. "Tinker. Hack. Invent. Saturdays" is an on-brand museum program and it starts with a name that's perfect.

The Museum of Contemporary Art, Chicago, holds a major fundraiser before a major art exposition. Two big branded events in a row, in a city loaded with galas and fundraisers. The fundraiser needed a brand name to distinguish it in a sea of black ties and glitter. Vernissage was born. In France, a party called the *Vernissage* (French for varnishing) takes place in the artist's studio the night before his or her gallery opening; it's when the final touch is put on the paintings. It's an art-appropriate name for an established art benefit that precedes a traditional (if contemporary) art show, and "Vernissage" tells the kind of story all brands crave.

A different story is told by the names of the annual fundraisers, respectively, of the Blanton Museum of Art, Dallas, and The Walker Art Center, Minneapolis. "Off the Wall" and "Avant Garden 2015" promise a certain hipness and spontaneity, images that a lot of museums want to project.

Ongoing activities acquire the patina of an event when you give them a name. Thus, the Museum of Natural History has Mineral Monday, Taxonomy Tuesday, and Fossil Friday. These days are announced on Twitter where they stand out in the sea of events. Naming days is a human thing, and it relates to how your audiences—who set aside Saturday Errands, Football Monday, and Wednesdays as Meeting Days—really talk.

The Harry S. Truman Library and Museum, like all famous-person museums, faces an ongoing challenge in getting repeat visitors. After you learn about the man—even when there's a lot to learn—what's next? For starters, every Wednesday there are "White Glove Wednesdays." This is where visitors figuratively put on the gloves that protect archived material and look at the artifacts that illustrate history. Visitors might not realize how many objects are not displayed, and locals might think they already know the museum; this event, with its distinctive name, brings them back for a second or fifth look.

If you're a small museum, you could be forgiven for straying off the brand path in search of event topics. The Winnetka Historical Society, however, never strays. Its 2015 gala fundraiser, "A Southern Belle's Birthday," might seem to wander afield, but a town's history is one of many homes and the museum's logo serves as a reminder. Used on all its marketing materials, including on the invitation to the Southern Belle's mansion, the logo is a window of the museum's iconic log house.

As you hash out event topics and names, for each one ask: Is this "On Brand" or "Off Brand"? Get down to the "nub of the idea," why it appeals to you, and then condense your reasoning into a simple statement that you can use in all communications. And think like a public relations professional and be prepared to briefly explain your event topic and speaker verbally, as well as in print and online media.

Step 3: Identify the Speaker or Honoree

Guests of honor make a splash and, unlike a lot of event flamboyance, boost your brand as well as attendance. The type of honoree, the name and title of that person, and the relationship of the honoree to the museum all serve to define your brand loud and clear. Caution: If you can't justify the shared values between your brand and the honoree, this is just another awareness-fundraising event. Not wrong, but not "On Brand."

The National Churchill Museum, in partnership with the Winston Churchill Center, chose a perfect honoree for its big gala. Former Secretary of State Madeleine Albright was the honoree in 2015, a highly visible star in international government relations, an intellectual heir to Churchillian statesmanship. What's more, she was a youth during the World War II, when Churchill's image was honed. And then the e-mailed announcement augmented that connection with these brand-perfect sentences from the event chairman and the honoree:

> Winston Churchill was a determined opponent of totalitarianism . . . . It is thus especially appropriate that . . . [we] honor Secy. Madeleine Albright, whose own life bears eloquent witness to the impact of these twin evils in our time.
>
> I am thrilled to receive the 2015 Churchill Leadership Award. As a child of World War II in London, I am truly honored to be associated with one of the world's most important and respected leaders.

Your museum selects a dignified event committee to enlist prestigious speakers, and you then hope for media attention. Be prepared with brand-appropriate—even scripted—statements from each.

Master Classes

Honorees or speakers who also teach a master class raise the value of your brand in ever-broadening circles. New audiences, who didn't buy a ticket for the main event, get to see the guest and, even better, interact with him or her. The event becomes more democratic with an educational component, and the "interpretation" part of your mission expands in prestige. Awareness grows, along with prospective new members.

The actor Phylicia Rashad was invited by Ten Chimneys, the historic home of actors Alfted Lunt and Lynne Fontanne, to speak to and to teach master classes for "The Lunt-Fontanne Fellowship Program." The event brings together theater professionals to exchange ideas and to learn how to be mentors in their community. In the process, of course, these fellows become acquainted with the mission of the museum and are in a position to be ambassadors for its mission to be "a national resource for theatre, arts, and arts education."

Step 4: Find Sponsors

Sponsors and major supporters present a combination of requirements and wants. Among the requirements that must be addressed is placement of their name and logo, how their and their representatives' names should be used, what you write about them in the materials, and what images you use to depict the sponsors. This could include everything from who is included in people photographs, to how much space you give to the history and mission of the company. Yes, it's your event, but they are also key to the branding of the event. A not-for-profit brand is known by the people it attracts, and it's advantageous to describe your supporters' relationship with your core values. If you're a local science museum, and one of your supporters has a degree in a science, it's worthwhile to list that under his or her name. If an underwriter company has just initiated an environmental program, it makes sense to mention that in the program biography.

When looking for sponsors, think about your brand and the sponsor's brand. You're looking for an image fit, as well as a financial partnership. Joe Waters, in a webinar on sponsorships, talks about a nonprofit organization's assets, and he puts a strong brand at the top of the asset list.

There are other aspects of your museum that will appeal to a sponsor:

- A history of successful events, which could be fundraisers, well-attended 5-K runs, a signature event, or a popular exhibit
- Existing donors and a healthy membership list
- Loyal employee base, because each one spreads the good word
- Visible building and/or location. Even if the business's audience don't visit museums, they'll know your brand
- Good relationships with vendors
- Large following on social media sites
- Emotional mission; businesses want to connect and engage, not just sell
- Rich (meaning mine-able) database

Each one of these aspects, when functioning well, results from a respected, trusted brand.

The creation and enrichment of your database is consequential to any event. Chapter 19, "Databases," covers this subject from a branding perspective. From the sponsor's perspective, one of the benefits is a well-managed list of names, and a record of your ongoing relationship with them.

Make it clear how your brand's reputation will benefit sponsors. Maybe it's the halo effect of partnering with an arts brand, or establishing a local presence, or gaining a more pleasing image. The large financial, automotive, and industrial firms that sponsor events like "Off the Wall," Blanton Museum of Art's gala, and "Avant Garden 2015," The Walker Art Center's annual benefit, want the humanizing image that museums exude. Remember that your museum, whatever its type or size, represents hands-on, thoughtful, imaginative enrichment for all people, all the time.

Flaunt your brand. Sponsors look for a hook that connects your museum to their brand.

Lucy Craft Laney Black History Museum in Augusta, Georgia, offers city tours highlighting black historic sites. Its website provides an interactive map to the sites with links to each one. It publishes a monthly newsletter, presents regular events, rotates exhibitions, and has a social media presence on Facebook, Twitter, and YouTube. Its website prominently features a sign-up to receive the newsletter. Every feature clearly indicates a willingness to maintain a regular conversation with the community.

No wonder this historic house museum of an early Georgia educator, born eleven years before the end of slavery, attracted sponsors running the gamut of Georgia industry: university, insurance, media and publishing, local and national broadcasting, banker, builder, marketing and design, power company, church, law firm.

Emotion

Don't forget the emotional aspect of your brand. Your story is what connects an institution to a person, and the decision-maker at your prospective sponsor is a person. Head for the top person, because these people allow their emotions to show; they are proud of their personal accomplishments and interests, and they have no business points to make with higher-ups. There are three types of decision makers—"thinkers" who are logical, "feelers" who are emotional, and "deferrers" who defer to public opinion. Joe Waters, the sponsorship expert, advises lining up the first two first.

Look for a variety of sponsors, one brand per category, if possible. Here are just some of the categories that sponsor events of big museums and small:

Financial
Legal
Automotive
Technology
Alcoholic beverages
Senior services
Insurance
Retail
Sports
Media
Higher education

These businesses aren't buying sponsorships out of charity; they are getting a lot of emotional payback for their money: your excellent brand and all the familiarity, respect, and trust it encompasses.

Step 5: Decide How You'll Be Profiting—Awareness, New Members, Revenue, Loyalty Building

Remember that amorphous thing called "emotion" when you evaluate the payback of your event. Don't plan on them all making money, even if they collect it. In many cases, greater value ensues from awareness, new members, and loyalty building among current members. However, there is a danger in giving events away. With free events, there is no commitment, no pondering one's calendar, no RSVP sent. According to "Shirley," a participant in a webinar on webinars, there's a 10% no-show for free events, diluting the brand glow for everyone—speaker, audience, staff, venue—that a good event should impress.

Revenue

What raises lots of money is asking for lots of it. With well-named events, you can make huge sums seem like fun. Arranging them by tiers also helps; it gives attendees a choice, which makes it harder for them to say no outright.

Different tiers of gift-giving gives you permission to ask for large amounts and gives donors permission to contribute less. The savvily branded Wild About Harry event for the *Harry S. Truman Library & Museum* has an excellent range of dollar amounts for underwriters:

Oval Office Underwriters—$20,000
West Wing Underwriters—$10,000
President's Kitchen Cabinet—$5,000
Cabinet Members—$3,000
White House Advisers—$1,000

The headings of each tier are witty, and they serve several serious purposes. They keep eyes from moving too quickly to the lowest level of giving. They impart significance to each level; you have to think a little about the value of each gift. And they're fun, which takes some of the onus off writing a big check.

If you're a small museum, profits look especially good if you don't have to invest too much at the outset. According to Christina Lister, in a LinkedIn post from December 2014, you could use your online store to also sell and manage event tickets and database. Shopping for merchandise and attending an event attract different audiences; however, they both live in an online environment. An online shopper may see a workshop that looks interesting; a webinar registrant might see a gift to buy. If your store merchandise is brand-appropriate, and the programs reflect your brand, this cross-selling is possible; and with sales come new names and consumer data.

Member Loyalty Reinforcement

At an event, the goal is more than one-time check-writing generosity. Events are enriching, as well as functional, and good events aim for ongoing involvement, increasing familiarity and trust. That's why Taxonomy Tuesdays (at the Natural History Museum in London), White Glove Wednesdays (at the Truman Museum), and Tinker. Hack. Invent. Saturdays (The Henry Ford) merit attention. They introduce the museum into your weekly agenda. Good brands become part of your life.

Since one of the reasons for an event is to thank your existing members, say so. Ask the speaker to acknowledge them; most speakers want to know the makeup of an audience, and will gladly focus remarks to them. Put something special on subscriber seats, like a small sign that states "Reserved for (fill in their name)" or even a flower. Add to the message about turning off cell phones this message: "We'd like to offer a special welcome to all members tonight . . ." Even at small events, the presenter can start the program with these words: "Thank you to our members who are here today." The more visible and acknowledged the members are, the more others in the audience will want to become one. These public displays of affection are definitely encouraged.

With its "Coffee Talks with Nan Colton," Museum of Fine Arts, St. Petersburg, builds loyalty among all visitors, who can attend the monthly thirty-minute presentation free with admission. Its performing-artist-in residence dramatizes current artworks and artists, a brand-appropriate event that encourages repeat visits throughout the year.

New Members

It's harder to acquire new members than to retain existing members. Marketing no longer attempts to promote to strangers, but rather to earn the trust of friends. Your new members will come from the ranks of people who know and respect you—and grow to love you. Sometimes, you have to show them a side they didn't see before. Plimoth Plantation utilizes the universal love of food in its event, "The American Plate: a Historic Dinner with Libby O'Connell"; it's a history of dinner, starting with the seventeenth-century colonial era of the museum. There's the scholarship that's the expected part of Plimoth Plantation's brand, and something more: relevance to people who enjoy informed fellowship that ensues around a dinner table. The speaker has written a book on White House dinners, and the topic is relevant enough to attract a wide range of people.

Awareness

All events garner some kind of awareness as long as they promise novelty, are priced reasonably, make sense for the museum to offer, and are well promoted. Anniversaries fit this template for several reasons. They honor a founder or creation legend; everyone enjoys the story of a successful person with a wonderful idea. Anniversaries reinforce stability and the enduring presence of your museum and their community. Anniversaries don't require expensive celebrity guests and speakers; the celebrity is the museum. You can make this a one-of-a-kind event with frankly garden-variety activities. Whether it's a concert or a lecture, a big party or a small series of workshops, a children's field day or an adult conference, the focus is the founding spirit of the museum. Keep all activities in sync with your brand message. Make sure the signage, venue, booths, merchandise, and speakers are all brand-appropriate. The popularity of such crowd-pleasers may tempt you to relax the branding effort. Don't. All those willing attendees are snapping photos, tweeting, gramming, posting, and pinning; their wide circle of friends will all know about your museum, if they can see it. Instruct your board members and volunteers to direct them to designated photo ops where your building or other recognizable artifact is part of the shot. This might be a good time for volunteers to don costumes for posing with social photographers.

Anchorage Museum of Art staged a November 2015 event to celebrate its hundredth anniversary and envision the next hundred years. It kicked off the event in a way beloved to engagement advocates—it sent an e-mail with a request for proposals, inviting anyone to propose a performance program to highlight the event. This is a profitable move on so many levels: awareness, member loyalty, new stakeholders—used here to describe vendors who themselves could be new members—and revenue, with engagement topping them all.

Also in the new stakeholder category are the craftspeople who populate the American Indian Marketplace, The Autry Museum's annual show of two hundred artists. Over two hundred exhibitors show and sell jewelry, pottery, weaving, textiles, handmade instruments, and ledger art. To promote the event's success, the web page list of participating artists includes links to each one's website.

Awareness Attracts Partners

Events are also ways to raise your visibility for partnerships. It's an unexpected consequence, because prospects could be parents at a children's event, guests at a gala, attendees at a lecture, vendors at the event, or even a person you contacted to be a speaker. You won't know all of them by name, but you will follow up with them, as you do with all the people you assiduously add to your database.

An exciting new partnership opportunity opened up by social media and the sharing economy is mobile/online businesses. There are social media entrepreneurs lurking in every corner, even at your events, and they see collaborations you might not have thought of. A good example is the data collection at the Natural History Museum's "Citizen Science" program at the Natural History Museum, London. This ongoing effort asks people all over England to "record . . . observations of wildlife, collect . . . samples [to help] . . . unlock the potential of our collections and gather vital data for our scientists." One activity collects seaweed to assess the effects of climate change. A web page link directs visitors to local nature and environmental groups. A blog keeps track of a wide range of proceedings. It's a good educational event, good for branding, and good for awareness among many segments. The new potential is sharing-economy ventures. And, of course, the school kid at today's event is the millionaire start-up founder ten years from now.

Be alert to potential partners at your events; as you collect names for your database, flag the ones who are as entrepreneurial as you are.

Step 6: Grow Your Database

How would you describe an event: fun, memorable, feather in our cap, dollars in the bucket, or names in our database? Go with the last one. Events do all those other things, but their lasting value, year after year, is an information-filled, rich source of people you can call on year after year.

The people who were heretofore known by:
name, address, and e-mail
Will now also be entered as:
Visitor, attendee, member, guest, local, tourist, student, educator, scholar, official, media
To which will be added fields for:
Mobile, postal code, country, # of tickets, donation, total price of tickets and donation, previous event A, previous event B, subsequent event A, subsequent event B, previous membership level, subsequent membership level.
Those people will now be known as data.

You will spend a lot of time and budget building and maintaining a database, and every cent and minute will be worth it. The goal of a brand is enduring interest and loyalty; you maintain that engagement by managing each individual relationship. You tenderly care for that relationship by monitoring how much and how often each member partakes in museum activities. The set of data you get from any program or event, small to large, is invaluable. For starters you have information on:

E-mail addresses for further communication
Membership levels
Other events attended
Whether attendee lives close enough to visit/attend more often
What attendees purchased in the store
Names of non-members you can target separately
Seasonality of interest
Place in the life cycle—teen, young adult, child, adult, family, depending on event

This data can be analyzed in many ways, starting with the unassailable fact that these are people who have already experienced and shared your museum. Keep them close. Before you collapse from event exhaustion, take a deep breath and complete the database.

Step 7: Schedule for Optimum Timing

Timing your event comes naturally. In February, when the Chicago Botanic Garden most wants to be indoors, the Garden's greenhouses open for the annual Orchid Show with a cordial "Cold outside? It's warm inside at the Orchid Show Greenhouses and Galleries."

Spring is an occasion to flaunt your gardens and homes. Summer is for connecting with families and children, reaching out to new generations and also to new residents who have waited for the end of school before moving. Summer is when the Albright-Knox Art Gallery heats up Buffalo Sundays with its Summer Jazz Series.

Traditional Christmas parties blossom like mistletoe in historic houses every December. And even if your brand doesn't fairly scream that it calls its October Unhappy Hour "the Spookiest one of the season," as the museum of Edgar Allen Poe does, take advantage of time-sensitive periods like Halloween, Thanksgiving, and Christmas to hold your events. This kind of shirt-tailing on already well-known events is smart. It doesn't dilute your brand's image, and it saves a lot of marketing costs. The four seasons and the innumerable calendar holidays are part of everyone's lives. Your visitors and prospective members are already engaged with them. They provide your members with a comfortable way to get closer and more attached to you.

Holidays and seasons are also strategic times. Fall is a time for renewed intellectual activity, a good time for lectures and book signings geared to the content of your museum. In the fall and winter, you're taking advantage of year-end philanthropy. Anniversaries of founders and founding dates remind the heritage-minded of your enduring place in their community. With each event, even while aiming for the largest ticket-buying crowd, you will be engaging discreet communities. Be assured that people without an interest in a particular author, or a fondness for house walks, recognize that these are manifestations of your brand. Never worry that an event might be too specific. The main danger is having an event so generic that it's boring. Generalization is off brand.

Step 8: Consider Alternatives Such as Trips and Webinars

Events are killers of staff energy and annual budgets. They end up in the asset column, but at a cost. Two less arduous alternatives must be mentioned, one traditional and one virtual. Both require less time of staff. They register high in visibility and appeal, and they attract a lot of your targeted audience, even if they don't bring in large profits. Trips are glamorous, webinars are enriching. Both enhance your brand identity with an immersive, engaging, shareable experience.

Paris, river tours, the gardens of Kyoto, the Indiana Dunes. Possible destinations are without bounds but your brand has a definite place in the mind's eye. Name a city and certain images spring to mind; they should reinforce your brand, not compete with it. The price of the entire tour says a lot about who you are. So do the hotels, restaurants, and other art venues you visit. In addition to the museums you tour, consider the connotations of private homes, villas, estates, castles, galleries, fairs, biennales, and expositions. Every detail conjures an image. Is it your image?

President Harry S. Truman's presidency spanned World War II and its aftermath, so the Harry S. Truman Library & Museum World War II History Tour of Germany in September 2015 (also, by the way, celebrating the seventieth anniversary of the end of the World War II) was original, educational, and absolutely on brand.

Vesterheim National Norwegian-American Museum & Heritage Center is touring nine counties in Norway—Oppland, Sogn og Fjordane, Buskerud, Hordaland, even the names are brand-evocative—to study folk arts.

You can target different membership levels with your tours, as Crystal Bridges Museum of American Art does. It offers trips to Tulsa, Oklahoma, and also major art shows in Chicago, Miami Beach, and Europe. Each is open to different levels of giving. Why, you may wonder, with Crystal Bridges's identity firmly rooted in American art, does it travel to Europe? Because many of the best artists in the world are American! For all museums, trips at the upper levels offer more than the objects for which a museum is known. They include lectures, workshops, panels, and private house tours. On the Chicago tour, a Crystal Bridges curator and board member are each giving keynote lectures. This is engagement of members who are positioned as donating the greatest amount of money. We tend to think of trendy "engagement" as belonging to phone-wielding Millennials. Think, too, of checkbook-wielding philanthropists in any age group.

Benefits of Travel Events

Trips are full of benefits that redound to your brand, and here are some of them:

New objects and artifacts to reinforce your brand
Lectures and workshops that deepen the knowledge of your brand
Getting to know museum administrators and curators that maintain the brand
Shared experience with other members of the museum community
Posting, pinning, and tweeting
Fresh material for blogs and YouTube
Augmented database, including inquiries

Webinars Attract the Scholarly and Professional Segment

After all the preliminary discussions, sometimes the question arises: Why are we doing this? It's a good question, and it's never too late while still at the discussion stage. If your reasons are finding new members, revenue, or a treat for existing members, you might well opt for a webinar. They're still new enough to set you apart from other museums, and that's powerful branding.

Webinars introduce the voices of experts behind your exhibitions and programs, so virtual attendees see the human side of your brand. They provide a format for photos of your building, galleries, and your objects, to familiarize viewers with the museum experience. The concept of a seminar allows your spokesperson to talk about the specifics that a visitor would never ask a docent or information desk employee. Most webinars are presented in a simple slide format that allows for a lot of information. The engagement part of a webinar is the Q & A, and these can be outlined into the presentation at least twice during a typical one-hour session.

If nobody asks a question, you have still brought them into the fold, made them part of an inner circle, connected them. If they do ask questions, two important branding successes happen:

The museum hears the concerns that every good brand needs to know.

Participants develop trust.

You have to be straightforward in presenting a webinar, and knowledgeably concise and clear with your answers.

Some topics around which to build a webinar are as follows:

- A guided tour of exhibits
- Summary of past, present, or upcoming programs
- Current events or trends that prompt an exhibition or program
- How to work or volunteer at a museum
- How your museum helps homeschoolers
- Demonstration of conservation project

Some other brandable additional benefits: You collect a lot of interest, even from people who may not actually sit in on the webinar. You can offer a discount for a future visit. You offer a replay link. You can send a follow-up reminder as Wild Apricot, an event management firm, does after one of its webinars:

> "Based on your recent visit, we thought you might be interested in these items."

Webinars and travel, because of their large mailing lists, are big ways to capture names and e-mail addresses, as well as big megaphones for telling your story.

Step 9: Keep Staff and Vendors Happy

Make sure your employees understand the significance of the event, strategically and from its branding perspective. They're spending a lot of time on it. Whatever their tasks or role in the event, tell them why their part is important to the whole. At a large city museum's cocktail reception for members, docents were assigned to act as "ambassadors," explaining any questions the guests might have. Their role this time was social rather than educational. The lavish party, a museum administrator explained, was a way to thank members and remind them of why they had joined in the first place.

Also explain the brand connection to caterers, musicians, and entertainers. Give them a written statement of your brand and, where possible, show them how to talk the brand. The wait staff can comment on how the community loves the museum. Face painters can refer to exhibits in the museum. This is no imposition. It actually eases the vendors' job of connecting with the guests.

Step 10: Emphasize Networking

An event offers networking opportunities almost by default; everyone there is potentially connected by mutual interest in the topic or raison d'être of the event. It's in the interest of the museum to provide this opportunity because the ripple effect of networking spreads your name. Networking increases your credibility within your community; it's a credential in your field. It also increases the value of any event by making attendees feel productive. Sure, they've donated to a large event, or enriched their minds at a smaller event, but by meeting people socially, they were collecting a kind of business card; they gained something tangible. It's the cheapest goody bag you can provide!

Think of networking in a much broader context than the professional, job-hunting one. Networking is sharing information, and that's what you want your loyalists to do. Social media has made it simple—even necessary—to join virtual communities for the purpose of sharing information important to them.

Gardeners, for example, can now find fellowship at the September 2015 Heritage Harvest Festival at Thomas Jefferson's renowned Monticello. It featured a full schedule of educational lectures, as well as celebrity farmers, to spotlight the Founding Father's role in American food culture. It was good branding for the museum, and it engaged visitors with the brand in down-to-earth ways with hands-in-the-dirt workshops, heirloom produce tastings, and seed preservation. Yes, it was a very real and actual event. However, for those who couldn't make it, social media tweeted excellent updates. And that was networking.

Staff at an event can interact with guests to prompt the sharing, perhaps suggesting photo opportunities or offering to take a group's photos. Of course, each photo gets tweeted, posted, pinned, or grammed. If guests weren't engaged before, the mere fact of being part of a photo engages them. Most museums now allow photography—with a few necessary restrictions—in the galleries, and the policy of the Figge Museum of Art in Davenport, Iowa, is just one example of how museums convey photo-taking rules: it's right out on their website's Plan Your Visit page, as important as Hours, Address, and How to Get Here:

> "Visitors are permitted to take still photographs of the building, galleries and artwork . . . with cameras or *smart phones* [italics are the author's] for personal, non-commercial use."

Preview Networking

Some events are so novel, prospective participants may not know how to handle them. Consider the summer hiking and camping trips offered by The Burke Museum of Natural History in Seattle. Another summer event, "Know Before You Go," introduces prospective campers and their families to the concept. This day-long series of workshops teaches families the fundamentals of birding, how to press plants, and how to pitch a tent. Think of all the sharing that takes place before the backpacks are packed.

Step 11: Promote Through Social Media

Events must announce themselves, and the social media platforms available to you are wondrous and varied. But you've got to be choosy. Different media reach different targets in different ways; they are as strategic as your event. Chapter 12, "Social Media," delves into strategy; here's the before-you-delve list of the major social media and their advantages. Each engages its audience in different ways, depending on the nature of your event.

To begin getting a handle on the many platforms, here's one easy classification, based on word count:

Few words—Instagram
Fewer words—Pinterest
One hundred forty characters—Twitter
Sixty-800 words—Blogs
Four-six minutes of words—YouTube
Infinite number of words—Facebook

Another way to assess the advantages of each is by audience characteristics:

Visual people—Instagram
Visual people who like to categorize—Pinterest
People who are at your event—Twitter
People who read about your event before and after—Blogs
Visual types who like to research a subject—YouTube
Everybody, including a lot of grandmothers—Facebook

This rundown is purposely general and not a little idiosyncratic. It's meant to stop you in your tracks before you try to engage everyone, everywhere. Events are not meant to be general; they are effective in engaging people because they are selective.

Step 12: Ask: Did We Do This Right?

Day-of Checklist

You see it all the time when you visit a museum on the day of an event: a room with rows of chairs; a bevy of well-dressed people leaving a lecture; confused visitors who arrive at the end of the usual hours of operation. Do these event attendees see the connection between their event and this facility? Make it clear!

- Leave brochures on a side table, unobtrusive but there.
- Designate Instagram photo opportunities.
- Offer to give a brief tour or a few words of welcome.
- Place a sign at the entrance, with the museum's name and logo, as well as the name of the event.
- Hashtag the event for real-time comments.
- Put a display case and object in the restrooms.
- Design a signature appetizer or dessert.
- Put your name on the podium, your name on a banner above the book-signing table.

Day-after Disaster Check

Soon after the event, take account of it. If the museum doesn't continue to grow in income, awareness, memberships, and renewals, the event is just eventful, not meaningful. Whether your event does, in fact, make a nice profit, requires an objective look at the books. Whether, in retrospect, the event generates increased awareness, new members, and continuing engagement are realities that can also be checked. Here's what to check:

- Database—count the new names.
- New attendance—have five to ten percent of new names that attended further events.
- Memberships—are renewals holding pace with, or exceeding, last year's?
- Social media—listen to what's being commented, posted, or pinned on Facebook, Twitter, Pinterest, Instagram, TripAdvisor.com, Yelp.com, or aggregators such as topsy.com.
- Sponsors—are you getting new sponsors for other, smaller programs?
- Visitorship—up, down, or holding steady; does it include new market segments?
- Surveys—in the months after an event, what do visitors say when you ask: "How did you hear about us?"

Follow-up

Finally, be assured that your event was, indeed, successful. The best way to ensure its success is to follow up. You wanted people to re-engage with your museum and the best way to do this is to reach out to them again. Remind them that just a day or two ago they were at a wonderful event at a museum they now know better than ever. Send an e-mail with the most engaging words in the English language: "Thank you for coming."

Chapter 5

Membership and Fundraising

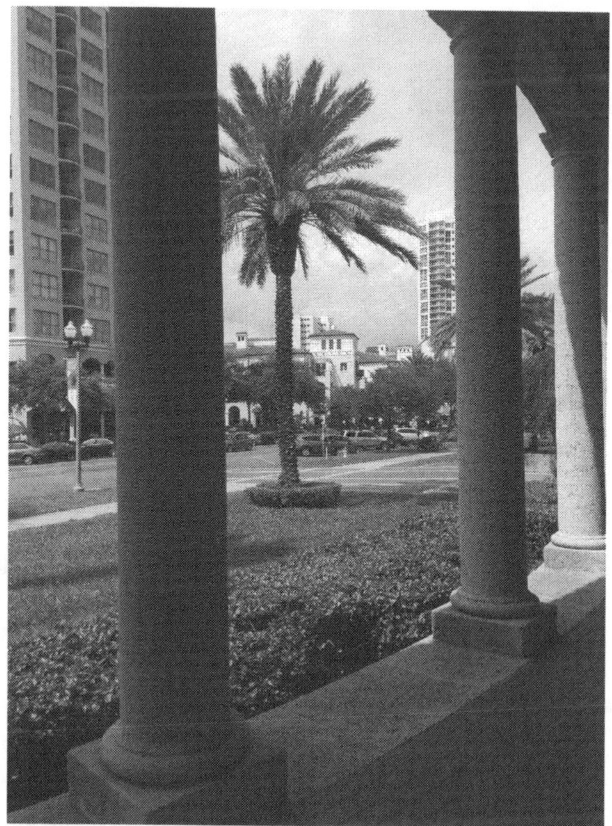

Figure 5.1 The Museum of Fine Art in St. Petersburg (Florida) offers a year-round calendar of events and programs, the kind of brand presence that aids fundraising. *Source*: © 2015 Margot Wallace.

Nancy F. lives in a suburb of a big city. She likes golf and symphony, her grown children and local theater, her book club and investment club, and her weekly volunteer job and museums. Nancy is nine niche markets.

Chuck is a college professor in a small city. He coordinates his schedule around his working wife's, and he drives his mother to her volunteer job at the botanical garden. His grown son joins him for camping trips. His real love is gunsmithing. Chuck is eight niche markets.

Do you speak to any of these interests besides the museum psychographic? Can you convince people who are museum-friendly to prioritize their habits and spend more time with your programs? And if you win them as members, can you inspire them to slide the credit card one more time to donate?

Your challenge is to demonstrate how your niche connects to theirs.

How to Identify Niche Markets

Niche markets are smaller segments of larger demographic groups. Think, for example, of all the different websites that are visited by the 25–40-year-old women demographic with interests in health, parenting, cooking, and fashion. Or the TV networks watched by the demographic of males 15–50 who like sports, politics, comedy, and the stock market. Then there are hashtags, which infinitely expand the number of niche interests and markets. Niche markets have always existed, but now, with digital databases, marketers can pinpoint individuals by their narrowest interests . . . and then send them an e-mail.

Find niche markets by finding individuals. Ask any staff member of your museum, director on down, to characterize ten people they know by their interests and habits. Once you have fifty-plus names, see if you can put them into five groups. Those are niche markets.

Or look at the hashtags on any of the social media your museum, or others you admire, use. Count the most popular hashtags. Those are niche markets.

Analyze the books that sell the most in your store. Their subject matter helps delineate a niche market.

With a more pinpointed sense of your audience, you can start to devise your membership and fundraising programs more sensitively. This chapter will first discuss branding's role in membership, an enduring relationship. Then it will discuss how branding can make additional demands on that commitment.

BRANDING FOR MEMBERSHIPS

These four activities and functions, properly branded, entice visitors—actual and virtual—to think ahead and pay a one-time fee to become a member:

1. Database
2. E-mail announcements
3. Chapters and affinity groups
4. Members-only benefits and trading up

Database

It all starts with a rich list of names, e-mail addresses, hometowns or ZIP codes, and the museum events that each name attended. You have to have a resume of your visitors, however sketchy—where they come from, what they did at your museum. Some people travel from far-away ZIP codes and you want to know what lured them so far from home. Some ZIP codes are within a twenty-mile radius, and represent people you can expect to return and perhaps become members.

Some people rack up a big total at the store, and you'll want to stay in touch with them. Some people came for family events; stay in touch with them at least unto the next generation. Membership cannot be achieved without regular and meaningful communication with museum-friendly folks who have already taken the first step in your relationship.

When the Vesterheim Norwegian-American Museum located in Decorah, Iowa, sponsors Nordic Markets in Minneapolis and Chicago, chances are its database has revealed a lot of Vesterheim-interested people in those areas.

Maintain your database weekly, at least. The major task is adding new names and e-mails as they visit, attend a program, buy a lecture ticket, purchase a store item, or complete a comment card. If you have the resources, add to the database fields, to get further insights into your audiences.

Everyone Is a List Maker

Collecting names eventually becomes a habit, with everyone on your staff being a list maker, and everyone else going on the list. Staff members should be encouraged to jot down the contact details of everyone who crosses their path: school trip chaperones to telephone callers to the archive manager, volunteers to vendors.

Because you'll be soliciting donations from people you've recruited for membership, it's important to consolidate your lists; too many requests are annoying and unprofessional. There are professional event management systems to collect your data and help you mine it, but in-house systems will work with simple spreadsheet programs. For a system that's less high-tech and less expensive, bring out guest books and comment cards, and ask that visitors print their e-mail addresses!

Chapter 19, "Databases," will help you dig deeper to get insights. For the purpose of membership, the main message is: Have one.

E-mail Follow-Up

The Tenement Museum succeeded mightily in a fundraising campaign that raised its larder over ninety percent, primarily with the simple and—in retrospect—obvious method of following up on donors and ticket buyers with immediate e-mails thanking them for attending and continuing e-mails announcing new events. If they bought once, and liked the product, they'll repeat the purchase: this is a standard marketing tenet. All it takes is regular communication, listening, and updating the product, so that it retains its relevance to the consumer.

Member Retention

The donors you take for granted may not take contributing for granted. Don't rely on anyone staying on the list, or staying at the same level of giving. Keeping the passion alive is a daily to-do list, never a routine, that museums address with every exhibition, every item in the store, every tour. But unlike marriages or sports teams, a museum seeking passionate loyalty may have to find new audiences. Attracting new audiences is creative and excruciating because it forces an exploration of market segments you have never known. The place to start is with your existing audiences; expand from them.

Chapters and Affinity Groups

Good membership initiatives are selective. They're not elite, but they appeal to very definite groups who by definition are cliquish. Young Adult Chapters and North Shore Chapters are examples that allow museums to target their members into narrow niches. The result is late-night parties for the former group, and chartered buses into the city for the latter group, both effective programs for retaining members.

Travel as a membership event is often categorized by level of membership; it is a very selective benefit of membership. Frankly, most travel programs are selective: certain kinds of people like foreign trips; others like insider house tours; yet a few others like history or music woven into the itinerary. The Harry S. Truman Library and Museum offered a brand-appropriate trip to WWII History sites: cities in Germany related to the war. The trip celebrated the seventieth anniversary of the war's end, under Truman's watch. This niche museum smartly created a niche trip that was attuned to several niche groups.

Travel has always been a popular event, yet it's fraught with peril, not the least of which is small numbers. All that planning for so few people! The upside is the networking and community building. People who commit large sums and a big chunk of their time are loyal to you or your mission, and they grow more bonded when they travel together. The Harry S. Truman Library and Museum offered an excellent trip, nicely suited to the brand, when it cohosted a ten-day World War II History Tour of Germany. This trip had an original theme and a rather scholarly agenda, and was well-suited to travelers who had probably already seen much of the world and were primed for a different perspective on it. Not for your typical tourist, but, then, a presidential library and museum is not for just any museum-goers. This is an elite group, a small but influential range of people that all museums need.

Single-focus museums have to be watchful that their brand-appropriate events don't limit potential memberships. The Poe Museum in Richmond, Virginia, hosts Poetry Nights, but lest non-poets think "nevermore," it also holds more general Unhappy Hours and Strange Stories Walking Tours.

One affinity group that is harder to define, but one of the more devoted, is the "crowd"; the people who crowd fund your projects. Your museum's followers and friends have a mind-boggling choice of causes to read about, and then support, but support their favorites, they do.

You don't have to be hard-charging startup. Many already-successful brands are learning new, more creative, more contemporary ways to interact with "The Crowd." And yes, this can mean asking them for money.

Members-Only Benefits and Trading Up

Never underestimate the power of exclusivity. Today, it means accessibility and speed in a crowded schedule. Members-only gets over-scheduled visitors into the fast entrance. Members-only scores seats to author lectures. Members-only means guests will get fed at after-hour programs that seemingly always happen on late-work days.

Benefits must be meaningful. All museum memberships include the magazine, entrée to special events, and passes for guests. Some, like the Chicago Botanic Garden, give green umbrellas, which are nice quality and great for walking in rainy landscapes. One of the most niche-sensitive lists of benefits is offered by The Baker Art Museum, Naples, Florida. Naples has a large snowbird population, and it can be expected that many museum visitors also contribute to museums up north. It is probable that many visitors are retired and travel a lot. So the Baker's member benefits include:

- Opportunities for day trips to other cultural organizations
- Invitation to book domestic and overseas travel tours
- Free or reduced admission to reciprocating museums in the United States, Canada, Bermuda, and El Salvador through the North America Reciprocal Museum Association

Prospective members can see the members-only benefits on your website, and here's where you can graphically show the value of trading up. At each membership level, the list of benefits gets longer. Even the brand-appropriate names of categories evoke the advantages.

At the Mariners' Museum and Park, the top donors sail at the "Leifr Eiricksson" level. Beneath that is the Lancaster Eagle group. At the lowest tier, the donor is called Donor.

BRANDING FOR FUNDRAISING

These five tools and techniques, properly branded, persuade members and other interested people to support the future of your museum:

1. Solicitation letter
2. Major campaigns
3. Grant proposal
4. Advocacy
5. Lobby donation box

Solicitation Letter

The reasons for asking for new dollars have also changed, commensurate with the growth of so many competing museums. Where once funding was for a new gallery, acquisition, or staff person, now it could be for a more environmentally sustainable habitat, or for an acoustically perfect auditorium. Frequently, prospects will have to be educated, and certainly they will have to be persuaded. Donors need a clear picture of what they're paying for, almost an itemized bill of sale. Amidst all the variables of fundraising, one principle emerges: You must clearly state your museum's brand. It justifies the new project and connects the project with the person you are asking to support it.

An example is the "Dear Garden Member" letter from the President and CEO of Chicago Botanic Garden. As a coda to her status report of construction on major new education and conservation centers, Sophia Shaw says "Both projects are part of the Garden's ten year-strategic plan, 'Keep Growing.'" She continues: "If you would like more information on supporting this important endowment . . ." At the top of the page bearing the letter, the museum's mission is stated:

> "We cultivate the power of plants to sustain and enrich life."

This is a project that will endure. Members are included in a long-range plan that reinforces the Garden's brand mission.

Writing the Solicitation Mailing

You might assume that a standard solicitation letter accompanies some printed marketing materials such as a brochure, or coupons to an event. But if you're asking someone for money, nothing should be assumed. That person is no longer on a member list, or past donor list. That person has individual interests that must be addressed. So don't use traditional marketing brochures, but one geared to members. For example:

> "Here are five recent additions to our Museum. We value your opinion and ask you to vote on the one you'd like us to exhibit first."

Also, the letter recipient is on several cultural organizations' lists. You can't assume that others haven't also been soliciting donations. Make your appeal and enclosed materials brand-specific:

> "In the next year, we will be updating the air quality systems in our storage spaces to better preserve our musical instrument collection. Music has enlivened the traditional holiday tea that you have enjoyed for so long."

Now that the enclosures are more brand-specific, on to the cover letter. All of us know how to write a basic cover letter. Or do we? "Basic" is the antithesis of "branded" and sometimes the cover letter is all the recipient reads. The letter must be steeped in the brand and not at all basic. The first paragraph describes several activities of the museum that exemplify its personality: a recent speaker or a new research finding. If the mission statement isn't printed on the letterhead, the opening paragraph states it. If the museum has a tagline that goes with the logo, it can be integrated into the letter, or added at the end. A letter can be witty or serious, scholarly or informal, detailed or anecdotal; your tone of voice adds to your brand identity.

Trustees who write their own letters should follow the above rules, if possible. They may be reaching out to their own contacts, but they're appealing on the museum's behalf. If they send letters on their own letterhead, decide how to include the museum's tagline, or a short version of the mission.

The requisite hand-written personal note at the end of the printed letter should avoid bland clichés. "The Farm's new Tool Shed and I thank you" is preferred to "thanks for your ongoing support." The outer envelope and return envelope, which are fast becoming curiosities in the postal service mailbox, should retain their dignity; use better quality paper stock and print your logo large and proud.

Solicitation communiqués needn't be grand, and a small example from a large museum comes from the Art Institute of Chicago. On the back of membership brochures that were placed on a special rack outside a members-only lecture, this simple request was printed:

> Dear Guest,
> One of my favorite things about the Art Institute has always been our community of volunteers, members, and supporters. As part of the inner circle, we get exclusive access to . . . . I'd like to invite you to join us and become a member today.

It's personal, from the director of membership and annual giving, and it's specific to the event.

Major Campaigns

When asking for money, specify why. People who give for the future, for a project that will take eighteen to thirty-six months to complete, want details.

Small museums have an advantage in capital campaigns: their single-minded brand image. Potential donors will likely know the museum, by name, by location, and as an organic part of the community they live in. They know someone who has visited there, works there, or has supported it in other ways. Knowledge and reputation validate the brand. Position your campaign on these three legs:

- Identifying the need
- Creating a campaign theme
- Appointing a message watchdog

Identifying the Need

For a major gift, funders need a museum-specific reason for giving. Foundations and individuals get many worthy requests and need to see what niche/need your request fulfills. The Tenement Museum offers a unique reason for funds, with supporting documentation for how they will address specific niches.

> As you know, the Tenement Museum at 97 Orchard Street tells the stories of the more than 7,000 European immigrants who lived in its 325 square-foot apartments between 1863 and 1934, when . . . [it was] shuttered . . . . The Museum now has the opportunity to move the story of immigration forward. Two doors away from 97 Orchard Street, the tenement at 103 Orchard Street remained open . . . housing Holocaust survivors, Puerto Rican migrants, and Chinese

immigrants in the closing decades of the 20th century. Our new exhibit . . . [will tell] about the experiences of asylum-seekers, the erosion of national origins legislation, and the impact of the civil rights movement.

Count the brand-building concepts that underpin this appeal: the museum's brand story, details of the capital need, benefits to stakeholders, and the personal approach to members.

Creating a Campaign Theme

A campaign theme is a rallying cry, short and dramatic. It's easier for a prospect to grasp "Bring the Seahawk Mask to Seattle" than to ruminate on the value of "capital campaign." This focuses the donor on a worthy cause, rather than neediness. More significantly, it focuses on the museum itself.

Here's the campaign theme of San Francisco Museum of Modern Art:
"Campaign to Transform SFMOMA"
This is the theme of the capital campaign for Speed Museum of Art in Louisville:
"Changing speed"

Campaign themes evoke the vision of their museums; they connote energy. More important, they are brand names that everyone can use. During the course of your campaign, everyone who works at your museum will be involved in some way or other. You need to rally their support, too.

Everyone in the museum is responsible for raising money, even those who have never asked for money before. A campaign theme keeps amateur solicitors from stumbling all over the subject and the less informed from giving incomplete information. A short, descriptive theme line helps the media write headlines, and it gives tweeters and posters a rallying point. It also gives unity to the steady flow of announcements, reminder solicitations, and financial reports that should be sent. As brochures, invitations, social media posts, pins, and tweets are developed, a campaign theme line ties them together. Costly marketing materials will go a lot further with a theme tying them together.

From the museum's perspective, a mission for your brand is irrefutable. Like a strategy, the prospect might not agree with it, but they have to respect it. It's an easier sell.

Appointing a Message Watchdog

Having a campaign line doesn't guarantee consistency; a human being does. Regardless of the museum's size, there will be a multiplicity of communiqués, created by different designers and writers, and aimed at widely divergent audiences. Also, a large campaign continues over many months or years, a calendar for mistakes that can be prevented by a watchful guardian of the message. Someone has to vet them and keep them on message. The message watchdog is a staffer or senior volunteer who peeks in everywhere, listens well, and has the standing to interrupt and correct anybody who strays off message. It sounds like a busybody job, and that's probably why it goes unfilled in most organizations. All printed materials should be vetted by the message watchdog, everything from solicitation letters to speeches at Rotary. Telephone marketing scripts should be cleared. Board members should be briefed and encouraged to use the museum's terminology, not their own. Curators and educators—professionals whose background gives them a vocabulary in their own field, but very few words for getting money from the public—can get a brief foreign language course in fundraising. Even guards, guides, and store personnel need to talk from the same page, because the capital campaign will be a big part of the museum's daily life, and the subject could come up at any time, from any quarter. And if outside grant-writers and professional funders are hired, they need to be relentlessly schooled in the specifics of the individual museum and its unique campaign.

Grant Proposals

Know your brand, have a firm sense of mission, and articulate it. These are the qualifications needed to write a grant proposal. Any staff member who understands the museum's mission has the ability to write one, and he or she should take a crack at it. Small museum staffers, accustomed to wearing many hats, are good at this. The reason so many proposals hit the wastebasket, according to executives in charge of corporate giving, is their failure to focus on the museum's individual, singular mission. They agree that articulating one's brand doesn't require the services of a highly paid grant writer.

A good grant proposal includes:

Description of what you need the money for. Be specific. If by shelving you mean bookshelves to hold a newly acquired and rare 150-book collection, say so.

Outline of how your project differs from similar ones—it's likely that your museum's core values and vision will be the distinguishing factor. Many museums offer STEM courses. If your plan centers on the mathematics found in Leonardo da Vinci drawings, say so.

Who will benefit from the project—think of your niche markets and remember that not-for-profit funders are legally bound to serve their own niche constituents. If your education program is designed specifically for immigrant parents to help them understand their children's homework, say so.

Goals of the Funder

Whether corporate, foundation, or individual, funders give according to their own goals, which are usually more stringent than what's written in their mission statement. Funders also like numbers. In lieu of numbers, they like an economic rationale. Cincinnati Museum Center addressed this funding reality when it commissioned an economic impact study, a measurement of how increased investment in the museum would benefit visitors, the public in general, and the vitality of the Cincinnati community.

Advocacy

When lobbying government officials, from the mayor to state and federal legislators, details are what's appreciated, and branding gets you thinking that way.

The Alliance of American Museums' suggestions for conveying the right message to your congressman also reinforce your brand:

- State what makes your museum essential to your community
- Highlight how much of your budget is dependent on charitable giving
- Describe the "unexpected" community programs you are reaching
- Enumerate the underserved populations are you reaching
- Note whether you have received any federal grants
- Invite board members, volunteers who have been inspired by your museums

Elevator Speech

The North Dakota State Historical Society devoted a newsletter to the best ways of lobbying governments, and the first article headlines this point: "Know your elevator speech."

The elevator speech is a short statement of your museum's brand mission, identity, purpose, DNA—call it what you will, you have to describe yourself perfectly in the course of an elevator ride.

Tell stories about your museum—vignettes about a school visit or a curator's process on a recent exhibition. Tell stories that will interest the official, so find out about his or her interests, what positions got him or her elected in the first place. Maybe with that information, you'd tell a story about the science class that visited your museum or about the museum's architectural history.

It's not enough to do good deeds; you have to publicize them. So take photos of your productive meeting and share them through social media. And then practice one of hardest rules of good branding: stay relevant. If there's a new program that will engage a new challenge for the legislator, e-mail it. Advocacy, like branding, requires regular updating.

Don't be shy about advocacy. It's legal and it's essential for legislators who want to adequately represent their constituency. At every level, local to federal, policy-makers appreciate that advocates are conduits between their respective niche issues.

Lobby Donation Box

From macro fundraising to floor-level donations, branding continues to be your friend. The value is not in the $1 to $5 level of giving, but in the reality that these prospective donors are already right in your building. They have seen your exhibits. They have shared space and ideas with like-minded visitors and docents. They have snapped photos and sent them, browsed the store, posed questions or comments on a gallery laptop, signed a guest book, picked up a brochure. Another value is end-of-visit reflection. Before visitors walk away, the donation box stops them, if only for a minute, with a reinforcement of the brand. As the Art Institute of Chicago says on its donation box:

> "Pitch In."

This is accompanied by a detail of American Gothic, the pitchfork-holding farm couple whose iconic image is one of many that distinguish the museum.

The National Civil War Museum, Kenosha, Wisconsin, says:

> "Help to Honor a Civil War Veteran"

It proceeds to tell a story about the soldier and his battle. Every $1,000 collected goes to one brick on the terrace of the museum. And then a new hero, a new story, starts. It perfectly fits the personality of the National Civil War Museum, which uniquely tells the story of the seven Upper Midwest states. This continuity, kind of a 1,001 Nights in museum storytelling, is exemplary.

At High Museum of Art, Atlanta, the donation box banner says:

> "Help us continue to make Atlanta the cultural capital of the Southeast!"

This positions the High as a culture linchpin in its city. It takes its obvious brand identity—art—and relates it to the niche that embraces The Arts. Its impressive architecture, with windows to every point of Atlanta's compass, reinforces a brand balance between the world and the community.

You picked a good field to toil in. Museums fill a need in every community. Your challenge is to drill down a little farther and discover your own niche.

Chapter 6

Education

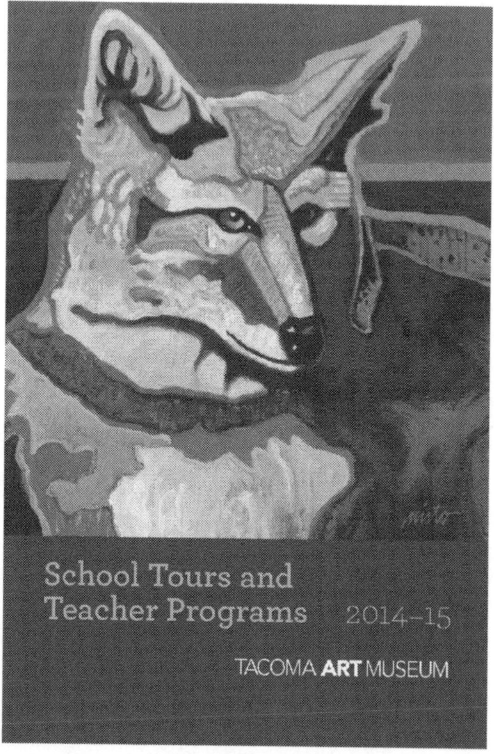

Figure 6.1 The cover for Tacoma Art Museum's school and teacher programs is a commanding image for the target audiences—schoolchildren and teachers, who are visitors, too. The Museum understands that every touchpoint reinforces its brand commitment to the communities and art of the Northwest and broader Western region. *Source*: Cover John Nieto, Coyote (detail), 2008, Tacoma Art Museum.

Problem-solve, say educators.
Innovate, says business.
Analyze and evaluate, says Blum.

You've heard it all because you've been doing it for years. Museums have always reinvented education in everything from tours to lectures to special events to new spaces.

Branding helps you get more credit for it.

This chapter talks about the goals and implementation of education and how branding augments your image from the generic "always-reliable" field trip to the specific "Your Museum." These are some of the ways branding keeps your museum from being taken for granted:

Depicts the museums as an exploration for schoolchildren
Envisions the museum as an adult destination
Elevates you above the 4'8" height of the average fourth grader to eye-to-eye level with adults, scholars, teachers of all grades, and the community
Augments resources with revenue from series tickets, purchases from the store and café, and facilities rental
Converts sightseers and program ticket holders to regulars and members
Gives you a name and a personality

By fulfilling many of the new education goals, museums add specificity and excitement to their brand identity. Here are some of those brand-enhancing goals:

1. Curiosity
2. Visual literacy and synergies of Visual-Aural-Read-Kinesthetic learning (VARK)
3. Problem solving through hands-on, project-based learning
4. STEM literacy
5. Peer teaching and learning
6. Lifelong learning adults

And here are some brand-enhancing ways by which museums implement the new education:

7. Flexible time periods, flexible walls
8. Stories
9. Helping the teacher
10. Catering to scholars and professionals

BRAND-ENHANCING GOALS

#1 Curiosity—Exploration

Curiosity and its partner exploration happen every time young visitors get a passport or treasure hunt card. They take a risk on this gallery, consider it, and try another. From curiosity flow sharing, comparing, and daring to evaluate. Museums make this brave new attitude possible, because they are safe environments, untied from grades and a grader at the head of the schoolroom. The exercise of curiosity is, by definition, glomming on to something that takes time away from the day's agenda. It must be encouraged and it can be taught. It requires a teacher to say:

"Sometimes the wrong train can get you to the right station."

Museums, when they open their doors in the morning, invite students to take a different train and see where it leads.

Let's give this word "curiosity" its due. Being curious, and having the motivation to follow one's curiosity, is a habit museums can help teach. In the taxonomy of learning that includes explore, investigate, and discover, Curiosity doesn't fit; it isn't a verb. But what a wonderful thing it is, and at the Spencer Museum of Art, the Cabinet of Curiosities has been resurrected. It's a big glass display case, allowing for 360-degree viewing and easy rotation as the spirit dictates. As a learning tool, it puts the responsibility on the learner who must not only imagine possibilities for the objects but also decide which ones appeal to his/her own curiosity, and then follow that line of inquiry. A student of any age might find rocks or carved marble, birds or places on a map interesting. I hope other museums find a place in their galleries and their programming for a Cabinet of Curiosity, because it sounds like a brandable concept for the Spencer. Where else could a teacher let students loose without ground rules to simply find something that makes them curious?

Children in Anchorage be forewarned: bring your questions. At the Anchorage Art Museum, each program, "whether it's a summer camp, school workshop or gallery tour [is] designed to let children ask questions and seek their own answers."

#2 Visual Literacy

Visual literacy is the "ability to construct meaning from images," says Brian Kennedy, who, as president and CEO of Toledo Museum of Art, took action on a cause that he'd been writing and speaking about for years. Because, the fact is that though we are a fiercely visual culture, very few learners have the vocabulary and grammar to speak Visual. Except for the so-called visual people—and they know who they are—most people trust words, not images, and that bodes ill for imagination, critical thinking, and visionary innovation.

Once again, museums are already saving Visual from becoming a dead language.

One museum docent remembers a first training session, which rightly focused on visual reading. It was difficult for every single one of the smart people in the docent group. The drill went something like this:

> Look at this painting.
> What do you see first?
> Describe it.
> What does it mean to you?
> What do you see next?
> Compare the two things.
> Why are they in the same picture?

One day I stopped to listen to a docent talking to a group of schoolchildren; she asked similar questions and instantly got a lot of answers. So visual literacy can be acquired, but it gets harder as we grow up and learn to be verbal.

When learners acquire the confidence to "read" visuals, they're ready to make confident evaluations. At the end of the basic 45-minute tour, docents ask:

> "What was the best part of this tour for you?"

The museum learner, despite many options, is empowered to judge.

VARK—Visual, Aural/Auditory, Read/Write, Kinesthetic

While more learners could and should be more confident in their visual literacy (the V of VARK), the synergy of learning styles—Visual, Aural/Auditory, Read/Write, and Kinesthetic—still works best. All good educators use the full portfolio, and chapter 2, "Tours," and chapter 1, "Exhibitions," detail the A and the R of VARK more fully from a branding perspective.

Tours—the A of VARK

Tours—school groups and adult—are inarguably the backbone of most museums' education programs. Whether conducted by a person who talks and answers questions, or by an audio device that talks and responds to button clicks, tours let learners use their ears while they look. For people unconfident about reading objects, the voice of a person is reassuring. A good script is not just descriptive but also explanatory. It offers examples, interpretations, and scenarios. If the narrator is skilled, his or her enthusiasm will inspire a similar curiosity in the auditor. An audio tour lets visitors curate their own tour, and that's instructive. A live person adds the connection and sharing that builds essential bonds with the museum. Tours let visitors become familiar with the museum; from this comfort and involvement, a brand is strengthened and a supporter is born.

Labels and Panels—the R of VARK

Visitors are used to reading words and learning from them, so good labels and panels are the basic comfort zone. When the information is presented in a hierarchy—from titling to explaining to evaluating—reading becomes easy and pleasurable, as much or as little as the learner wants. Some labels tell a great story. Some expand the information to the artist/maker and his or her era. Some leave a lot to one's imagination and intellectual powers. Labels and panels can be designed to reflect a museum's personality, so they make the learning an integral part of its core values.

When the High Museum puts labels on the floor on one gallery section, it says a lot about the power of looking. It's not the only museum to place labels in unexpected places, where visitors have to look twice at the exhibit. When the Museum of Contemporary Art, Chicago, Illinois, placed the labels for its Richard Tuttle exhibition up high, down low, and wherever the artist specified, they showed a new relationship between visuals and verbals; one had to think and ask: Why?

Kinesthetic Experiences—the K of VARK

What museums excel at is the kinesthetic approach to learning. Museums get people up and physically moving from idea to idea. Museums encourage visitors to talk to each other, sharing comments, questioning docents, interacting with everything from their cell phone camera to the merchandise in the store.

A most kinesthetic experience takes place every day at the tours offered by the Tenement Museum on the lower east side of New York. As visitors grab the banisters of the century-old building, climb the steep wooden steps, and peer into the bare rooms where immigrants once lived, they start to feel and connect with the way of life that's the mission of the museum. It's effective learning for students: In programs like *Meet Victoria Confino*, they get to see Vicky's world, learn from a costumed interpreter about the life of a fourteen-year-old immigrant who immigrated to America with her family in 1913 from southern Europe. They get to talk to Vicky about her challenges and, maybe, fears. It's learning that fuels curiosity and imagination, and demands evaluation. There's no other museum quite like it. And that exclusivity, rigorously adhered to by the Tenement Museum, is exemplary branding. Thanks to the education department for bringing the brand to shining, meaningful life.

Introverts and Extroverts

An interesting exploration into learning styles by Susan Cain, in her book *Quiet*, gives pause for thought. We think of kinesthesia as motion, but the senses can also sense calm. Calmness is a sensation that is especially valid in a museum. *Quiet* is a book about introverts and their place in a Western world that seems to favor talkers, doers, and group exercises. For the one-third to one-half of all students who are introverts—Cain's estimate—museums are a haven for studying. Museums provide quiet nooks and their visual stimuli all have labels, which can be quietly read. However, I could argue that museums also welcome extroverts, who thrive on stimuli, motion, and wide-open spaces. Introverts are sensitive to change, and like to explore carefully. Extroverts are risk-takers, and venture forth assertively. Museums are magical places that offer all kinds of experiences for widely divergent young people. Importantly, they are special places, unlike any classroom yet designed. Your learning place can own its unique space.

#3 Problem Solving through Hands-On, Project-Based Learning

Critical thinking, the beloved objective of K-16 education, is already a valued component of museum Education programs. And it's not just the "So What?" aspect of school and adult tours. Programs such as conferences, summer camps, and family weekends all provide the time and facilitation to think through an idea. So do some basic tours.

A wonderful example of hands-on learning comes from New York City's Tenement Museum, and it's firmly based on the brand of the museum:

> "Tenement Inspectors . . ."
>
> "Take on the role of housing inspectors in 1906. The assignment: investigate 97 Orchard Street to see if the building is up to code, and interview actors portraying the building's landlord and tenant to get both sides of the story. In 1901, New York State passed the landmark Tenement Housing Act, responding to hazardous and unsanitary tenement conditions. Come find out if 97 Orchard was in compliance, and delve into the broader questions of social justice and housing."

And this kind of problem solving is relevant for lessons in fields ranging from sociology to science. All courses intend to teach relevance—the lessons of history, the insights from literature, the meaning of scientific inquiry. Encouraging students to ask "So What?" puts the burden of finding relevance on them. In a museum, your museum, where every exhibit is new and a little strange, docents always say: "What does this mean to you? Why do you think it's important? How was this person's experience like your own?" Museum educators understand that relevance is a great tool.

#4 STEM Literacy

It's time to acknowledge the elephant in the room, the curriculum changer that comes in capital letters, STEM. If you're an educator, in any institution, your administration is exhorting you to bring students to science, technology, engineering, and math. The lure is one that museums know well—hands-on, problem-solving activities that foster critical thinking and innovation. Science museums will cheer, and the other museums will learn some tricks from them, as museum show students how creative science can be.

The Science Museum in London acts on its words. A challenging e-mail titled "Exciting new exhibition inspiring future engineers" opens to a web page that continues "Engineer Your Future" and an opening paragraph of text that asks "Could you shape the world we live in? Find out if you've got the problem-solving, big-thinking, team-working skills to be a globe-trotting engineer of tomorrow."

The e-mail, web page title, and text all state loud and clear the curiosity expected of tomorrow's innovators who will, at the museum:

- Design something (in this case, a space vehicle) that solves the problems of a strange terrain.
- Not just create something, but a thing that's better than their friends' creations.
- Test and question the existing truths, in this case a baggage-handling grid designed by experts.
- "Make the best better" and not settle for the first brilliant concept.
- Never expect, always finding new solutions in unexpected places.

Along with science museums, anyone who appreciates branding should be interested in STEM projects. STEM symbolizes all that is responsive and relevant; the way to prove you have a vibrant brand is to show that you face forward.

Many museums integrate science, technology, engineering, and math into their education programs.

At the National Textile History Museum in Lowell, Massachusetts, the mission is to survey the range of American endeavor through textiles, including the science of textiles. When you read this enticing description, the excitement of science reinforces the brand, and vice versa.

> Textiles impact every moment of your life in ways you may never have imagined. The clothing we wear, the clean water we drink, the sports we play, the cars we drive, and the roads we drive on are all possible through the innovation in textiles.

The Burpee Museum of Natural History states that students will "measure, estimate, observe, predict, classify, gather and record data." With that, the always-been-there museum housed in another old mansion takes on a new and vibrant personality of its own.

Taking a holistic view of STEM learning, Berkshire Museum in Pittsfield, Massachusetts, offers middle- and high-school teachers professional development courses in local, inquiry-based water science.

Art museums are showcasing science in their conservation labs. Examples are at The Ringling in Sarasota, Florida; Indianapolis Museum of Art; and Cleveland Museum of Art.

Children's Museums are natural places for inquiring, analytical, evaluative learning. At Mississippi Children's Museum, a core science module on heart health reinforces the permanent Healthy Fun Gallery with hands-on exhibits about "making healthy choices and learning about the human body."

And local historical museums can introduce their science side to their most loyal constituents—members who receive notices of their annual meeting. A 2015 annual meeting of the Winnetka Historical Society featured a talk on preservation.

#5 Peer Teaching and Learning

All you have to see is a docent talking to a tour group to see how museum education is changing teaching and learning. The docent, no matter how well trained, is, after all, a peer. And when the docent asks the people in the group to give their opinion, most people ante up. And that's not where the peer-to-peer learning starts.

As Future of Museums writes:

> There are strong indicators . . . that the next era of education will be characterized by . . . distributed [learner to learner, distance, hybrid] learning that is designed to foster the twenty-first-century skills of critical thinking, synthesis of information, innovation, creativity, teamwork and collaboration.

And, indeed, some time before the visit, the tourer has already called upon comments, tweets, and posts for peer information on your museum. During the tour, one visitor might turn to another for clarification. Sometimes the docent brings a printout that references other sources; it's all part of the shared learning. At the end of the tour, the docent might ask:

> "Twenty-four hours from now, what will you remember about what you saw today?"

End-of-tour comments and follow-up let tour-takers hear what others saw and thought. In a few days, many will receive and spend a few moments with a brief e-mailed questionnaire from the museum (their data has been collected from a ticket sales, store purchase, or auxiliary program) about their opinion of the visit, which input will be used by the education department to hone the tours and programs.

Exploration before, analysis during, and evaluation after the tour—all done with peer help—are educational triumphs that museums have performed for years, and which they do better every day. They are also feats of branding, because with each peer mention, validity and trust accrue.

Homeschooling

Museums, large and small, are fulfilling homeschooling parents' wish list with **élan**. At the same time, this new market segment builds the brand. Once again, by being demonstratively relevant, the brand is enhanced. Like STEM courses, homeschooling is a cultural badge of honor. Entertaining homeschoolers and their children distinguishes museums not only from other museums, but also from other cultural institutions, including schools.

Plimoth Plantation relates homeschooling to seventeenth-century Massachusetts, its brand focus. On its web page for homeschoolers, the introductory paragraph says: "Did you know that the Pilgrims taught their children reading and writing at home? Did you know that the Wampanoag used the natural world as an outdoor classroom where they could teach life skills? The Museum is an ideal place to let your children explore the past by being curious, interacting with Museum staff, and trying new things."

Like so many excellent aspects of the museum, homeschooling needs to be promoted. If your museum offers specific homeschooling tours or courses, give the program a name. If you can, relate course content to schooling of another era, as Plimoth Plantation does. If you set aside a day of the week for homeschoolers, call it Homeschooler Monday. Also, any tour that is offered to traditional schools can be branded with a line added to the description that echoes that of the Carnegie Museums: "Designed especially for enhancing the inquiry skills of home schoolers."

#6 Lifelong Learning Adults

Visitors come through your doors in many sizes and degrees of willingness to learn, so the opportunities for meaningful communication are many and varied. At the same time that museums are interpreting their exhibits, they are introducing the museum itself, and beginning a beautiful friendship. Lavish as much of that attention as possible on adults; they buy the memberships.

Education, of course, is not just for children; while everybody embraces that thought, the Anchorage Museum says it out loud. Its website states that its intended audiences are adults and educators, as well as children. This may be partially a marketing decision, given that the median age of Anchorage citizens is young, as compared with other American cities. However, it's a wise one for all museums to note, because of all the adults who support you: donors, members, corporate and community partners, facility renters, and everyone who presents a credit card at the store and café. And it's easy to reach a broad swath of adults socially because their social network growth is so steep. All you need to see is the number of comments on social networking sites like Yelp, TripAdvisor, and OpenTable to appreciate adults' willingness to learn from their peers.

Peer-to-Peer with Docents

Look at your docents carefully; they're adults, sharing their learning with other adults, and this is where training your docents, guides, and interpreters pays off in branding, as well as education. Adults cross your threshold with positive expectations far more precise than those of an eleven-year-old. Adult visitors have many years of museums to compare you with, and docents should try to discover those expectations. One way to get the adult-to-adult learning off to a good start is for the docents to arrive at the tour starting point 10 minutes in advance and be prepared to answer informal questions. On the dot of Start, they ask the assembled group where everyone's from. If your docents are museum-traveled, they might be able to say, with authority, that they know and admire that city's museum(s). This warm-up exercise starts the bond that grows during a tour, the familiarity that builds a brand. At the end of the tour, docents can make the bond lasting by staying around to answer questions. Many times, other tour members will join in. This time for shared reflection is also, by the way, a hallmark of the new learning. Education enriches your brand at every point.

Training Manual

The training manual reminds docents why the museum needs them, and elucidates the education message they are to deliver. Many guides lapse into platitudes about the love of learning or the majesty of museums, but this happens only in the absence of information. While docents are conveying the specifics of your museum's exhibits and mission, they must relate them to the museum as a whole. State the mission prominently in the manual. Show the logo proudly. If you have a signature line, use it prodigiously.

Use the manual as a way to talk professionally to your docents. Make it informative but collegial. Trust them with lots of facts, but don't micromanage. When docents understand your brand and mission, they can be fluent with the give-and-take that's so important to establishing relationships. The tone of voice of the handbook is as important as the details; scholarly or conversational, textbook or workbook, it sets the stage for how docents portray your brand.

Given the professional expectations placed on docents and guides, consider professional training in presentation skills. Local colleges have the names of Speech professors who can help you find coaches for communicating in the media age.

During every tour, docents, guides, and interpreters should connect the objects with the mission of the museum. Sometimes it's as simple as starting a topic with:

"Here at the Smith Jones Museum . . ."
"The Smith Jones Museum acquired this piece . . ."
"Musical instruments have always been a key part of the Smith Jones Museum mission . . ."
"This is an unusual plant in our area, and the Smith Jones is proud to display it . . ."
"Has the Smith Jones convinced any of you to become zoologists?"

Internal Branding

The manual serves another function besides training: it's an internal marketing piece. Marketing to one's own staff is an old and not-to-be-underestimated tool. Don't be shy about selling as well as telling. Your docents will take their enthusiasm home to family and friends. That same attitude will keep them from taking their enthusiasm to other nonprofit organizations. It's worth the effort to produce professional training and materials for these valued unpaid employees.

Chapter 7, "Boards and Volunteers," covers the branding significance of non-paid staff, but there's special resonance when they're interacting with peer visitors.

BRAND-ENHANCING IMPLEMENTATION

#7 Flexible Time Periods, Flexible Walls

Picture a graphic of a square factory building, clang lines radiating out of an illustrated bell, and regimented lines of workers walking in one door and out the other side. Nineteenth-century education is what Sir Ken Robinson illustrates and decimates in a TED talk, and what The Future of Museums terms "industrial-age learning."

Now observe how students move around a museum: wandering, stopping, or passing by, they curate their learning much as you've curated the exhibits. If, a week later, they wanted to return with their parents, they could skip ten grades and take the adult tour. Watch them teach their parents something they see. Observe how they share an item of interest with their virtual community. There are no physical or curricular constraints on their curiosity.

This flexible attitude is right out in the lobby at Tacoma Art Museum, which doesn't pigeonhole its education into school days or special programs. Just past the entrance is a big, open room where visitors of any age can fill a mesh basket (looks like a French fry cooker) with supplies and start to learn. They'll select from open shelves and racks full of pencils, water colors, sheets of high-quality paper, and go to work. There are frames for framing your work, and lots of uninterrupted peace and quiet. It's subtle branding, because art-making is such an integral part of an art exhibition. It's the new education to learn by doing, hands-on from the get-go.

Then there's the education department printed schedule of programs. The generic photo of touring children is included, but first comes the cover, where it's a bold brand statement. Three-fourths of the cover is a daring painting of an orange-eyed wolf coyote, artist John Nieto. Open the piece to a half-page painting of a bucking brown horse and rider, artist Bull Schenck. Big western art is the brand of the museum, and it's the big promise of the school tours, too.

In any education program, the whole museum plays a role. Classrooms could be anywhere, and no bell clangs, no stopwatch plays a ring tone, to mark the time period. This flexibility is essential to contemporary learning—the actual rendition of multiple screen media from television to mobile devices.

On a school or adult tour, the more exhibits or galleries passed, the more doorways promising different paths, the more chances of engaging a learner's interest. And the more opportunity to brand! Students will see all aspects of the museum's identity and unique personality. Brand loyalty starts with affinity for a few exhibits, and develops into a bond with the entire environment of the museum.

To create cohesion within the whole museum, the guide can point out galleries passed but not visited, note recent acquisitions, talk about the architecture and landscaping, and supply anecdotes about the people who make the art and artifacts. This whole-museum narrative works when introducing lectures or workshops, which also may cover just a portion of your mission. The total picture embraces not only space but also time, so visitors might be told about past and upcoming exhibitions. A museum has a full and rich story, one that helps attract and enfold all who enter. And it is a unique tale, so guides should be reminded to refer to the museum by name, the whole name, as they wander amongst many different exhibits and visually alluring panels. Encourage guides and other speakers to look beyond the script at hand, think of the museum in its entirety, and use phrases like "here at the Zoo," and, "when the Museum first held this conference . . ." One further step: always use the full name of the museum. It's your brand and it shows pride.

Niche Market—The No-Wall Learner

Museums educate not only through tours but also with lectures, courses, conferences, summer camps, seminars, videos, performances, and travel. Each of these attracts people who want to learn, and the learner is a niche market within your typical categories of visitor, member, series ticket holder, and student. The learner comes to you not just because you're a trusted museum, but because you stand out as a learning place; this is high praise, and it is fertile ground for branding. Make sure the museum's name and logo are on or near every learning resource. Learning resources and their accoutrements, in this context, include, but are not limited to:

- Lecture mailings
- Workshop materials
- Podium in lecture hall
- Folders holding handout material for courses and conferences
- Summer camp materials—print, online, mobile, and t-shirts
- Background in videos
- Trip materials—from one-day excursions to week-long tours
- Theater tickets
- Opening remarks from speakers introducing lectures, conferences, and performances

The energy of these teaching occasions carries a danger for your brand. Programs that appeal to Learners are appreciated as different from the traditional four-wall museum. That's what you wanted, but they will acquire their own identity if you don't continually link them to the museum that created them. Naming rights also steal some brand identity from the museum. When new performance spaces and auditoriums emblazon their names on tickets, website pages, and above the doors of the spaces themselves, the museum name gets lost.

Some of these topics are discussed in chapter 4, "Events."

#9 Helping the Teacher

Field trips, which are perhaps their first trip to any museum, accost students with new smells and sounds, new ways to socialize, new structures for the school day, and new people, not to mention new sights. Branding actually helps sort out all that stimulation. Branding gives museums a name; now you can build familiarity with a tangible thing, and not just a strange concept. From pre-trip preview materials through the actual visit to post-trip follow-up lessons, learning benefits from relating objects and interpretation to the mission of the museum; it puts the visit in context. For instance:

"We're visiting the Smithville Museum of the American Indian because it has a lot of objects that show what we're studying, how American Indians lived around Smithville, 400 years ago."

But wait. Before you put the museum in context for the children, learn more about the students, their educational environment, and the teachers and chaperones. That includes knowing the neighborhood of the visiting school, and how familiar its students are with museums.

It's not only the students who should be researched but also the teachers and chaperones. Learning their experience and level of involvement will improve the success of the tour and the chance of making a strong branded impression. When guides know the other players in each day's program, they do a better job of weaving the museum's personality into the fabric of the tour.

Once you discover the curricular niche your visit will attempt to fill, define it in your own words—as learning outcomes, the learning students will take away. Emphasizing these is a powerful way to imprint the mission and brand of the museum from the outset. Here's how Fort Worth Museum of Science and History describes some of its summer programs:

> Take Apart, Make Apart . . . . Enjoy taking things apart? How about repurposing one thing to create something new? Who knows what kind of machinery or electronics you may find in the Maker Studio to take apart as you design and invent an entirely new creation!

Chain Reactions . . . Create a Rube Goldberg inspired chain reaction with other museum guests.

By the way, note the analytical thinking in the first program, and the teamwork component to the second program, both excellent examples of what museums can offer education.

Learn About the Teachers and Chaperones

The teachers and chaperones are your allies in learning. Their enthusiasm for the museum and its exhibits will help seal the students' approval. Learn their names and call them by name; it aids collegiality and puts everyone on the same side. A written sign, welcoming Mr. Brown's class, is another way to recognize the teacher and make the students feel more at home and ready to learn. Learning names will remind you to add them—correctly spelled!—to your database. It also serves to introduce other people in the museum to the class, spreading the word about your interesting education programs to other stakeholders.

Some museums ask the teachers and chaperones to help in teaching and that's smart. You'll learn from each other, and they will experience the museum as participants.

Asking the teachers their interests and course load is more than professional politeness. It helps docents understand the importance of the field trip in a teacher's schedule, both at school and in his or her personal life. By discovering teachers' interests, hobbies, and special skills, the department can better adapt the tour and follow-up materials. When docents find common ground with their visitors, and vice versa, it's another link in the connection. Of course, after hours, teachers are just adults who are prospective repeat visitors and members. It's the same name in your database, but entered in a different data set as prospects for membership.

By the end of the visit, teachers and chaperones should buy into the museum and everything it stands for. They will have had a stimulating experience for their students, a pleasant change of pace for themselves, and an involving introduction to the institution. The goal is not only making this field trip successful but also establishing a foundation for many future visits—by these teachers and their peers, through the school or individually.

Providing pre- and post-visit materials serves the two purposes of familiarization: education and branding. Your first materials will give the museum's name and location, so students and parents know what's ahead. Preparatory readings or exercises give a flavor of the exhibits to come, and also a sense of the personality and mission of the museum. Follow-up lessons build on the memories that were begun on the trip.

Follow-up

It's important to frame the exit as carefully as the introduction. Ease up to the finale. Don't take away the crayons or project sheets right away or funnel them into a dark coatroom: It suggests that when the visit ends, the museum disappears. A cheerful debriefing space helps the students discuss what they've seen, or even act it out. A little energy expending is good—congratulate yourself that the tour has stimulated the children so much.

At the end of the tour, the memories start to form. Even the most stimulating education sequence will fade like exhaust from a departing school bus without follow-up from the museum. Before the field trippers ever leave, guides can ask students what they're going to tell their parents. This puts the visit in a familiar context and helps children recall their impressions. It's both a teaching and a branding tool, because it suggests discussion at home and ongoing reflection about their experience. If there's budget, send each student—and teacher—home with a memento of the museum. At the very least, facilitate photographs around a designated—brand reinforcing—museum space, object, or prop.

And then thank the teacher and chaperones by name, and invite them to return another time.

After the visit, a letter sent directly to the schoolroom, thanking the class for their visit, reminds everyone of the trip and the museum. The letter could thank students for asking such good questions, include some new information about the exhibits, and remind the class and teacher about upcoming events. It's both politic and brand-smart to copy the school principal. And so the database of contacts grows.

To reiterate, education programs open your museum to an ever-wider circle of interested people. The name of every educator, from lowest title in the hierarchy to the highest, should be in your database; they're particularly good prospects because they've already tried your product.

#10 Catering to Scholars and Professionals

The first professionals to embrace are the classroom teachers. We tend to think of them as existing only in front of twenty-five students. As customers of your museum, they are invaluable stakeholders.

Science Museum in London installed a special place for teachers—one that opens like a speakeasy—on selected Friday nights during the museum-wide Science Museum Lates.

Actually there are three brands involved with the Science Museum: The Museum Lates series of evening programs open to all; the Teacher Zone, which is a tangible room for teachers; and the MasterCard corporate sponsorship. All reflect the brand of the Science Museum. The events aren't just clever names. Their regular schedules have the consistency that strengthens a brand. They offer something new each time, always on theme but different enough to keep people returning and reconnecting; they bring like-minded people—teachers—together to bolster community. There's even a logo for the Teacher Zone, with a type font that's consistent with that of the Science Museum's logo.

The individual branded activity should always point back to the museum that created it and that maintains it. As museums become annexes to the schoolroom, they run the danger of becoming a commodity—the good old museum, always dependably wonderful, always professional, always there. They can't take you for granted if you're branded. With a brand, the museum is an associate professor, not just an adjunct.

The Teacher Zone gives itself that authority. Brilliant!

The Science Museum practices another good branding habit: good writing. Recognizing that creative teachers are an audience it wants to retain, its web pages never get tedious. Its writing is lighthearted and adult-appropriate. The headline on "Ice Balloon" page says: "Watching ice melt couldn't be more interesting." The subhead tempts the teacher: "Just the tip of the iceberg."

Artists and makers are another important adult constituency, which the Anchorage Museum addresses constructively. "POLAR LAB: Collective" is a (2015) program for emerging Alaska Native artists to study objects and collections of the museum. The program provides "an opportunity for artists to find inspiration, insights, and technical information from the collections, through close-up research and documentation, advancing their development as an artist and contributing to the relationship between artists and museums."

Teacher Education and Certification

Professional development courses are a natural for museums with research and scholarship bonafides, and that powerfully enhances the museum's brand.

When The Mariners' Museum offered a course on deep ocean life and exploration, it would naturally appeal to teachers of zoology, oceanography, and maritime history, to name a few disciplines. Thus, it will naturally be publicized to other teachers, their administrators, and the school board. Now an entirely new audience, who may have known the museum only by its wave-design logo, understands that this is no ordinary sail through the seas, but a real science museum. The logo, by the way, is a fine piece of branding. But no logo tells the whole story. Your whole museum tells the whole story.

When the Virginia Holocaust Museum teaches about the Holocaust and genocide, that's a natural. And because the course is part of state education requirements, offered in cooperation with the University of Richmond, it connects its brand to a much wider audience of students, academics, scholars, and everyone who reads a college catalog.

The museum's brand is burnished by the way it is recognized by the funder of the program:

The Holocaust and genocide are two curricular topics now required by many state departments of education. The reasons for this statewide mandate are well described by the State of New Jersey's 1994 legislation, titled "An Act Mandating Holocaust Education In Schools." It states, in part:

> The State of New Jersey is proud of its enormous cultural diversity. The teaching of tolerance must be made a priority if that cultural diversity is to remain one of the State's strengths . . . . The instruction shall enable pupils to identify and analyze applicable theories concerning human nature and behavior . . . [and] shall further emphasize the personal responsibility that each citizen bears.

Note the language: Cultural diversity, identifying and analyzing, personal initiative. All the goals of the new education, all amply manifested in a museum's learning scheme. This topic is taught in conjunction with Holocaust museums throughout the United States, in chapter 6, "Education."

Police Departments and Medical Schools

Students come in many ages and disciplines. Many are medical school students, part of a cohort that is not new, but increasingly interesting if you're serious about new audiences. One popular tour has beginning doctors diagnose figures in paintings, testing their diagnostic skills on "patients" who may have lived centuries earlier, and certainly aren't usually seen in a typical waiting room. The possible diseases on the wall run the gamut from dermatology to pediatrics, endocrine and rheumatic disease, leprosy, syphilis, and polio. If your museum was a science, children's, history, or art museum, you could teach the course. At the Metropolitan Museum of Art in New York, a course taught NYPD detectives to be more observant.

The possibilities for connecting your objects with a niche group of people with an intense calling, such as medicine, are the stuff of branding.

Much the way improvisational theater companies have developed courses to teach teamwork, leadership, and listening skills to businesspeople, museums will find that art, artifacts, and the process of curating help all professionals with observation, critical analysis, and "what-if" thinking.

Closer to your museum are the observation and analytical techniques used by docents for public tours. Select one painting—preferably a large one—and have your professionals observe and analyze it for, say, 15 minutes.

Then discuss it in small groups. Participants are encouraged to speculate, develop scenarios, and, upon reflection, change their minds. The only rules are those used by the teacher of the police course:

- Two words are not allowed—"obviously" and "clearly"— because what's evident to one person may not be evident to another.
- Don't read the labels—they're not relevant to this exercise. The artist and title aren't meant to tell you what to think.
- No pointing. Communicate verbally. Describe.

Academic Museums

Variations of these courses would give academic museums and galleries the much-needed curricular material for the programs demanded by their college or university at Columbia College, Chicago, whose students major in theater, cinema arts, business and entrepreneurship, and dance, as well as the graphic arts. The Museum of Contemporary Photography uses a similar technique in its talks, workshops, and written guides. For example:

- How can a portrait communicate information about our identity and standing in society?
- What do you notice about their body language and facial expression? How do they present themselves to the camera?
- How did . . . [the photographer] use techniques such as framing and composition and vantage point?
- Are there clues in the image that suggest when and where this portrait might have been made?
- What might we learn about the subjects based on where we find them?
- How does what we see here challenge, or conform to, our concepts of these places (nations/states/cities)?

Should Education Programs Have a Fight Song?

Think of every educational institution you've ever been part of. It's not the pennant, the seal, or the fight song you remember—though they are powerful symbols—but the experiences and the fellow students, the courses and the professors. Hands-on, experiential, hashed over, critiqued—each had a brand, a vibrant identity by which you value its importance in your life. Your museum's education programs perform the same brand function. Wave their banner.

Chapter 7

Board and Volunteers

Figure 7.1 Chinatown Gate frames the building housing the Wing Luke Museum—visible down the street. It exhorts prospective volunteers to "be a part of the community and volunteer at The Wing!" *Source*: © 2013 Margot Wallace.

"People like you liked . . ." It's now accepted that consumers listen to people like them for advice on what to buy, or what museums to visit. Yelp, TripAdvisor, and Facebook have become confidantes and experts they treat as friends. But long before the sharing economy was born, these friends were people they knew, like museum volunteers, or experts in their community, like board members. There were, of course, other sources of advice on how to spend an afternoon or where to donate money, but board members and volunteers carried a lot of the advocacy burden. They have always been brand ambassadors and they labor diligently and without pay, because they believe deeply in your brand and what it stands for. The two groups have hugely different responsibilities and functions in what they do for museums, and this chapter will discuss each group's range of activities that reinforces the brand.

Branding is very much a heartfelt thing. Many people work hard and smart at jobs they like; for nonprofit trustees and volunteers, it's a labor of love.

That said, there are guidelines for keeping loyal unpaid workers on brand. Just as employees have written job descriptions, those who work without a paycheck also need a checklist.

WHAT ALL BOARD MEMBERS AND VOLUNTEERS SHOULD KNOW

The following list identifies what museum professionals already know. It forms the foundational knowledge for trustees and the volunteers:

1. Understand the concept of branding
2. Respect the competition for visitors' and supporters' time and money
3. Use to the fullest the skills brought by trustees and volunteers
4. Think new
5. Have a script
6. Keep meetings on brand
7. Select appropriate agenda items to discuss at board meetings
8. Solicit
9. Support all events
10. Know when to say no (to donated services)
11. Meet the media intelligently
12. Play like a team
13. Governance
14. Pass the baton to new trustees and volunteers

This chapter explores internal branding, as it affects two special groups of non-employees, who work primarily for your brand mission and reputation.

Understand the Concept of Branding

Brands and branding must be taught. The first goal of brand-smart museum professionals is to teach the concept of branding in a nonprofit organization. The people who lend their expertise to boards and sign on as volunteers may already understand the principle of branding without realizing how it applies to museums. Remind members of your board and volunteers that a brand has two main purposes: to differentiate one product from others in its category and to build trust with its consumers. Tell them that branding is everybody's business. The concept of brand distinctiveness is put into practice every time board members solicit funds. The concept of brand bond is developed whenever a volunteer answers questions on a tour, chats about a store purchase, or directs a visitor to another part of the part of the museum.

Here are some of the branding verities that you, the professional, can impart to your trustees and volunteers:

- Your museum's core values, founding principles, personality, and image, and the singular features are what distinguish it from the competition.
- Your understanding that whatever other nonprofits they devote energy to, they will keep your museum's mission and vision distinct.
- Your reason for selecting them as board members was that you saw a match between their interests and the museum's brand.
- Your reason for accepting them as volunteers was that their skill and attitudes truly made them the human face of the museum brand.

Most museums look for prospective board members who are lawyers, accountants, media geeks, and connectors within the community. Museums look for volunteers who won't be bored by doing jobs ill-suited to them. When it comes to volunteers, the Chicago Botanic Garden multiplies that formula by ten and asks applicants to match skills ranging from data entry to public speaking. Good branding includes recruiting people who will be on the same page with you. They will be superb brand advocates if they feel well utilized.

Respect the Competition

In a culture and economy where consumers have finite amounts of money and time and unlimited choices of where to spend them, museums have to compete for visitors and supporters. You know this fact of museum life. You need to share your understanding with board members and volunteers who, in their loyal benevolence, may not stop to examine the many activities that steal business from you.

An excellent event from Plimoth Plantation demonstrates where competition could come from. Friends of Plimoth Plantation were invited to taste craft beers at "Living Proof—Celebrating the Makers," as part of the museum's ongoing exploration of seventeenth-century crafts. Of course, the museum's friends could just go to the local brew pub. It's your job to tell board members and volunteers how much their support is needed for museum events, because good brands know they're not the only game in town.

Nurturing trustees and supporting volunteers are equal priorities: one is the hand that signs off on brand-appropriate budgets; the other is the face of the brand to the public.

Recruit for Skills

A glance at the professional titles of the members of the board of Cincinnati's Contemporary Art Center is informative: attorney, banker, community volunteer, college professor, artist, interior designer, small business banker, elected city official, gallery owner, contractor, media executive, professor of theater, brand consultant. All these are credentialed, experienced minds, and that's before you consider personal skills and interests.

The main purposes of a board are to approve budgets, sign checks, and raise money. Whether or not they also advise and pitch in, their skills must be aligned with the brand. Money frees up more easily when the money-person understands the core values of the brand. Patron relations proceed more smoothly when all eyes focus on the brand vision.

Board members are spokespeople for the brand who operate at highly visible levels; they must understand the museum's brand and how they will help project it.

Volunteers are truly the face of the brand, because they are on the floor and in the field, interacting with many kinds of people (including prospective donors!) at less guarded moments. Both need acculturation to the museum's values and personality.

Many museums utilize a questionnaire to ascertain degree of interest of prospective volunteers. You want them to respect the brand, not add to their own resume. The same thinking applies to prospective board members. Some questions to ask them are:

1. Name three of our museum programs, activities, or amenities that interest you the most.

2. How do you think the museum adds value to the community?
3. If you have volunteered at museums or other organizations before, how would you rate these experiences:
   - It was what I expected based on the description given by museum staff or in published material.
   - I was given the help and supervision I needed to be successful.
   - I felt that I made an important contribution to the museum's work.
   - I felt that my volunteer time was well utilized.

All volunteers, the generals and the troops, are visible in other ways: they talk to their families, chit-chat with buddies, and share their opinions with thousands of friends. Click. Send. And without divulging any secrets, your brand is disseminated worldwide. Your board and volunteers need to understand how to keep their communications on brand, and the repercussions of veering off brand.

Sometimes it's a matter of new vocabulary. Of course, you want to encourage spreading the word, and with a little rehearsal it can be done with the right words.

Think New

Loyalty has two edges to its valiant sword. In protecting their beloved museum brand, trustees and volunteers may unconsciously resist new directions. Creative destruction to directors and curators may feel like chipping away at the foundation to them. One such change is the switch to storytelling, to painting a broad idea around selected objects. For those who have long loved the museum, according to the experience of one director, it will merely put old favorite displays out to oblivion.

Have a Script

One of the informal filters that separate good trustees from so-so board members is their ability to communicate. They usually speak well and relate to others admirably—a notable exception being artists, whose verbal skills are usually placed second to their visual-musical-theatrical talents. Well-spoken or clumsy with words, board members need a script. Often called an elevator speech, it's a concise, confident mantra of your museum's brand. It takes many tries before you'll write a good one. Plan on several trial runs to make sure the lines are, indeed, deliverable in a short but meaningful slice of time. As board members talk to prospective donors and community leaders, they will comfortably talk the talk. Most dealings with prospects are informal, and loose brand messages can capsize the underwriting and solicitation process.

The script is useful when dealing with all stakeholders. Vendors should understand your brand. So should educators, scholars, and local governments. Considering that volunteers also speak regularly about the museum—to family, friends, prospects, the media—make sure they also get copies of the script.

Here's another tool for your trustees and volunteers. Whether you're advising a board member on fundraising or training a volunteer, prepare a one-page handout for them to use in preparing their solicitation, giving a docent talk, or just conversing casually with customers in the museum store:

- Be direct. If you keep your talk short, you won't be tempted to stray off strategy.
- Ask for feedback. That's how you'll know if your message got through.
- Be informed about details around the museum. It's assumed that if you're involved, either as a powerful trustee or a regularly scheduled volunteer, you have all the answers. Branding is not just about vision; the best branding is in the details.
- Sense when the others have not understood your point and rephrase what they are saying so that it better represents the museum's message. Don't put words in their mouth; speak words that others understand.

Keep Meetings on Brand

No rubber chicken lunches. No rubber stamps. Make every meeting count, and that includes deciding up front whether this is a social event—with chicken—or a brown bag meeting. You might want to provide sustenance but, unless you're a food museum, a big meal is off brand. Most people today appreciate such frugality. The through line of every board and volunteer meeting, regardless of agenda, is: "Is this part of our brand?"

To keep to the agenda, and also stay on brand, heed these meeting guidelines:

- Updates from the museum staff. If news breaks between meetings, the president of the board should send an e-mail or pick up the telephone, and outline what's going on. All board members are responsible for keeping the museum on track.
- Attendance is essential. The expectation of their individual donation does not exempt a board member or volunteer from meetings. Woody Allen echoed centuries of wise leaders when he said: "80% of winning is showing up."
- Introduce board members and volunteers to each other—job, volunteer activity, hometown, interests. This is not just good team management.

When everyone sees the variety of personal brands, it sets the stage for brand thinking about the museum. One corporate manager disallows people citing their children. Everyone has children, she admonishes. Tell something different.
- Keep task forces and committees relevant. The director of volunteers doesn't let just anyone serve on the aquatic plants team or the docent corps. Use the same restraint with trustee committees. You need breadth of viewpoints, but not all the views, all the time. Get in the habit of curating your committees. The "anyone can do this" attitude is antithetical to the rigor of branding.
- Strategize the first meeting. With regular board turnover, the first meeting of the year sets the tone. It's a perfect time to present and readdress your brand.
- Keep branded minutes. Whoever writes the minutes is well advised to include the brand message. Minutes are official documents, and it's appropriate to also record the museum's identity. However they're distributed, in print or electronically, minutes should carry the museum's logo, tagline, or mission statement.

Meetings occupy ninety minutes. Museum work weeks cover forty-plus hours. Keep the former on brand, and you stand a better chance with the latter.

Select Appropriate Agenda Items to Discuss at Board Meetings

There are many subjects a board can and should put on its meeting agenda. Use valuable board meeting time to discuss brand-building ideas. Eschew busy-work projects that can better be done apart from board meetings.

Brand-Enhancing Agenda Items

- Deciding on an appropriate personal message that members can hand write on benefit invitations.
- Planning the theme and location of the annual benefit.
- Discussing new board members you want to recruit—an ongoing project.
- These are all subjects to discuss at a board meeting; they affect the museum brand.

Brand-Irrelevant Agenda Items

- Envelope stuffing is a busy-work function doable by staff or volunteers.
- Arranging the benefit flowers, bringing the event food, and purchasing the projector are tasks that many small-museum boards shoulder, but they're additional, not key, to board meetings.

- Calling a list of names is a tactic; if telephone solicitation is necessary, it's a personal task, to be done outside of meetings.

Solicitations

Although some experts feel this is the bailiwick of the development office, not the board, soliciting funds comprises some portion of every board member's time. It is essential for anyone who asks for money to describe the product impeccably. This is a sales call and you have to know your product. Know the museum's brand promise, and if this is a specific campaign, articulate the mission. Use the tagline or slogan if you have one. Talk about "the brand." Corporate donors will understand, and funders will recognize it as the distinguishing niche they require. Having a brand makes all financial transactions more credible.

Grants are pure branding. A funder receives dozens—hundreds?—of similar requests from like-minded institutions, often from comparable museums. They are obliged by the terms of their fund to be selective and then discriminating. What unmet need does your museum uniquely serve? How do your programs and rationales set you apart? If your project isn't uber-distinctive, they won't find a reason to fund it. Good grant writers understand brand thinking, even if they don't use the term itself. They deal with the specifics and inherent values that distinguish your project from any competitor's.

Support All Events

Boards, to a large extent, are accountable for big events, and select small events. First, they approve their budgets, based largely on their adherence to the mission.

Second, they promote and attend the events, always framing them as exciting ways to engage the public in the goals of the museum. Volunteers may also be enlisted functionally the day of the event. Both groups, because of the huge added effort, need to know how the "event" reinforces the museum brand. As discussed in chapter 4, "Events," your events are highly specialized initiatives that target groups of like-minded people to better draw them into your brand. Think of events as dynamic branding opportunities that reaffirm loyalties and motivate deeper involvement.

Benefits and Galas

The gala, with its attendant publicity, excitement, and cost, is the perfect place to flaunt your brand. The name, venue, food, guests of honor, invitations, and décor all combine to augment your brand statement. The board will, of course, support all events, with attendance, perhaps funding, and always with brand messaging. Board members should never promote an event, even casually, without linking it to the brand and mission.

Hosting a Table

Whether the event is a gala or an afternoon tea, you may be asked to bring a group of eight to ten friends. This is engagement at a personal level, with invited guests who appreciate the museum's mission and your role in it. They aren't spending a lot of money on the event, but they will be spreading the word to friends. By all means, utilize dinner conversation to talk about the museum and introduce your brand-appropriate friends to each other.

Honorees

Of course, guests of honor and celebrities are selected to rigorous criteria, even if they're good friends of a board member. Give them a short script, so they can pay tribute to your museum and reiterate why they are a fit for your brand.

Members' Tours of the New Exhibits

Board and upper-tier members' previews of an exhibition are a perk for, and a way to thank, your highest donors. Relatively easy to organize, behind-the-scenes tours are very much on brand. Since exhibits and exhibitions reflect the mission of the museum and its brand, make sure all board members understand the connection between exhibition and museum brand, and can articulate it to anybody at the event. This is especially important because the media might also be present. Smile and say "branding."

Nametags

Board members and volunteers are your ambassadors, so give them a sash and a medal—or at least a well-designed, logo-imprinted, permanent name badge, to be used at all events. We are an ID culture, with lanyards and magnetic pass cards in the real world and @ addresses in the virtual one. At events, nametags also visually identify the museum's brand.

Visitors at events, like those at the museum itself, always have questions, and they need someone with credentials to give answers. A docent at a museum's member event once noticed that many guests were asking the guards, the only people at the swank soiree who looked like museum employees. Board members' nametags might additionally say: "Ask Me Questions." This is a prime time to engage guests, and board members are particularly good at learning talking points.

Know When to Say No

Board members are well placed to hear about in-kind donations. They may get naming rights inquiries. They must know how to say "no." Volunteers also can be asked about donated items. It's best to forward all such inquiries to the museum director. Here's the way to nicely say "no":

> "We're so sorry, but that lovely item is not consistent with our brand mission."

Follow up with a recitation of IRS policy on not-for-profits adhering to the terms of their 501(c) (3) designation.

Meet the Media Intelligently

Fortune smiles on you if the media calls you for a story or quote. You can hope for media interest in an event, but be prepared for out-of-the-blue calls. Especially if you're the local expert on a topic—photography, or prairie recipes, or Civil War battles—you should expect calls. Don't just answer the question, but also link it to the mission and identity of your museum. Be brand-ready.

Play Like a Team

Trustees are part of a board. Volunteers are part of a corps. They have the same relationship with each other as they would in an office; the only difference is that they aren't spending two thousand work hours a year working together. It's the museum's job to simulate the common cause of a job with the shared values of the museum. Remind them with regular conference reports and e-mail notices. Send all communications on your letterhead or in e-mails with a logo signature. You might want to consider having business cards, e-mail addresses, or letterheads available for trustees and volunteers, as appropriate. When on museum business, they represent the museum, not themselves and certainly not any company that sends them a paycheck.

Create a volunteer newsletter that keeps them informed and involved. Mention volunteers' names in the newsletter. They'll remember to talk the brand message if they're regularly reassured of how important they are to your brand.

Write all instructional materials that go to volunteers with verve. Unpaid workers work too hard to be bored, or to think you're bored. Your communications to the volunteers should be as thoughtful as the materials you create for visitors, donors, and sponsors.

As you talk to trustees and volunteers, formally or informally, state the name of the museum, so that they remember to do the same for contacts and visitors. It's inclusive to say "we" when talking to trustees and volunteers, but it's smarter to say the name of the museum. *The Chicago Botanic Garden: Volunteer Handbook* puts its mission on the first page and its logo on every sheet in the volunteer packet. It notes that the institution is "popularly known as 'The Garden'" and, indeed, that is the term used in all volunteer materials. A nice extra touch: the store-bought folder is bright leaf-green.

Materials for the board of trustees should be businesslike at all times. And that includes business letterhead and museum e-mail addresses.

Make sure the board meeting-space or volunteer sign-in area is branded in some way so that trustees and volunteers feel a part of the museum while working there. Post a logo and mission statement. If you supply notepads, or worksheets, use your logo or letterhead. Pass around name tags, with museum identity. "Hello My Name Is …" labels should be avoided.

Rule of thumb: Never go cheap with the people who donate valuable time.

Governance

The Alliance for American Museums endorses the following, which were written by the Minnesota Council of Nonprofits, among the many responsibilities and legal obligations of the board of trustees:

- Determining the organization's mission and purpose
- Determining which of the organization's programs are consistent with its mission and monitoring the effectiveness of these programs
- Clearly defining and articulating the organization's mission, accomplishments, and goals to gain support from the community and enhancing the organization's public image

Your mission is your brand. It's everything your museum stands for, aims for, and wants to be perceived as. Your mission and your brand are the identifying values by which you are understood and trusted. Mission statements are lofty; your brand is exercised and reinforced every day.

Pass the Baton

At the end of the board year, as you assemble and organize the notes from your committee chairs, document how each agenda item, each initiative, each budget line reflected your brand. Whether on paper or online, your brand now becomes law, *de facto* if not *de juris*. When put into words how your brand was deployed, it can be easily explained to next year's board. Some members will be continuing, of course; it's also wise to reflect in May and review in September.

The volunteer corps also turns over and, as with boards, its members move to other organizations, other towns, other commitments. At the end of the year, leave them with a strong impression of your brand.

INTERNAL BRANDING AUDIT

Periodically, sit down and review your branding with your board and volunteers:

- Have we recruited, integrated, and trained our board members well?
- Do we have a brand and can everyone define it?
- Do we know our competition?
- Is there a script to use when talking to our constituents?
- Do we solicit with a coherent sales message?
- Do we tie the exhibitions and events to our mission?
- Are our benefits good branding tools?
- Do our vendors and pro-bono suppliers understand our mission?
- Are we prepared for the media, new and traditional?
- Does every board meeting reflect and reinforce our mission?
- Does every volunteer reflect and reinforce our mission?

Chapter 8

Marketing

Figure 8.1 The Log House, an iconic structure in the Village of Winnetka, is an apt signature visual for the Winnetka Historical Society. Its windows form the stylized graphic that goes forth in all materials—from program invitations to newsletters to the website—with total branding consistency. *Source*: © 2015 Margot Wallace.

The responsibility of the marketing department is to guard the brand image and identity in marketing pieces disseminated to your museum's diverse stakeholders. The watchdog doesn't let anything leave the museum that isn't "on brand." It barks at anything that is "off brand." Marketing communications include brochures, newsletters (online and printed), magazines, logo, website, social media, blogs, booklets, posters, invitations, and ephemera.

The people in the marketing department, by function, have the training that guards the brand: the instinct for consistency and brand-specific communication. They also have the computers that hold the files of type fonts, logos, and images that represent the brand. In a small museum, where much of the marketing is contracted out, the watch dog is the person with the authority to say "Stop, let's look at this again."

While this book thinks broadly about branding at every touchpoint in your museum, it's in the marketing department that your identity transforms from "what we do" to "what we say"; from the fulcrum of the marketing department that message gets disseminated very far, very fast. The branding opportunities and dangers will be flagged and examples of other museums' on-brand marketing pieces will be described.

This chapter will deal with print content. Digital Content brand strategy and challenges are covered in chapter 12. The unique brand opportunities in publications such as magazines, annual reports, and exhibition catalogs are covered in chapter 17. If you're interested in delving more deeply into actually writing these communications, that's a chapter the size of a book; I refer you to my recent publication, *Writing For Museums*.

The watchdog responsibilities of the marketing department covered in this chapter are as follows:

1. Noticing and speaking up about what's On Brand and what's Off Brand
2. Developing, selecting, and using images consistently
3. Using your verbal message with consistency
4. Consistency
5. Invoking strategy and relevance
6. Brochures
7. Booklets
8. Newsletters
9. Posters
10. Ephemera—invitations, tickets, program handouts
11. Signs and environmental graphics
12. Business cards and letterhead
13. Local radio and television

RESPONSIBILITIES OF THE MARKETING WATCH DOG

Noticing and Speaking Up About What's On Brand and Off Brand

A watchdog is trained to sense danger; to simply get a little snarly in something seems foreign to your brand message. This marketer might not know everything about the brand, or how its message should be written, but he or she has the instinct to ask the questions: Is this On Brand? Does this seem Off Brand?

The real problem in questioning brand relevance is that many marketing people are interns, part-time or freelance. They can't be expected to know the brand look, and may not have the courage to question the person who gave them the job. Small museums must take time with freelance designers to explain and monitor the brand image.

Honing an ability to gauge On Brand and Off Brand requires that the marketing and graphics people know what's happening, all over the museum. They should tour the collection and special exhibitions, experience the programs of the education department, hear the goals and means of development, read the plans of the board of trustees, and understand the scholarly research that informs the museum. This is a lot of knowledge, but brand marketing cannot proceed uninformed.

Conversely, those other departments should be aware of what each is sending through marketing and graphics. Curators must see the mailers that development is mailing out. Trustees need to know what's on the cover of press kits. Sales associates in the museum store must see what the website is selling. And everyone, every so often, should ask the marketing folks for their opinion.

When the various departments within a museum have their own budgets, and can deal directly with the marketing department, the results are predictable, with every department getting its own table tent, brochure, or event invitation. Small museums might envy this "problem," but they have their own danger zones: One person wearing too many hats tends to deal too quickly with jobs as they pop up. Take the time to pause and reflect: Is this really On Brand? Some typical On Brand-Off Brand questions that writers and designers should ask about are:

Newsletter: Is this story relevant to our brand personality?

Brochure: Do these photos reflect our brand distinctiveness?

Store sign: Is this item description meant to sell a piece of jewelry, or a memory of the museum?

Invitation to Opening Night of Exhibition: The party sounds fun, but what's the connection to the exhibition that the curators so carefully thought out?

Developing, Selecting, and Using Images Consistently

Look at any ad, poster, or brochure: the ones you actually stop to read attract your attention with a good visual. When art directors and designers talk about "the look" of a marketing piece, they include every visual element from the typeface to the colors. Although it takes a visual person to see all these details, museum people have the advantage of working daily with visuals, and it's not difficult to train yourself to learn how to think visually. To teach yourself this graphic form of communication, take a brochure in one hand and a pencil in another and drag the lead down from the top to the bottom of every page; everything your pencil encounters is a visual, and each one influences your brand. By the way, the type in which words are set are also visuals. Look at the schedule of tours on the sign at the information desk and see if the type font is your font. Thumb through the employee and volunteer handbooks to see how often the logo and other design elements are used, and whether the paper is the same quality as you hope for from your workers. Pick up a media kit or facilities rental packet and see if the folder bears your logo, color palette, and type font. Every marketing piece, external or internal, sends a message about the museum and must be brand-conscious. Never let the reader wonder for a minute what museum they're looking at.

Choosing the right photograph presents challenges, because there are either too many or too few. Select photos that best represent the mission, that show the building, that contain relevant props. Smiling heads are a constant in all newsletters, so try to shoot people in front of an exhibit, or holding a prop, or in front of a sign with the museum's name. If no photographs adequately depict your brand identity, write a caption that elucidates it.

The Steelworks Center of the West, the former Bessemer Historical Society, has a look: It uses industrial colors of orange and brown, not the big blue sky of cowboy country. The Steelworks Center logo shows stylized silhouettes of silos, not cactus. The photographs on its pages depict steelworkers in factories and mineshafts. The photograph on one of the Museum Store pages achieves a new high in good branding. Instead of showing stuff that can be found on any museum store shelf, it selects a photo showing the original company store that served the industrial community that formed a large part of Pueblo in 1900. Every image reinforces the look of the brand.

Color

Colors are hard to keep, aside from those in your logo. Brochures must revolve around strong, communicative visuals, and the strength of the photo trumps its color. Websites must sacrifice color if it makes the text illegible. However, recognize the branding power of color in distinguishing one museum from another. For a good demonstration, access the website of

Historic Charleston Foundation (SC) and on the first page watch the homes scroll laterally: some are surrounded by pink azaleas, some by black wrought iron fences; and the ochre and green of Rhett-Aiken House Museum contrast starkly with the bright white pillars of the Elizabeth Thompson House and the apricot walls of the Nathaniel Russell House Museum.

Keep a watchdog's eye on large visual areas, as well as the small ones. For example, invite a visual person to check out the lobby, which is, after all, the visitor's first and last impression of the museum. The information desk in the lobby of the Franklin Institute in Philadelphia features overhead panels with science video. The visitor knows immediately what kind of a museum lies ahead. When your meeting rooms are used by business or community groups, identify them boldly. This could be wall signage, with your logo, or notepads and pencils with your logo. At the very least, provide a stack of brochures that identify your museum's programs. If you have bought space in kiosks in airports, malls, convention centers, or other heavily trafficked area, use the logo double strength. It will be competing with dozens of other visuals for the attention of an easily distracted audience. At Chicago's O'Hare airport, a fifteen-foot dinosaur towers next to the souvenir shop of the Field Museum. Busy travelers buying last minute gifts for the kids can identify the origin of their purchase.

Logo

Your logo may be the first visual you design, and even if it only hints at your brand promise, it is charged with the huge task of personifying it. Viewers of any marketing piece—poster, ad, video, e-mail news—know from experience that the logo identifies the sender. It is a shorthand communication that says volumes about your brand personality and heritage. It's your signature. The months of effort spent on developing a logo also helps your staff coalesce around your brand distinctiveness.

St. Augustine Lighthouse and Museum positions itself as a museum, not just a tourist site as so many lighthouses are, and its stylized logo shows a lighthouse tower with the light emanating from its window, not its beacon; this is a welcoming place to enter and learn.

The logo development task is best given to experienced designers who know how to create an identity program usable on all materials. It's not just a matter of creating a unique mark, but of finding one that will be reproduced on all materials, in all sizes, and in black and white as well as color. It must look as good on a glossy magazine as it does on a merchandise label or visitor tag. Whether seen on a wall label, podium, or board minutes, it must be seen as the embodiment of the museum. The typeface that carries the tagline must work with the logo and be both distinctive and readable. And the logo and tag line entity must travel well, by electronic file, photocopy, or fax.

Choosing a Designer

The process of selecting a designer is key. Interview several, get recommendations from other clients, and study their online portfolios. Ask if the candidates have experience working with not-for-profits. Make sure the designer understands your brand and is willing to live with it over a period of time. Most logos take longer than expected to complete, and designers end up making less money than they thought. You don't want them to feel frustrated. Realize also that designers like to display logos in their portfolios and might design something too creative (and insufficiently On Brand) for your requirements.

A successful logo, and logo designer, will go through many iterations. After the initial concept has been selected, there are choices of style, period, or technique. The same image can be modern, colonial, global, or grunge. A logo created with a paintbrush look will convey a different identity than one that looks chiseled, and computer software has made the variables of design limitless, with very little effort. Good graphics professionals, by nature and training, look at simple ideas from dozens of perspectives. They try and discard, and try again.

When the typeface is used accurately, and the palette of colors is established and adhered to, the look, logo, and tagline are ready to go on all materials seen by the public. This includes all the usual marketing pieces, plus overlooked surfaces such as exhibit labels, every page of the website, invoices, store merchandise tags, café menus, all educational material (even those handed out to grammar schoolers, which are seen by their teachers and parents), audio tour wands, employee manuals, the printed agenda at board meetings, and the podium at lectures.

The power and communication value of a brand logo also depends on its size. If you're co-sponsoring events with corporations, local businesses, or other not-for-profit institutions, negotiate the size and placement of your logo. Neither partner should be overshadowed by the other. At all events, provide name tags, with your logo. Remind event and meeting attendees of where they are, and whom they're sharing the experience with. This applies to volunteer meetings, garden walks, and small programs, as well as large public events or benefits.

Do a preview test of the size-clarity effectiveness of your logo. Photocopy it in black and white and reduce the image to the size of a postage stamp. Can you still identify your identifier?

Every surface is a marketing tool and some, such as business cards and name tags, are very small. Here's where your logo and color palette prove their power. When used with consistency, they will identify your museum, and the person representing it, as grandly as if they were a sandwich board.

A fine is example is the 3" square red lozenge identifying French historic homes. France owns the best nation brand in the world, and has earned it. Museums have earned one of the best culture brands in the world, and in France, every other building seems to have historic value. In the case of Illustrious Houses, they are branded with a crimson seal from the minister of culture, signifying to passersby and visitors their heritage and reputability. Instant communication, reassurance, distinctiveness, and consistency in every city in France: this epitomizes good branding. There may well be a similar organization of culture attractions in your region.

Using Your Verbal Message with Consistency

Marketing pieces are ambassadors. You set them loose and hope the messages they deliver are perceived the way you wanted, that they accurately reinforce your brand. Every single piece that leaves the marketing department—even if the department is just a photocopying machine—reflects your brand's core values, identity, and vision.

At the outset of writing a brochure or newsletter, words may come with difficulty, and the tendency is to fall into the comfort of mushy clichés. Quality, excellence, engagement, and commitment are some of those clichés. Get in the habit of using examples. When you are struggling for your distinctive brand message, the accumulation of specific details will help you through.

The Museum of Contemporary Photography at Columbia College, Chicago, fills its letter from the director in one of its print pieces with details of accomplishments: names and descriptions of exhibitions; the debut of a booth at EXPO Chicago 12, a major international art show; a candid explanation of donor benefits; and the high school mentorship program, "Picture Me." The specifics of your staff's hard work are fascinating: flaunt them. Details are describing a recipe: it could be summarized as delicious, but could be so much yummier when the ingredients are named.

Tagline—The Little Words That Sum Up Your Mission

If all branded marketing materials start with a look, they end with a tagline. The tagline is a short phrase that appears below or beside a logo, a short form of your message. British marketers call it a strapline, which nicely suggests a tight wrapping up of your valuable brand. The tagline proclaims what your institution stands for, not only on brochures, flyers, websites, and magazines, but also on letterhead, signage, menus, merchandise tags, and other printed and spoken communications.

A few rules pertain to taglines, the first being: Keep the same tagline and keep it to one. Despite the fun and ease of cranking out lots of clever slogans, after the brainstorming sessions end, just one line must emerge. It's inclusive and effective to open up the tagline process, inviting the suggestions of staff and volunteers, and testing one line against others. This puts thoughts on core values out on the table, where all concerned parties can debate them. It may be the only time that everyone in the museum has a chance to discuss brand and mission, and come together with a common goal. The danger is compromising a clear-cut branding position by flattering everyone and combining several taglines. However enticing multiple taglines may be, they split your personality into pieces. Choosing just one is staggeringly difficult, but stick with it and then band together to use it. It's your signature.

The need for a tagline becomes evident at the beginning of a capital campaign, when strangers want to know who you are and why you're more deserving than other institutions. Going through the tagline process provides the concise answer. Foundations also want to know your unique place in their deliberations, and grant writing begins with a point-of-view that should be as clear as a tagline.

The tagline is an inexhaustible ally. When a prospective donor, or employee, or editor says, "Tell me about your museum," all you need say is the tagline.

A tagline ties your multifaceted marketing efforts into a coherent whole, and each individual piece is seen as a continuation of the main message. The tagline is a memorable, shorthand expression that extols your museum wherever it is seen. A small budget stretches much farther with the same tagline on every piece. If the recipient of an e-mail then visited a website, then visited the museum, and then brought home a brochure, the following taglines would continually reinforce the brand message:

Smart Museum of Art, Chicago: Small worlds. Worldly art. So Smart.
The Autry (museum, Los Angeles): Go West. Explore the Unexpected West.
Burke Museum (of natural history and culture), Seattle: Discover . . . the life before you.

At any stage of the tagline and logo process, focus groups are a good idea. Internal groups, chosen from administration, curators, board members, employees, volunteers, and even visitors, cost little and provide valuable insights on the effectiveness of the communication.

With a good logo and tagline, and a history of consistent marketing pieces, museums can multiply the effectiveness of each piece, save on production costs, and easily stamp their identity at innumerable touchpoints.

Consistency

Brand consistency would be easy to enforce if museums realized how much effort and money is saved by always using the same message, logo, tagline, typeface, format, and style. When the brand look and message are used consistently, brochures stand out on tourist racks, website visitors always know where they are, links connect to known places, posters are worth the printing costs. Museums save money, time, and aggravation by following the amazingly efficient law of consistency: Stick with one message, don't change the look, and don't reinvent the wheel.

While everybody is responsible for maintaining the brand, the marketing department has the greatest opportunity to lose it. The brand look, or visible image, is so potent that, when it deviates from the established, it's as good as gone. Every time a museum changes its taglinc, or trics some new design formats, or varies its writing style, it feels like a different museum. On the other hand, every time a marketing piece reiterates its tagline, repeats its design format, and hews to its writing style, it feels like the old, familiar museum. No marketer can afford to keep switching its look; there isn't a big enough budget in the universe to keep customers loyal if the image keeps wandering.

The Vesterheim National Norwegian-American Museum and Heritage Center, Decorah, Iowa, does an uncannily consistent job of proclaiming its brand identity, and its website is worth noting here. Every photograph on every page contains a Norwegian flag, Norwegian craft object, or Norwegian ski sweater. Every paragraph of the text refers to heritage, history, connection, or experience. It's a small museum, in a small Midwest town, yet its presence is grand because of this proud consistency.

There are many decisions made as a branded piece works its way through the marketing and graphics department. First, consider a museum's many publics—including visitors, members, donors, sponsors, educators, the community, the business community, the neighborhood, scholars, employees, suppliers, government, and the media. Then imagine all the different marketing materials produced over the years for each one. These many pieces frequently come from the minds and hands of different designers, writers, photographers, illustrators, and printers. Even experienced marketing experts need to watch out for brand wobbliness.

How to keep everyone on brand? Experts recommend good communication between personnel and departments, so that the brand message is conveyed to all vendors. This works well in a small museum; just remember to take a time out to talk! For larger museums, a style book is essential. One excellent online guide that you can access is that of Georgia Museum of Art. This page is instructive:

"Do not use Georgia Art Museum or University of Georgia Museum of Art. When it is necessary to indicate the museum's location at the university, use 'the Georgia Museum of Art at the University of Georgia'. Do not refer to it as GMOA. Note that the museum presents exhibitions, not exhibits."

Budgets face the worst dangers when museums try to reach all their audiences separately, when each department wants its own material. It's better for the budget and for consistency to use the same material for multiple audiences. Teachers are also parents. Donors also take classes. Your many stakeholder groups overlap, and everyone should see the same message. An invitation to a gala might be seen by a teacher; a school tour guide might land on a donor's kitchen table.

Considering the range of materials a museum produces, maintaining a consistent brand identity across the board is a huge job that relies on one mantra, repeated as often as necessary: "Is this piece On Brand?"

A good glimpse of brand consistency comes from the Steelworks Center of the West, a museum in Pueblo. Colorado, whose mission is to tell the world about the industries that built the west. No cowboys, no big sky ranches—all factories, and immigrants' hard work, and technology from the days when something new was really something. Here's the snippet, to be found throughout the Steelwork Center of the West website:

"The Industrial West"

In one version or other, the core value of western industry, industrialization, and continent-building industries is present on every page of the site.

One of the first pages a visitor might seek out is Education, where they'll see:

"At the Steelworks Center of the West one of our primary goals is to educate students and the community about the cultural and historical significance of the steel and coal mining industries in the development of Colorado and the West."

Invoking Strategy and Relevance

Understanding your museum's strategy actually occurs first thing in a watch dog's Day, reoccurs approximately every hour, and never really goes away. It informs every piece of communication. To strategize is to first know the goals of your project, and then to select the most effective marketing media. Before putting together a booklet, brochure, newsletter, magazine, local radio announcement, direct mail, banner, or billboard, ask "Why?" In fact, learn to verbalize "Why?" and "So What?" when any of these materials are requested. The strategy for each marketing piece is different and plays a part in each one's design and execution.

When you stop—and you should do this frequently—to think about why you're producing a specific marketing piece, also ask this question:

"Are we being relevant?"

This isn't an automatic reflex for professionals who have been at their posts for a while. They rightly focus on the task at hand; they spend a lot of energy keeping up to date on the museum field as a whole, and their genre in particular; they are over thirteen years of age. No excuses, though for marketers: they have to stay relevant with all ages and trends.

Staying relevant and staying consistent may seem to fight each other, and, indeed, this balance takes careful thought. Brand watch dogs can learn some new tricks from social media, whose audiences demand content that is meaningful for them. It's no longer acceptable to speak from the castle; the one-to-many format just won't fly. Although you invent new topics for your audience, you never reinvent your core values.

"You" is a key word in marketing, on the printed page and certainly in the mind of the person approving the marketing materials. The Winnetka Historical Society did an amazing job of relevance by promoting a "Researching Your Winnetka Property" booklet on its website. It's a fascinating document outlining how to describe your house's style, where to find documents relating to your property among the Winnetka Historical Society museum archives, how to use the county Recorder of Deeds office to find the chain of ownership, getting information on the architect, and exploring old newspapers to learn about other residents of your community. It's a fascinating and easy tutorial in learning about something historical societies are good at. It's good for the brand image, especially because the museum is being helpful and interested in you.

Fortunately, the human mind is excellent at absorbing the motes and memes of its environment, and accessing the brain's file of knowledge can be as easy as saying:

"Why?" "So What?" "Are we being relevant?"

Brochures

Brochures sell hard because they are short and sweet, four-color beauties as beguiling as a box of candy. More expensive than a booklet, they entice strangers to your museum to give it a try on trips, during conference free time, or for a new exhibition. Brochures are attention-getters. They should assiduously reflect your brand and accurately preview what they're announcing. It's this care, as well as the cost of a glossy piece, that makes them more expensive. They usually are produced on quality paper, are usually 8½ × 11 sheets folded twice into six panels, and fit into folders or a #10 envelope.

Strategically, they go to every possible consumer for your museum who is still shopping around for where to visit, from destination city to actual sight once in town. Brochures are found in sales meeting packets, hotel and visitor bureau racks, the racks of other sights, and as a follow-up to any marketing that says: For more information, contact us.

A brochure is frequently the first piece produced for a new branding or rebranding effort, after the website. As such, it becomes the informal template for the rest of your marketing efforts. Some going-in rules are as follows:

1. Select an appropriate and distinctive typeface you'll want to use on all subsequent communications.
2. Find a palette of colors that reflects your brand image, and stick with it. You will use the same palette everywhere—from the business cards to visitor tags.
3. Make sure your logo enlarges and reduces for all the subsequent marketing. This includes all the usual marketing pieces, plus overlooked surfaces such as exhibit labels, store merchandise tags, tray liners, educational material (even those handed out to grammar schoolers, who take them home to their parents), Twitter, audio tour wands, employee manuals, the printed agenda at board meetings, and the podium at lectures.
4. Stop! Does your just-finished brochure convey your brand's message verbally and visually?

There are six features of a brochure that will adhere to your brand. The cover visual, the headline on the cover, the three to six photographs or other images inside the brochure, the six paragraphs of text (six is recommended to say what you need, concisely), and the back cover specifics.

Back Cover

You may relegate this information to the Easy Task File, but don't. There are only two covers to a brochure and both should communicate your brand promise immediately. Look at your locator map and see what other points of interest also appear. Show other cultural institutions or unique city landmarks; don't show pizza joints or gyms. Make sure your typeface is the same as used in all your pieces. This is no place for the standard font that is copied and pasted from Word. Put your logo as large as possible on the back cover.

Front Cover

The front cover frequently appears on brochure racks and conference folders, so it's the top part that shows first. The photograph should clearly reflect your brand mission, whether it's a general brochure or one designed to promote a special exhibition or event. Write a headline that communicates something relevant to your target audience: people who are considering adding you to their tourist agenda.

The front cover of the brochure for the Museum of Electricity in Mulhouse, France, is titled "The Adventure of Electricity." What shows above the rack is a young girl's hair standing on end, and a harmless halo of light around her head. There's a small logo of the British flag to signal the English language version. On the back, the locator map shows Mulhouse's relationship to other French and German cities in the Alsace and westernmost Germany. This is consistent with France's commitment to a global worldview; it also reflects its ongoing policy of connecting all French cultural and heritage sites under the France brand.

A subgenre of the brochure is the rack card, a two-sided piece with a strong visual on the front, and condensed information on the back. The membership card of the Museum of Glass, Tacoma, Washington, has a visual of the museum's famed glass furnace filling two-thirds of the cover; the headline reads: "Join the Hottest Club in Town." The back is filled with information, but it still carries a visual of the plaza of glass sculpture that fronts the museum.

Of all the pieces you print, the membership brochure should carry your brand promise. Why else would someone pay money to become part of your family? I'm dismayed at how many museums lose this opportunity to connect by simply saying "Join."

Booklets

Booklets are informational, usually at least eight pages, and frequently produced in black and white. Line drawings are often used, and photos don't have to be reproduced perfectly. Many are inexpensive, and they inform so meaningfully that they should be used liberally in the galleries, or in educational packets. They are frequently targeted to people who are already in your museum, and they function as wonderful retention pieces. Tourists may keep a brochure for address and website, but visitors save booklets for further study.

Some booklets are exhibit-by-exhibit tours of a museum's galleries, with some photographs and complete, label-like text.

Some are written more creatively to promote an exhibition. An example would be a botanical gardens booklet showing some of its orchids supplemented with vanilla recipes, or a historic house holiday booklet appendixed with written songs of the season.

The History Museum of the City of Strasbourg booklet is elegant, a history book of a crossroads city that belonged to two countries and a thousand years of marching populations. Its outstanding brand feature is the thoroughness of its research and the role of Strasbourg in world geopolitics. It is important information that the museum wants its visitors to understand fully.

Newsletters

Newsletters don't need to contain breaking news, but e-mail, Facebook, and Twitter make it possible to publish the news often. The fundamentals are the same as with a printed newsletter, minus the hyperlinks. Because, as will be seen in chapter 12, "Digital and Social Media," it's so easy to scoot Off Brand in the rush to hit the Publish button, we'll look at branding from the more stable position of a printed piece. Many organizations find a print newsletter very much to their liking. Newsletters deliver news, and that keeps your brand relevant. Newsletters consume time of staff, but they connect a wide range of people to your brand through stories, people, tidbits, and previews. Newsletters come out regularly, so they remind prospects and members alike of what you stand for. The caution with newsletters is brand identity: it's easy to splash out fun stories without regard to brand aptness.

The *Gazette*, newsletter of the Winnetka (IL) Historical Society, balances attention-getting headlines with relevance to the community's main park and local elementary school.

The newsworthy headline "Historic Civil Rights Milestone in July 2015" has this subhead: "Celebrating the fiftieth Anniversary of Martin Luther King, Jr.'s speech on the Village Green."

The provocative headline: "When Art Was Threatening" adds this subhead: "The Hidden Works Progress Administration at Skokie School."

Well-branded newsletters strive for news that's relevant.

Academic brands have a parent company—the college or university—they need to distinguish themselves from. Spencer Museum of Art, the University of Kansas in Lawrence, deftly accomplishes this in its newsletter. In its "Director's remarks," Director Saralyn Reece Hardy carves a position for the museum brand this way:

> "More than anything else, it is our collection that defines our mission and vision."

She remarks in detail about an ambitious expansion that includes service to new—the museum's own—audiences. Two major donors of works are credited as "collectors" and "collector and professor." The University is not excluded, but in this case it is part of the museum, not the other way around.

Names of newsletters should reflect your brand. *Update* and *News* and *Courier* are generic and, worse, if those names are in the Subject line of e-mail, they could be ignored. When readers actually do open your e-mails, they should see a brand name like these:

Postmark—Newsletter of the National Postal Museum
What's Next?—Newsletter of The Autry, whose tagline proclaims "Explore the Unexpected."

Posters

Your museum goes to the expense of hiring a designer and printing in four color on heavy paper stock only when you have an important event or initiative to announce locally. Posters work well in local retail establishments, school and college bulletin boards (the actual kind), and public buildings. The poster design, without the printing, can be used in electronic kiosks in malls or airports, above your information desk, and as the image for invitations to the event.

Posters should follow the same concept they did in the Art Nouveau and Art Deco periods, when they were popular advertising media: big, bold graphics, and few words. You've seen vintage posters advertising liqueurs and fashion, entertainments and art galleries. The latter were very affective in cities for leading people to local attractions.

If you go the poster route, look at designer's portfolios—local colleges have career centers for their art students, and any good designer will have an online portfolio—to find the style that suits your message. Posters will brand your museum best if the style of art compliments the look of your museum.

One caution with using big, splashy posters: make sure your logo and identification are large enough so that they don't get submerged.

Ephemera—Invitations, Tickets, Program Handouts

"Ephemera," roughly defined, is any printed material that isn't meant to last. It is not bound like a booklet, dated like a newspaper, or meant to be kept on a kitchen table like a catalog. Today, almost everything not uploaded is ephemeral, and that raises their value a lot. They might not stick around for long, but there are strategic reasons to use them.

Some examples of these flighty objects: invitations to events, children's find-and-paste "passports," giveaway bookmarks, lecture and performance handouts, menus, tickets and guest passes, study guides, gallery maps, weekly event handouts, and more. This chapter will discuss three of the most used types of ephemera: invitations, guest passes and tickets, and event program handouts.

Invitations

These are usually member mailings, and they carry the weight of all member communications. They can lead to more visits, word-of-mouth advertising, donations, community and corporate partnerships, and board involvement.

Consider an invitation to an opening reception. This piece of paper, which will be out of date the day after the reception, speaks directly to a prized audience: people who already know and have shown some fealty to your institution. For them the brief event proffers uncrowded access, networking possibilities, perhaps a conversation with the artists or exhibition designer, and a catered buffet; all these will increase their involvement. For you, this time-sensitive piece of paper lets you identify your best customers, sharpen your database, renew contact on a personal level, and nurture new relationships.

Let's look at how one museum leveraged what is usually just a folded piece of paper. It's glossy paper stock, printed in glowing color, and shown to me by a museum member with the preface: "This is different from their usual mailings." The museum referred to is Spencer Museum of Art at The University of Kansas, and the reception is a real coup, a preview of a James Turrell installation with the artist in attendance. This event, in Lawrence, Kansas, took place in the same year (2013) that the artist had exhibitions at the Guggenheim Museum in New York, the Los Angeles County Museum of Art, and the Museum of Fine Arts, Houston. It was an occasion for pride and the invitation reinforced the brand in several ways:

A brief biography of the artist describes him as "the pre-eminent light artist of our time," so upfront the recipient learns the artist's medium and how important he is.

The time of the event is not just 7:30 p.m., but, because this is a light artist, beginning "after sundown."

The back of the invitation provides a website address for anyone who wants to better understand this unusually beautiful announcement.

There are other ways an exhibition invitation can burnish your brand, if it is a large invitation, or if it uses multiple inserts:

- Authoritative quotes about the artist and his/her significance
- List of complementary programming during the exhibition
- Names of exhibition lenders and supporters and their affiliation with the museum
- List of event committees, so people know whom to network with
- Statement of the museum's mission and why this exhibition—and preview party—fulfills that goal.

Tickets and Guest Passes

Most museums print quantities of guest passes and hand them out freely. Hundreds, if not thousands, of people see them. Remember the people who get the passes first: members, visiting speakers, and volunteers. They are reminded of their connection to the museum, and their pride in being able to share it.

Most passes are large enough to accommodate a large logo, a photo of an iconic artifact or your façade, so guests will recognize it when they get close. If you have a tagline, use it. This is a golden opportunity to sell yourself to a person who possibly wouldn't visit at all if it weren't for the free ticket. There's also space for the visitor's name and address, which is good for data collection. If funds allow, put the passes in an envelope, so it looks like the gift it is.

Here's what shouldn't take up the 2" × 3" space: mission statement, sponsors, bad photography. Hold a staff meeting to select just the right artifact or photo to use. If several tickets are given at one time, have different photos on each one, the better to tell your story visually to the people who will, probably, visit together.

Everything that appears on a guest pass can be printed on your regular tickets or, if you offer free admission, tickets to special exhibitions. Strategically, these tickets are targeted to people who are already in your museum, or are predisposed to make a special visit. These tickets stay around for a long time before they are used, and each glance at them reinforces your image. Even an entrance ticket will get tossed out slowly if it looks as good as your exhibits. A non-branded ticket looks like any entry receipt, from a high school football game to a cash bar.

Event and Program Handouts

If you go to the effort to offer programs such as lectures, book clubs, and family days, provide a reminder of this museum-specific event. A program handout can be simply produced and should include:

Title of program
Time and place
Description or program notes
Name and bios of speakers, where applicable
Reason why this program furthers the core values of the museum

There's one surface that also sees a lot of traffic and is unequaled in branding power: the museum store shopping bag. It should be designed with panache and supplied with even the smallest purchase. This is potent word-of-mouth advertising that buzzes for a long time, over a long distance, even if its initial use is impermanent.

Signs and Environmental Graphics

On the façade of the Snite Museum of Art at Notre Dame University is a sign that says "Inspiration for a lifetime is seconds away." At the point at which a visitor is close enough to read the sign, he is standing outside Gate 9 of Notre Dame Football Stadium. It must be tough being an art brand less than four downs from the Shrine of Football, and the museum's brand bravado deserves a cheer.

A frequently publicized environmental graphic is the Bridge of Glass leading to the Tacoma Glass Museum. Its walls are made of display cases holding glass art objects by Dale Chihuly, Tacoma native son and art glass pioneer. It's actually a full-dimensional graphic that serves as a welcoming preview of what's to come.

The Aga Khan Museum, Toronto, fills an entire lobby wall with a map graphic that indicates the many overlapping cultures through the Muslim world's history. As an introduction to the museum, it visualizes the arts, education, and lifestyles of many peoples, across many borders.

We've always seen environmental graphics on the doors to the ladies' room and men's room. Some are more brand-specific than others. Kudos to the Strasbourg Museum of Modern and Contemporary Art's doors: They have eight-foot brushstroke sketches of the familiar gender symbols. Functionally, these are visible from afar. From a branding viewpoint, they're one more reminder of a conceptually attuned art museum.

As you think about signs on stands around your museum, think twice and take the time to add your logo, or a visual, that gives not only directions, but also brand reinforcement. Some places for these signs that are part of your interior environment:

Notices announcing group tour starting points and times
At the restaurant and leading to it (hungry visitors will thank you)
Shelf strips in the book section of your store
Wall panels that list the names and logos of exhibition sponsors

Cleveland Art Museum devotes a full wall to post-it note style questions from visitors. It's near the open conservation gallery, but displays questions on all kinds of questions, and answers from the museum. It's not part of any exhibition design, it's part of the environment, and it communicates that this museum believes in open inquiry and one-to-one answers.

Business Cards and Letterhead

After you've decided on a logo and designed your business cards and letterhead, feel the paper. Check your letterhead stationery and make sure you haven't switched to lighter, cheaper paper. Check your business cards to see if the most recent printer captured the ink color correctly.

Because business cards are such a frequently seen surface, they deserve special graphic attention. They should deliver not only the identity of the museum but also its personality. Many companies now state their mission on the back of the cards.

It's tempting to think that all contact information is on a museum's website, and that anyone you meet can find you there. But this ignores all the museums who eschew individual e-mail addresses and telephone extensions. Part of brand strategy is to reinforce it with everyone—everyone!—you meet, and that is difficult. If your new dentist asks where you're working, give him or her your card. If you meet your child's fourth grade teacher in the supermarket, give him or her your card. Maybe it's your cable TV guy, dog walker or someone you chat with at a long table at the coffee house—dig in your wallet for your card. This kind of networking doesn't come naturally to many people, but it's a lot easier than referring a new acquaintance to your web page.

Local Radio and Television

Radio has a local audience, costs relatively little, and a commercial can be written and aired quickly. You can place radio ads on stations that appeal to your target audience, at times of day when those people are most likely to tune in. They're much quicker to produce, and can be used in emergencies to bump ticket purchases. If you don't have the creative power to write a commercial, write talking points for the local radio personalities to read; these have the advantage of coming from a known person in the community. Because of the selectivity, radio relates better to your brand.

Television is expensive, reaches a large geographic audience, and often airs with big brand national spots. If you look amateurish, you resemble the local car dealership, and that doesn't help your brand image.

If it's a television public service announcement (PSA), it may run at odd hours, probably not reaching the audiences your museum appeals to. And the likelihood of getting one of few PSA spots made available is not good.

Radio PSAs offer a slightly better chance of being available. Here is where your tagline earns the trouble it takes to create. A shorthand expression of your core values, it identifies you quickly, and there's usually not much time on a PSA. For a thorough discussion of the strategies and tactics of PSAs, visit the Community Tool Box website of the Work Group for Community Health and Development at the University of Kansas.

On public radio, your museum may want to pay for a "brought to you by" segment. Pick a brand-appropriate program. For instance, business and financial news programs are frequently "brought to you by" business programs at local colleges and universities. Again, your tagline is important; it will complete the on-air mention, "brought to you by the Smith-Jones Museum . . . Explore, discover, dream . . ."

SWOT ANALYSIS

SWOT stands for Strengths, Weaknesses, Opportunities, and Threats. Marketers use the SWOT analysis at many decision-making junctures. For a museum, it is essential when rethinking your brand because it forces you to focus on what's distinctive (strengths) and what the competitor brands do best (weaknesses). The ultimate value of the SWOT lies in opportunities, for here is where you take charge of brand core strengths and use them in your marketing efforts. If you're redesigning your web page, analyze the current one with a SWOT. If you are assigning an intern the job, work together to identify strengths and opportunities. If you are writing a solicitation letter, demonstrate your strengths and assess your threats. If you are selecting items for the museum store, buy to your strengths.

For a major marketing plan, conduct a complete assessment of strengths, weaknesses, opportunities, and threats, and include as many of your staff and other stakeholders as possible. Community partners will have a perspective on threats that you don't. Educators can point out opportunities. Vendors will know something about the competitive marketplace, and help you strengthen your weak areas.

The textbook SWOT analysis looks like this (see Figure 8.2). Your job is to fill in the spaces. It's a simple template and immeasurably helpful in cutting a daunting job into understandable parts.

BRANDING TIPS

The following checklist will help everyone in the museum remain consistent, on brand, and in the good graces of the Brand watchdog.

The following series of warnings is a reminder that even the best marketing piece is only as good as its contribution to the brand. It is an extensive list, but not an exhaustive one, and the ingenuity of marketing will find new ways to address new opportunities as they arise.

1. Select an appropriate and distinctive typeface and use it on all communications.
2. Find a palette of colors that reflects your brand image, and stick with it.
3. Know your budget and marketing costs so you're not tempted to switch messages—verbal and visual—as you start a new project.
4. Use your logo on all materials seen by your public. This includes all the usual marketing pieces, plus overlooked surfaces such as exhibit labels, every page of your website, invoices, store merchandise tags, tray liners, educational material (even those handed out to grammar schoolers, who take them home to their parents), audio tour wands, employee manuals, the printed agenda at board meetings, and the podium at lectures.
5. Stop! Does your just-finished brochure, invitation, or sign have the same look and tone of voice as all your other marketing materials?
6. When co-sponsoring events with corporations, or other not-for-profit institutions, negotiate the size and placement of your logo.

Strengths	Weaknesses
Opportunities	**Threats**

Figure 8.2 SWOT.

7. Pay attention to the announcer's voice on radio commercials. If it's a station announcer, make sure you like the sound of his or her voice; you may have a choice. If it's a pre-recorded spot, you can guarantee that the voice reflects your museum's brand.
8. Have a visual person check out your lobby. Remember, this is the visitor's first and last impression.
9. Use different sizes of envelopes for your mailings. Unexpected snail mail buried amongst the junk mail enhances your brand in nice envelopes.
10. If you have kiosks in airports, malls, or convention centers, use your logo and signature visuals double strength. They'll be competing with hundreds of other visuals.
11. Design your shopping bags with panache, and supply them with even the smallest purchase. This is potent word-of-mouth advertising, albeit soundless.
12. Send school groups home with a memento that relates their trip with your museum, as well as with their school day off. And other members of the family will also see it.
13. Mail out postcards with some frequency. These can be one-color pieces with seasonal reminders about your collection, as well as event notices. Postal rates on postcards are relatively inexpensive. Postcards always draw attention because they're so rare. And their glossy surfaces reproduce your signature visuals beautifully.
14. When your meeting rooms are used by business or community groups, leave a stack of brochures at the door.
15. Don't let your ads be dominated by visuals of the exhibition. Give your logo plenty of space.
16. You're part of the community, so look for local places to put your ads: ATM receipts, lighted taxi signs, store window displays.
17. Advertise in college publications. It's inexpensive and you're reaching a highly motivated target.
18. Don't squander the good fortune of a television interview. Put a large sign with the name of your museum behind your spokesperson. The station may not mention your name, but they can't edit out the sign.
19. Give directors something at every meeting that reminds them of the museum on which they're spending so much time and prestige.
20. Put your logo on visitor tags; they are part of the landscape that other visitors see, and if they are taken home by mistake, consider that viral marketing.
21. Design t-shirts, signature scarves, or other types of apparel for your guards. They must never look like police, and always look like members of the museum family.

22. Always have signage present at lectures and conferences, whether to the general community, or at professional conferences. If possible, have a permanent graphic on your home podium. At out-of-town conferences, remember to hand out your business cards, and small brochures if appropriate.

Chapter 9

Partnerships

Corporate and Community

Figure 9.1 The Musée Bartholdi in Colmar, France, is branded as one the "Maisons des Illustres," houses of the illustrious, that France honors and that honor France. This seal of excellence exemplifies the symbiosis between a museum and its community, one brand reinforcing the other. *Source*: © 2014 Margot Wallace.

When Vesterheim, the National Norwegian-American museum and Heritage Center, sent a curator to give the commencement address at Luther College, that was a community partnership. When the Decorah, Iowa, museum opened a one-day Scandinavian Market across the border in a Minneapolis hotel, that was a corporate partnership. One was decidedly a local partnering. The other shared enterprise, though privately sponsored, utilized a corporate partner. In both cases, the museum added a new perspective to its brand, and so did its partner. The college gained real-world, professional expertise from the museum. The commercial venue gained the cultural patina of an arts institution. All the parties gained new awareness in new sectors, among people with an affinity for the values each espoused.

The relationship with your community—business, social, educational, geographic—lends identity to your museum. It locates your focused institution in a wider context. Surprisingly, it lends you credibility; sure you're smart and helpful and wonderful, but you're also one of us.

Partnerships are entered into willingly by both parties. Sometimes there's a contract, frequently a financial advantage, often an in-kind exchange of goods or services; it is always a cultural handshake as well, and when a museum has a strong brand, it's easier to find like-minded partners with shared values. It's also easier to maintain your brand soul, even with strong partners with equally strong brands.

Partnerships are sought and consummated for a variety of reasons; if they're based on mutual brand building, they will work. This chapter shows how museums can partner to advantage with corporate brands, government and civic brands, global issues brands, college and university brands, regional brands, and association brands.

This chapter will discuss how to maintain your brand's distinctiveness and identity as part of a partnership. But first, here are some definitions of partner brands.

CORPORATE BRANDS

Corporations have many cultural organizations that they can support; and corporate social responsibility demands that they be responsible to their stakeholders as well as to the community. When a business partners with your museum, it's because they know your brand personality and values; they understand the types of consumers you reach and the exhibitions and programs that reach them; they see a brand fit. For their part, museums must realize the same compatibility. They, too, must benefit perceptually. The reason Solar Express pajama parties have succeeded wildly at museums as diverse as the San Bernardino County Museum in Redlands, California, and the Antique Automobile Club of America Museum in Hershey is this meeting on the brands: on the one hand, a beloved and superlative corporate product, perfectly marketed to not-for-profits all over America; on the other hand, museums, known and respected as safe places to dream and discover. Both partners contribute an emotional journey from home to discovery and back.

The beauty is in the branding: museums retain their own distinct identity, tying fun and entertainment to their own displays and stories. Some include visits from Santa and photographs that create memories to take home. They all engender a family intimacy in which connection is made; it's good branding for everyone.

The same feeling is produced when a local marketer sponsors an event. In the museum setting, the bank or chain store looks different. With the imprimatur of well-known businesses, thc museum has a new look. Both brands change a little in the consumer's perception, and that's the kind of evolution all brands must undergo.

Museums housed in corporate headquarters are another breed altogether. The implicit partnership is with the museum field, an unstated agreement that if the Household Name Brand calls its showroom a museum, it will observe the guidelines that govern a traditional museum. However, many of these so-called museums are more curio shops than cabinets of curiosities. Many household brand names tell the story of their brands loosely connected to popular culture, but few seem burdened by curatorial practice. One that stands apart—that could be a model for other corporate museums—is the Wells Fargo History Museum, San Francisco. The bank's mission emphasizes its roots and commitment to its community and its galleries integrate Wells Fargo history as a transportation company into the development of the west. The museum has a strong education component, and its curriculum guide states that ". . . the history of Wells Fargo & Co., the Gold Rush, and life in the nineteenth century . . . [is] intended as a classroom aid for the study of California history." The archival material is to be used for analysis of original sources, which certainly hews to the critical thinking directive of current pedagogy, and the lessons listed are provocative:

"Wells Fargo and diversity: African Americans, Chinese, Latinos, Women"
"How fast does a stagecoach travel"
"Reading a historic map"
"Microhydraulic mining"

Museums built by wealthy individuals are a subset of the corporate museum, but with a much firmer handshake with standard museum policy.

Vanity museums of rich men are always suspect, yet these museums are just scaled-up versions of the grand salons installed in the stately homes of eighteenth-century grandees with exploring minds. The best of them, such as the new Louis Vuitton Foundation museum in Paris, hire acclaimed curators and hang otherwise inaccessible art. They are dedicated to mission-oriented exhibition, open discussion, and analysis. As a symbol of success, they may not be as accessible as, say, a professional sports team, but they are an incontestable boon to culture in an era of impossibly high artifact prices. When these museums also showcase local artists, and raise civic profiles, they advance the cause of all corporate-museum partnerships: responsiveness to society. If your museum has a Name museum in the neighborhood, consider it a good partner.

GOVERNMENT AND CIVIC BRANDS

Partnering with a government brand brings all kind of halo benefits besides funding: credibility, prestige, awareness, and hometown pride. For example, in 2014 Congress passed legislation titled "The Lower East Side Tenement National Historic Site Amendments Act" that designated a second building of the New York's Tenement Museum as an affiliated site of the National Park Service. Although this designation didn't include funding, it was prestigious; the power of a brand like "National Park Service" always helps attract donors. And a government validates a museum whose brand is intertwined with social issues. The Tenement Museum's identity is based on immigrant stories, from the decades when the tenement buildings were immigrants' homes, to current stories, as well. New York Congressmen were looking for tie-ins with immigration, their signature issue. The lesson here is this: know your government and its representatives, learn their issues, and then see if your brand's story meshes with theirs.

ACADEMIC BRANDS

Partnerships with colleges and universities provide expertise a museum couldn't otherwise afford, nowhere more critical than in scientific research of your holdings.

One transatlantic alliance had the University of Missouri analyzing over two hundred pieces of black-glazed pottery from the Capitoline Museums in Rome. The American students get a chance to work with artifacts from a celebrated brand in Rome (a great place brand in its own right); from the

Capitoline Museums' perspective, "the objects will return to the museums with a scholarly pedigree," formerly unaffordable.

The more common academic partnership exists with academic museums on college and university campuses, originally built as learning adjuncts to the more established institution, but now expected to carry their own brand weight. Academic museums are partnerships that go back centuries, and their robustness is a credit to both institutions. There are over three hundred academic museums in North America, according to the membership lists of the Association of Academic Museums and Galleries (AAMG). From the largest, such as Yale and UCLA's Hammer, to the smallest, all have individual identities that need preserving. This evolving brand partnership will be discussed in chapter 18.

GLOBAL ISSUES BRANDS

Some issues are too big to be encased in one institution. Some are still at the "what-if" or "why-not" stage. Most big issues need the vitality of collaboration to keep them spinning and sizzling. Sustainability in environments is that kind of issue and Zoo Miami is the kind of museum needed. Zoo Miami is, at its core, a conserver and espouser of global environmental sustainability. Its partners—including National Park Service, Tropical Audubon Society, Belize Division of Forestry, U.S. Geological Survey, and Puerto Rico Department of Natural Resources and Environment—invigorate the subject with their breadth of activity. One can only imagine the places and challenges that these partners represent, and with imaginations come the engagement that a museum brand craves. It would be easy for a tremendously popular museum, such as a major zoo, to rest its brand on excellence of practice, superb education programs, a worthy mission, family enrichment, and fun. But a lot of museums can make those claims. Where's the brand vigor? Sometimes, institutions stand out by the company they keep. And the lengths they go to forge the ties.

REGIONAL BRANDS

An enduring example of partnership with an entire region is the Connecticut Art Trail, a consortium of thirteen Connecticut museums that banded together—branded together—to increase tourism. That's a winning collaboration for each museum, the State of Connecticut and its towns, and the tourism providers all along the route, from lodging and restaurants to stores and other sites.

Old Sturbridge Village, a living history museum, counts among its holdings examples of Nathan Lombard furniture, and that led to a partnering with furniture historians for an event designed to "encourage fresh conversations about the history, design, and construction of New England furniture." Suddenly, a museum in one town is a factor in an all-state partnership among eleven strong institutional brands celebrating "the craft and industry, tradition and innovation of Massachusetts furniture-making." Boosting the State of Massachusetts brand is a compelling concept, because of its far-reaching benefits. Place branding—of cities, states, provinces, shires—helps those places attract new trade, factories, major meetings, graduate students, scientists, technology centers, tourism, Olympic games, and a place at policy-setting meetings.

ASSOCIATION BRANDS

Associations are like corporations, but without the profit goal. These not-for-profit brands are dedicated to growing their businesses and improving the communities that work for and with them.

Livestock breeders, heritage seed farmers, and wetland management experts are three strong brand partners of the Garfield Farm Museum. The Campton Hills, Illinois, institution reaches out far beyond its patch of farmland to connect with agribusiness brands. The museum uses the credentials of these groups to support its programs of school field trips, adult professional workshops, and internships for college students. In return, the museum gives these groups a different kind of forum for sharing and disseminating new ideas.

ADVISORY COUNCILS

Advisory councils collect all kinds of partners in one conference room whenever the museum needs their advice. Advisory council members from corporate, academic, government, civic, and global issues groups are advocates for your museum and your initiatives; they are independent voices helping and supporting your brand mission so that your choices of programs, exhibitions, or events don't seem arbitrary or out of touch. Unlike elected boards, according to Annie Storr, a former museum administrator, advisory councils don't have duties or powers; rather, they have insights and the freedom to share them. You will make the best use of these advisors when you understand their backgrounds, the entities that form their core values and inform their vision for the museum. For your part, of course, make sure they understand your brand identity and core values. This cooperative group can be a stumbling block if you don't understand each other's brands; it can benefit you immensely when all sides do.

When you understand the brand image and values that different partners want to augment by partnering with your museum, you're ready to wisely augment your own.

Wisdom #1: Beware the Dazzle of Big Partners

Sometimes, the lure of meaningful dollars results in flamboyant partnerships, where the scholarship of exhibitions gets buried under in the surface glitter, and a basic truth is endangered. Dazzle brings in the crowds, but depth keeps the museum in business, so keep your exhibits and interpretations intact. Museums will not be appealing partners for business if they start to resemble theme parks. When and how to collaborate with corporate America can be examined as a business decision, but it also must be considered from a branding perspective. Will the alliance enhance the museum's mission and image? And, frankly, will the alliance support the corporate partner's marketing strategy? Museums need money, and businesses need respectability. Museums need more people in the form of attendance and members. Business needs more people in the form of new and diverse markets. This symbiotic relationship looks so good that it's easy to forget the branding aspect: the link-up must fit comfortably with the museum's organizational culture, its personality, and its brand.

Wisdom #2: Know Your Strengths

When selecting any ally, keep in mind the reasons this group is interested in your museum. It may be the type of objects you collect, the reputation of your collection, your physical plant, the reputation of your curators, your location, your membership list, a new project or acquisition, or your name. All these assets must be protected in the new alliance. The solid reputation, creativity, exploration, and high-mindedness that define museums are the intangible properties that corporations covet. Which is simply to say that they need you, and you can afford to be picky. The caveat is to work only with groups that share your goals. The corporate-cultural partnership is based on a similarity of philosophies and goals, a meshing of the brands. The danger is not losing your soul, but losing your brand.

Wisdom #3: Know Your Brand

Before you talk to any business, know your brand and be able to define it in one sentence. Everyone in the museum family should know the importance of brand and image, and be able to convey it to any visiting partner. Partner brands, from the CEO to the lobby guards, know their own story. Make sure your story is part of your organization.

Wisdom #4: Be Selective with Sponsors

Note the true definition of a sponsor and beware of adopting just any guardian angel. When someone sponsors someone else—think individuals for now—each is supposed to share the other's dreams and mentor him or her toward an agreed-upon goal. This shared interest must be maintained in today's high-priced sponsorships. When two logos appear on the same exhibition catalog or panel, or web page, both must reflect the spirit of shared initiative. It's harder today to find a match with so many partners and museums pairing up, but wait for Mr. Right.

If you're looking for exhibition sponsorship, those are of limited scope and duration and the timing has to fit the corporation's marketing schedule. Selecting the right exhibition at the right time can be very strategic for the corporation, so it behooves the museum to be as flexible as possible. Ongoing sponsorship usually involves operational support for the museum as a whole, rather than an individual event, and you have to be more eloquent in describing your mission; there's no program visual or exhibition title for the partner to hook onto. Don't be timid about asking for large funds; it shows you're serious and have long-range plans. Remember that the cost of sponsorship is usually small compared to a marketing budget and when it comes from the partner's community relations budget, it frequently is a very good tax deal.

An ongoing partnership brings in more than money. Through their employees, shareholders, and vendors, businesses bring many new people into your circle, and new databases for membership. Good businesses contribute fresh ideas, from vastly different perspectives. Some museum diehards say that the business of business is business, and should stay that way. But smart businesspeople know a lot about history, trends, art, science, technology, research, and display. They are valued long-term partners.

Wisdom #5: Watch Their Logo

If your partner's name is better known than yours, it will help you get awareness, and raise your stature. On the other hand, you might get lost in the shuffle. If you put their logo next to yours on a brochure or your web page announcing a collaboration, it will function as a seal of approval. Or it might dominate and make readers wonder whose exhibition it is. Having a partner representative appear at your benefit will seem glamorous; but their trained spokesperson might speak better than your scholarly director. Be aware of these realities, which happen in any partnership, and be prepared to work them out in advance. Again, choose your teammate wisely.

Wisdom #6: Know the Corporate Culture

Also pay attention to the corporate culture, or inner workings, of your proposed partner. The product or service might be a perfect match, but the way of doing business might be too divergent—too cautious, too entrepreneurial, too structured. A business that's just cut back on staff might not move as adroitly as your highly adaptable staff. A company with an unadventurous board of directors might jettison your collaboration that the marketing manager initiated. A business with staffers whose only job is to facilitate community relations might work too efficiently for your small, multitasking staff. These warnings fall in the forewarned, forearmed category. Just be prepared.

Wisdom #7: Do Your Due Diligence

As in any business venture, do your homework. Ask friends and advisors about the company. Find out what other not-for-profits the company has teamed with. Visit the company website to learn more about their products and services, and research past activity in their online Press Room. Send several of your staffers to the business itself—its offices or stores—to get a sense of its image and personality. Ask to meet with the people who will be implementing the partnership, in addition to the marketing people who brokered it. Invite their people to the museum and see how they respond. Do they understand your mission and seem to fit in? Do you like each other? After all, you'll be working together for a while. Do all this in addition to studying their offer, guarantees, and protection.

Wisdom #8: Learn All the Tools of Partner Promotion

Business marketers have long experience with many kinds of marketing, online and off, so borrow from it freely.

Cause Marketing

This form of corporate sponsorship offers advantages to everyone, a win-win-win deal you can wholeheartedly put your signature to. The marketing plan usually stipulates that a percentage of all product sales be contributed to the museum, in return for the right to place the corporate name in museum literature and advertising. This earns goodwill for the sponsor and for the museum, tax deductions for the corporation and increased visitors for the museum, new audiences for both, and real income for the charity. A little thought and both sides will discover truly synergistic ideas.

Product Placement

Several museums struck a good deal with the *Night at the Museum* movies. You don't have to be the Smithsonian Institution in Washington, DC, the American Museum of Natural History in New York, or the British Museum in London. If you have an interesting building, or evocative landscaping, or peculiarly photogenic exhibits, your location may be perfect for a movie; with all the different media platforms available, movies are more numerous than ever. Talk to your local business and tourism bureau. In addition to enhancing your brand, movie crews boost business all over town.

Sponsored Prizes and Awards

Explore presenting awards to partners—corporate, governmental, education, or association partners—similar to the Wright Museum award to U.S. Representative John Conyers, Jr. (D-Michigan). The "lifetime achievement award from the Charles H. Wright Museum of African American History for his work in promoting and preserving jazz and the arts in Congress" accomplished several branding goals. It named the museum; it tied the museum to the Government partner, and it went on to explain the mission of the museum in language that any group could appreciate: "Jazz grew out of the unique experiences of African Americans in the United States. It is one of America's truly original art forms. . . . The arts are an invaluable educational tool that help inspire children to learn about the diverse contributions Americans from all walks of life have made to our national culture."

Or give an award to a local student, teacher, promising artist or scientist, or successful project in the name of one of your partners. Of course, the partner whose name is used will be selected for appropriateness to your mission. Awards to individuals, or with individuals' names, always garner a lot of local publicity and, when they do, offer the perfect platform for stating your mission. Also, there's no limit to how many people you can honor, or how often the prizes are conferred.

Wisdom #9: Work with Human Resources at local business and associations

The booming training industry has benefited for years from the insights of non-business groups such as improvisational theater companies. Museums can follow suit with programs that teach business skills such as communication, leadership, teamwork, and problem solving—but in the context of curating, interpreting exhibits, developing displays, and writing labels. In today's business climate, human resources (HR) departments are charged to develop talent internally, as well as to retain employees through enrichment and morale-boosting activities. Professional HR managers and museum professionals are kindred spirits who understand how to challenge people and stimulate creative thinking. Through your expertise in various education programs, you can train employees to:

- Think visually
- See familiar objects from new perspectives
- Look at unfamiliar objects with understanding
- Solve problems in groups
- Think creatively
- Imagine situations outside their own cultural parameters

You also have conservation labs, visible storage, costumed interpreters, and interactive displays to use in adult workshops.

Surprising though it may seem, the techniques used to guide schoolchildren also teach adults to perceive, think creatively, communicate, work together, innovate, think strategically, and imagine scenarios. Remember, as you devise exercises specific to the partner group to also reflect your own brand's personality and identity.

Straightforward lectures or presentations are welcomed by HRs as bonus offerings and morale boosters in a time of overwork and stress. They are also looked upon as career enhancers, continuing education points that look good on a resume and push the employee up the ladder. Name your programs carefully so that they can be referred to quickly and also look good on a handout. "Shared Journeys" is the name of a workshop series of English for Speakers of Other Languages (ESOL) offered by the Tenement Museum in New York to help new arrivals learn English and American culture. It uses the same immigrant stories researched and used in museum tours to help newcomers unravel the mysteries of a new culture, learning English and making friends at the same time, and strikingly reinforcing the museum brand.

Check and double check that your popular programs do more than entertain, that they enhance your brand message. Make sure that whoever gives the presentation understands that there's more to the talk than what is on the slide. Outreach programs geared to local employees do a good job of creating awareness for, and suggesting a visit to, the museum, but the real advantage is having a whole hour to create an affinity.

After the 1-hour lecture or workshop is over, there's a residue of goodwill that you can build on with great effect. The employees have friends and families, and they'll probably spread the word about your talk. HR professionals have professional groups where they report their activities. And the person in the corner office will be kept informed of enrichment programs. Cultivate these three groups and send your good name even further.

To maximize this branding effort, supplement the program with:

- Brochures for employees to take home to family and friends.
- Material describing volunteer opportunities. HR professionals are always looking for ways to help employees serve the community.
- Business cards—hand them out to everybody at the lecture, including any support personnel like the audio/visual person, or the assistant who checks off names at the door.
- Signage on the podium. Have a graphic design person, or your printer, design a simple sign that can be taken to any speaking event and hung on the podium, or placed on the wall behind. It reminds the audience of the institution that's giving the talk. If you're lucky enough to have photographers or cameramen at the event, your name will be publicized.
- Video presentation. Any video your museum has produced brings the brand to life; bring a laptop and have it available before and after the presentation.
- Logo on name tags or table tents. Everybody who presents should wear a large, visible name tag. If the venue consists of tables or conference seating, instead of auditorium seating, use table tents to identify the speaker.
- Logo on all slides of a presentation. With interesting lectures, it's normal for audiences to love the show and forget who's bringing it to them. Identify every slide or overhead with either your logo or the museum name.
- Discount coupons, calendars, or passes. Hand them out at the end of the presentation—all with museum logo, address, and telephone number.
- Follow-up letter to the HR coordinator. Tell him or her how much you enjoyed the experience. If possible, mention and compliment some specific participants' questions. Ask for suggestions to improve the talk, and give assurance of your willingness to come back.
- Letter to CEO commending the good working relationship with the HR coordinator.
- Comment cards for participants to fill out. Make sure there's a logo on the cards.
- Questionnaire to the HR contact on the effectiveness of the program—on logo stationery.
- Periodic reminders to the HR department of new programs—on logo stationery.

Diversity Programs and Heritage

Museums with vibrant employer outreach series look to expand the franchise with other types of programs. Diversity is a huge issue that many businesses are trying to address, and which museums do an extremely good job of addressing; museum collections, by definition, are assembled with a goal of inclusiveness. Heritage programs branch out of diversity, and their attentiveness to individual histories also make likely topics for museum speakers. If your community is recognizing or honoring ethnic groups, you could develop programs that not only speak to their heritage, but also enhance your image as a responsive community institution.

Wisdom #10: Navigate the Proposal Traffic Jam

You aren't the only cultural institution that craves funds from the new headquarters in town, or from the new foundation, or the new multi-millionaire. So don't rush to get your solicitation on their crowded calendar unless you have a strong brand pitch. You should have your own brand message honed to a ten-minute presentation. You should understand their brand and current marketing goals. Then you must demonstrate that your two brand visions interlock seamlessly. Even with a proposal of that mutuality, your timing may work against you. Remember the rules of good salesmanship: pick your contact and your timing as carefully as you pick your words.

Wisdom #11: Take Small Steps

Liaisons can be initiated at any time, and with small measures. You don't have to plan a major event or program to solidify a partnership.

1. Invite small groups to lunch. Working men and women looking for new places to spend their lunch hour will welcome your café. If you don't have a restaurant, consider a regular catered lunch in a space that gives a glimpse of the museum's exhibits. Brown bag lunches, accompanied by a lecture, are an informal option. Participants bring their own food, and get a free lecture, a particularly useful format for garden or farm museums.
2. Loan exhibits to local business offices. A cross between a traveling exhibition and a site lecture, a museum display in corporate lobbies, offices, and conference rooms, is a wonderful way to advertise the museum.
3. Schedule spouse tours during trade shows and conferences. Most meeting planners now schedule city tours for spouses, male and female, as part of a conference agenda. Contact your local conference and tourism office to get on their list, or to help them develop a city tour for conference planners.

4. Provide guest passes for employees. Develop a once-a-year mailing of free admissions to employers in your area. It's an easy list to acquire, and employers, as well as their employees, will thank you.
5. Organize cultural exchange programs. Confer with local colleges, Rotary, and other organizations about partner programs with other cities around the globe.
6. On your Job or Careers web page, include local partners among the amenities of working in your town.
7. Contact local businesses for volunteers. This is a subtle way of getting your brand known, because by outlining the kind of volunteer you're seeking, you're also describing the personality of the museum. If you have a volunteer brochure, include it with a letter to the human resources director.
8. Show your local vendors your brand and mission. Since they're already on the premises, they can see the museum's personality for themselves. Take a few minutes to explain the museum's goals and answer their questions. Remember, everyone who comes in your door has ten friends, relatives, or business colleagues that they'll spread the word to.
9. Join Rotary.

Always have a stack of business cards in your wallet and pass them out as if you were the local ballpark hot dog vendor. Museums are perceived as cultural leaders in their community when, in fact, they are happily just a part of the culture. Sure, visitors come to your door, but you aren't their host or hostess, any more than the real estate agent or the county commissioner or the college history department is. Your brands are all in the community together.

Chapter 10

Finding Your Brand

Figure 10.1 From a collection of dolls and toys to a portfolio of artifacts, interactive exhibits, programs, research and partnerships, The Strong in Rochester, New York, refined its mission and rebranded to the National Museum of Play. *Source*: © 2015 Margot Wallace.

After 10 minutes of a conference workshop on museum branding—mostly theory at this point, not so much workshop—a museum director at the back of the room raised his hand and asked: "But how do we find our brand?"

Let's get down to business. You can't just design a logo and become a brand. Branding is a deep-digging process out of which brands will emerge. Your museum already has a distinctive collection, personality, and core values that distinguish it from others. Once you identify these, you'll find your brand. This chapter proposes some methods for getting there:

1. Remember your story
2. Dust off the founder legend
3. Translate the words of children
4. Analyze departing visitors
5. Plumb the online conversation
6. Discover what your stakeholders think
7. Explore and dig down with your staff

These methods are adaptable for museums of any size and type, at any stage of the branding or rebranding process. The goal is to have the brand emerge, and there are many ways to ferret out your brand's distinctiveness.

REMEMBER YOUR STORY

Any staffer of the above-mentioned pioneer museums would have told the same story, if they were asked. Most of their donors probably could tell it, as well, if prompted. That's what makes the story an unbeatable branding starter: deep down, everyone understands it. It combines vision and mission—the basics of your brand that are smack dab in front of you, just waiting to be discovered.

The mighty Smithsonian has a story. So does the Wing Luke Museum of The Asian Pacific American Experience, in Seattle, and the New England Quilt Museum, in Lowell, Massachusetts, the "historic center of the nation's textile industry."

The real brand emerges when you ask people to actually write out their version of the story. Here's the format:

- Tell a group of staffers, volunteers, or board members to write a story about the museum.
- Remind them that stories can take many forms—oral, written, sung, danced, dramatized, or communicated by correspondence.

- Point out that some stories are nostalgic, some funny, some dramatic, some memoirs, and so on.
- Give them fifteen minutes.
- Ask several volunteers to read their stories.

If there are five people in the group, with luck you will hear five different stories, five tones of voice, five narrative arcs; you will also hear a cohesive message in all of them.

The next step is to agree on the one story that *best* captures the heart and soul of the brand. That will be a problem, but a high-class one.

DUST OFF THE FOUNDER LEGEND

Go back to the founding of your museum, because that's where the vision and the mission began. Frequently, it's a single person, or cohesive group, that created the first spark, but it's the first ignition of an idea that counts. The legend is different from the story because it's older and somewhat haloed in romance. Not all museums have a founder legend, but it's worth looking for.

At an American Association of Museums workshop, I conducted some years ago, a museum director lamented the fact that her pioneer museum was right across the state border from another pioneer museum. If visitors were driving west, she said, they'd stop at her museum; if they were driving east they'd stop at the other one.

I asked for the story of her museum's beginnings: it was founded on the dedication of pioneering farmers. As for the museum across the state line, it was founded on the dedication of pioneering ranchers. They each had a very distinct brand; each was worth a stop.

"Founder Legend" is a term used by corporate brand marketers because, despite its aura of nostalgia, it works; relate the founding reasons for developing Coca-Cola, Nike, or Amazon and their unique identities emerge quickly and clearly.

Sometimes the founding legend is called the founding story, because stories are boundlessly popular, and help to market a product started by a known person: Chanel, Walt Disney, and Kentucky Fried Chicken are examples. If your museum has a founding individual with legendary appeal—Mt. Vernon, the Whitney Museum of American Art, and Mark Twain's House come to mind—that's your founding legend. However, many museums have humbler foundations whose origins are equally distinctive.

The founding story of Mystic Aquarium is pure science and no drama. One of the founders was a practicing chemist who developed an "artificial seawater" product for aquariums worldwide. Good stories are found, not made. And in cases like this, one distinguishes the museum from the lifestyle Mystic Seaport nearby.

TRANSLATE THE WORDS OF CHILDREN

Children get to the point. They say things that are funny because they're surprisingly true. Children are honest. And what's salient for museums, children see things that adult eyes miss.

A ten-year-old American boy stopped in front of a statue at the Musee d'Orsay in Paris. His American grandmother, a former docent, asked him: "What do you want to know about this sculpture?" And the floodgates opened. The boy wanted to know how long it took the artist, how did he get up to the top, why did he decide to make a sculpture, and (remember, this is a child asking) what did his friends do? There are at least four stories there.

At Brooklyn Museum, a young father, whose three-year-old was watching a video about Caribbean ceremonial dances, was asked what his child liked about the museum. "She just loved the masks," the father said. "We had to go upstairs and see them again." There's a story there, although with this one, you must be able to translate a three-year-old.

Not everyone is a born storyteller, but children are pretty reliable. They may not understand museum missions and brand identity, but they get to the heart of an exhibit and from small details, great plans are revealed. Stories are a technique, especially when you want to educate, and they build your brand in a unique way: they make it relevant. No story ever survives to the next telling unless it talks true.

You don't have to query children. Listen in on any school tour going through your museum. Use your quiet Mondays to chat with homeschoolers. After collecting several weeks' worth of raw data, discuss the verbatim with colleagues. You will find some distinctive identifiers of your museum that might add up to a brand. As with all children's pronouncements, you'll want to edit them. Or maybe file the words of wisdom as diamonds in the rough for future polishing. You can also query teachers after the tour, or propose a follow-up critique—written or drawn. Publishing the Thank You letters of children is not a new idea; what's new is reading between the lines.

ANALYZE DEPARTING VISITORS

Don't conduct a new branding survey. If you distribute questionnaires at the end of a visit, add at least one of these "Exit Interview" questions to your existing visitor survey:

- What was your favorite part of your visit?
- What specific exhibit—artwork, object, and display—was your favorite?
- Thinking of all aspects of your visit today, what will you post or tweet to friends and family?
- Did you take any photos during your visit? Which one will you send to friends? Why?

This is primary research, giving you only raw data. Now you have to analyze it. Plan a one-hour meeting of your staff and/or volunteers to evaluate the answers. The perceptions of visitors—the image they form of your museum—tell you what your brand is.

If you distribute your surveys at the café, or museum store, ask at least one of these questions:

- What part of the museum will you discuss with friends?
- What specific exhibit would you like to return to?
- Any questions about what you saw today? Write them on this card, with your e-mail address, and your server [the cashier] will give it to the person who can answer it.
- Did you purchase a souvenir that reminded you of the museum? Please explain.
- If you could purchase a book that described one object or exhibit, which object or exhibit would it be about?

The answers to this informal research will be sketchy. They aren't the whole picture and are usually hastily written. Think of them, though, as invaluable gifts because they've given you insights into how visitors perceive you. The next part is much harder because you'll have to analyze this data; just remember that your analysis will be based on genuine visitor input.

PLUMB THE ONLINE CONVERSATION

Everybody's talking, and many of those millions of talkers are saying things you should hear. Get online—or on social media—for a few minutes every day and hear what's being said. In an ideal world with a lot of budget, you will hire a media consultant who can help you mine the tons of data that courses through our lives every second. In the real world, you can offer internships to young people who need real-world research projects on their resumes.

Read the comments on the social media that you use. Read comments on social media that other cultural institutions use. Go to Yelp.com and TripAdvisor.com and read what people say about any museum. Use Google to find some websites that aggregate social media comments; use the search term: "social media aggregator." Topsy.com is interesting and free. Tweetdeck.com from Twitter is free and useful for searching tracks and hashtags. Any monitoring services will flood you with fifty times (an underestimate) as much information as you can use, but it's a gateway to understanding how the consumer thinks.

Monitoring social media is not for the faint of heart; all that intensive reading yields only teaspoons of actionable insights. However, you will be taking the pulse of contemporary culture. Remember that social media is a shared activity and not one-to-many advertising. If you post, it's with the understanding that everybody listens and responds, and that you are listening, too.

DISCOVER WHAT YOUR STAKEHOLDERS THINK

Marketing consultants call it "stakeholder discovery," which simply means talking to the people who have a stake in your success and a view of what you stand for.

Talk to staff, volunteers, and board members, at the very least. Depending on your specific situation, there might be an external expert or community leader whose perspective provides insight. If your museum is based on the work or ideas of an individual, talk to the family. Often, the best insights come from vendors, the folks who have done business with the museum over the years. These professionals are astute observers and counselors.

The hidden value to stakeholder discovery is early buy-in from people whose support you need.

Donors

For a concise, bottomline expression of your brand, talk to major donors and the fundraisers who reach out to them. The former are people who require solid reasons to support you, because they get a lot of solicitations and can't give to everybody. The latter are the people who make that sale. Does it make sense to find your soul in the give-and-take of money talk? Yes; money people are pretty sensible. Here's what the Arab American Nation Museum, in Dearborn, Michigan, says about its brand on its donor page:

> "Support from donors is a vital resource as we continue to document and share the Arab American experience, work toward dispelling stereotypes, and open the minds and hearts of people of all backgrounds across the nation.
>
> *Alif shukran*! That's Arabic for 1,000 thanks!"

For comparison, read what the Aga Khan Museum in Toronto describes as its mission, to its donors:

> The Aga Khan Museum in Toronto, Canada, offers visitors a window into worlds unknown or unfamiliar: the artistic, intellectual, and scientific heritage of Muslim civilizations across the centuries from the Iberian Peninsula to China.

Each does an excellent job of positioning of its middle-east culture's Diaspora.

This is not to say that you should task your fundraisers with crafting a mission statement. Just ask how they make your case when talking to prospects.

Sponsors

Talk also to the people who line up event sponsorships; and then talk to the sponsors. Sponsors see a mutual benefit in doing business with you and, since they have a corporate familiarity with their own brands, may articulate nicely what they like in your brand. These businesspeople are about to lend not just money but also their name, and they know exactly why they value your name.

Board of Trustees

Because it brings together members from all professions and walks of life, your board as a group is a kaleidoscope of opinions. Talk to one board member. Get that person's input and it will likely encompass some board thinking. Don't, however, make this a board project. In good time, the board will have its chance to sign off on your branding proposal.

Volunteers

Volunteer docents and store personnel are your face to the public, and these are discussed more thoroughly in chapter 7, "Volunteers," and chapter 19, "Databases of Supporters." Some have been personifying your brand for a long time, and your brand persona has emerged—accurately or not—through them. Hear what special place they think you hold. Ask them to compare your museum with other organizations they've volunteered with. From the twenty-year achievers, listen to how things have changed; change reveals brand strengths.

Talk also to the volunteers who aren't "people people." They are quietly documenting down in the basement or researching off in the archives, and they see deeply and widely into your soul.

On the application form you distribute to prospective volunteers, ask prospects why they've favored you. You may unearth some branding language glowing in their answers.

Museum Staff

Most importantly, talk to everyone, from director to educators, curators to guards. This will be a long talk, a deep-digging exploration when you bring the whole group together, preferably for several discussions. First, you will assay your own people as you have assayed other stakeholders. Then, as a group, you will all discuss and analyze the gathered information.

EXPLORE AND DIG DOWN WITH YOUR STAFF

At some point, preferably at several points, gather a group together and talk. These are no ordinary staff meetings. There will be no problems or issues, and only the briefest agenda:

Why Are We Doing What We Do?

For this meeting, you'll need adamant questioning and resolute answering, because everyone is encouraged to explain why they're doing what they're doing. There are no right answers or wrong answers, but there will be a lot of Questions and Answers.

Everyone will tell what he or she does.
Each will give an example of his or her job.
Curators will explain how they conceive and design an exhibition.
Educators will describe their various programs.
Marketing people will explain how events are selected and run.
Volunteers will tell what they heard on tours or at the store.
Administrators will share the results of any research.
Appropriate people will explain how objects are added to the collection.
Everyone will tell his or her version of the museum story.

The Five Whys

The rule of the five whys will govern all proceedings. This means that every participant's comment will be followed by another participant asking, nicely, "Why?" The concept of using five whys was introduced by Taiichi Ohno, a Toyota systems pioneer, to get to the root of any problem. It has been cited for decades as a way to dig down deep and find useful solutions.

After each person tells what he or she does, ask “Why?” Whatever answer he or she gives, no matter how logical it seems, ask “Why?” Do this five successive times. It’s tough, but surprisingly effective at digging down to the core reasons why the museum does what it does. Each of the following sample questions could be followed up with five whys:

Why was this particular theme selected?
Why do think that visitor said that?
Why are those souvenirs so popular?
Why is one of our versions of the founding legend different from others?
Why was this object purchased for the collection?

After five questions, you will have greater clarity on your unique identity. Strong brands emerge over time, based on their reputation and the trust placed in them. Museums with strong brands attract visitors, members, donors, sponsors, and community support at many levels because they are found—found—to be worthy.

Chapter 11

Public Relations

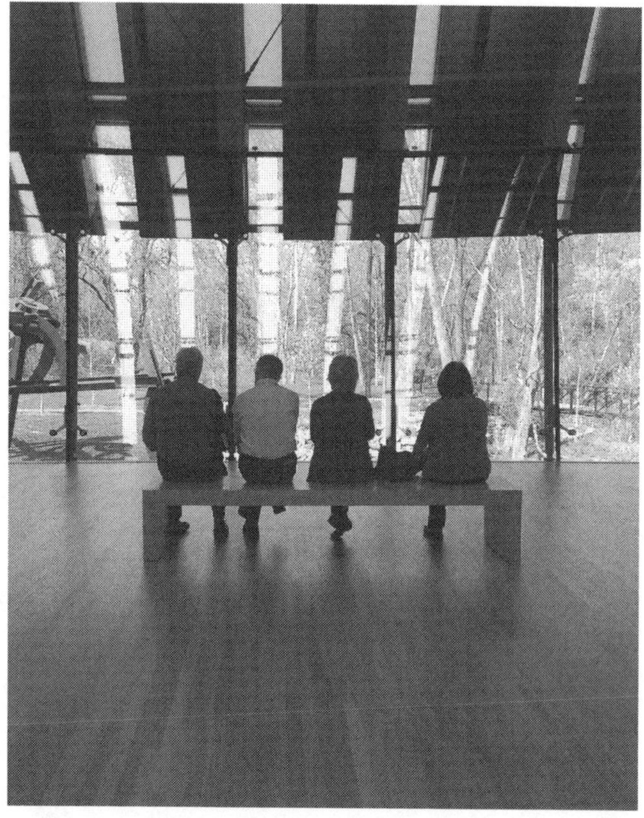

Figure 11.1 The Crystal Bridges Museum of American Art, Bentonville, Arkansas, attracts many publics to its distinctive collection and location in the Ozarks. *Source*: © 2012 Margot Wallace.

Every year in April, the Chicago Botanic Garden in Glencoe, Illinois, becomes a haven for interior decorators, antique lovers, lecture-goers, and big ticket spenders. That's a lot of consumer species for a garden, and it epitomizes how public relations works.

It's all about publics—plural—and maintaining a relationship with them. A museum has many publics, many types of visitors, members, and donors to be sought and nurtured. Public relations (PR) is the ongoing process of identifying specific publics and communicating with them in appropriate ways.

The Chicago Botanic Garden two-day event has keynote lecturers who, in 2015, for example, were a celebrated interior decorator and an expert on historic American gardens. It has an antiques and arts market. It has glorious gardens. It appeals to the home decorator, garden clubbers, lecture lovers, people who will pay \$65 to \$70 for a lecture ticket, antiquers, collectors, craftspeople, nature lovers, walkers, motor coach tourists, winter-weary Midwesterners, and home gardeners. This is one big museum, but any museum, of any size, has a similar roster of publics.

Many big public relations efforts fail because they are directed at the wrong market segments. And, sadly, small museum events, expensive in time and treasure, fail for the same reason. Some events should have been planned for members who bring guests; these leverage the loyalty of members in signing up new members. The purpose of the chapter is to introduce you to market segments that may have walked through your museum unremarked. By communicating with them more specifically, you'll instantly expand your audience and develop more fully the desired stair-step of visitor-member-donor.

Where did all these different publics come from—the architects at your history museum, or the scuba divers at your maritime museum? The Internet! Once upon a time, when museums used newspaper or radio or direct mail, they aimed only to reach mass markets. The traditional media didn't die so much as digital media sprang to life and sliced and diced those mass markets into smaller niches. PR professionals were ready: long trained and practiced in communicating with small, targeted groups, they mastered digital and social media, and still lead in employing them in identifying and reaching out to special-interest niche markets.

For a primer course in finding and relating to various publics, skim through the list of programs available at the Lower East Side Tenement Museum:

> "Exclusive evening program exploring . . . the architectural layers of history buried in the tenement's physical fabric . . . and how paint experts, wallpaper conservators, and urban archeologists "read" these layers"
>
> "Hard Times . . . Discover how immigrants survived economic depressions . . . ."

"Sweatshop Workers . . . Explore how immigrants balanced work, family, and religion at a time of great change."

"Irish Outsiders . . . Experience the heart of the immigrant saga through the music of Irish America . . ."

"Shop Life . . . Family-run stores filled the lower level of 97 Orchard for over a century. . . . use interactive technology to trace the stories of turn-of-the-century kosher butchers Israel and Goldie Lustgarten, 1930s auctioneer Max Marcus, and 1970s undergarment discounters Frances and Sidney Meda."

Your museum also has a varied slate of communities to which your brand identity and promise must be made manifest. This chapter discusses the various publics that PR efforts address, and suggests the specific ones that promise growth for your museum brand. For a discussion on how to plan a brand-specific event, see chapter 8.

These are the essential publics a museum needs to develop relations with:

1. Visitors, members, and donors, the stair-step of supporters
2. Community businesses
3. Civic and governmental communities
4. Educators
5. Scholars
6. Industry practitioners
7. Media
8. Internal market: staff and volunteers
9. Under-represented communities
10. Interest groups and social communities

Thanks to social media, there are thousands of other publics, often no larger than the hashtag trend of the moment, to embrace. Throughout this book, the term "community" encompasses a wide range of actual and virtual groups.

#1 VISITORS, MEMBERS, DONORS

Visitors are your first and biggest public, and the foot-in-the-door first step of this goal: attract visitors, convert them to members, and commit them to donors. Each level of engagement—casual, loyal, committed—must be treated with the best relationship management techniques. The basic tool is your database, which can be as basic as the e-mail address. With just that information, you can stay in touch with continuing news of the museum. Ideally, even if all you have is a handwritten guest book, you'll capture name, date of visit, and ZIP code. Now you can time your mailings, limit mailings to those living at a distance, and start to track repeat visits, store purchases, and event tickets to get insights into their individual interests.

This is how the general public gets routed into their specific publics by The Putnam Museum of Science, Davenport, Iowa. On its website's Visit drop down menu, the Putnam asks "Who Are You?" with the choice of identifying yourself as Adult, Parent, Educator, Grandparent, Teen, Pre-Teen, Kid, and Member. If you're a Grandparent, the Putnam understands your mind-set and offers an educational yet fun experience. If you're a Kid, the museum reassures you or the person reading the website that "you'll never get bored!" If you're a valued member, the museum wants to keep you engaged, and your page of the Visit menu emphasizes: "Think you've seen it all at the Putnam? Think again! Every visit is a new experience."

When your museum has a narrowly focused mission and brand, your vitality comes from programs—the more imaginative, the better. You leverage your programmatic creativity by connecting it to likely groups who will appreciate it. Frankly, this includes most groups; by calling them out, you engage them more fully. Your brand need never be limited by its single-mindedness; rather, it is enriched by showing its stretch and adaptability.

The Eisenhower Presidential Library, Museum, and Boyhood Home, in Abilene, Kansas, obviously has a singular identity. But the range of the Eisenhower legacy is shown in just a few 2015 exhibitions, such as a Smithsonian traveling exhibition "Patios, Pools, & the Invention of the Backyard," a look at 1950s America when suburbs and backyards became iconic, and the Eisenhower administration was credited with the prosperity that made them happen. The web page description makes it meaningful for today's homeowner public: "Many contemporary backyards still boast the pristine lawn, low-maintenance plantings, patios, outdoor furniture, grills and play equipment that first emerged after World War II."

Another exhibition, *Eisenhower: The Public Relations President,* had a decidedly contemporary appeal. The description of the program showed its relevance: "He revolutionized America's political communication process, forever changing the president's relationship with the Fourth Estate, Madison Avenue, public relations and ultimately, the American people."

Both reach publics that differ in interests and attitudes, and both point out their relevance in well-written web page summaries. Note that if your museum invests time, money, and brain power in an imaginative exhibition, go the extra step and find a good writer.

Visitors are a public that needs constant attention because their demographic changes daily. For one thing, they keep getting older and, of course, younger. They come from farther away. Members put down roots in your community, and they want to belong. New donors are born all the time.

One museum that connected well with its visitor public is the Columbia River Maritime Museum, in Astoria, Oregon. It moved beyond merely telling about the River and addressed real concerns of North Coast residents—one of its publics—with its 2015 lecture "Beyond Geology: How to Deal with the Risks of Living on the North Coast." The event emphasized "how people on the north coast can grapple productively with the threat of a large earthquake and tsunamis." Maps of vulnerable areas were included with the lecture. Several branding opportunities were utilized. The lecture reinforced the maritime mission of the museum. It related the museum to its physical community and its residents. And the "inundation map" was a take-home reminder of the museum that could last for months or years after the actual visit. It spoke meaningfully to a specific group of visitors.

#2 COMMUNITY BUSINESSES

"Business" and "museum" didn't always appear in the same sentence, but they've always been part of the same community, and they are as linked as salt and pepper at the local restaurant.

The Tenement Museum on Manhattan's Lower East Side embraces the businesses in its neighborhood. It holds a regular series of "Tenement Talks," and attendees at each program are invited to "continue the conversation" at a local eatery, a fourth generation business on the Lower East Side. That's good business for the neighborhood, and equally good for the museum brand because of the engagement inherent in a good discussion over food.

Look, also, at the good relations nurtured—or managed—by events such as the one at Plimoth Plantation. Plimoth plantation brought in local distillers for an event held in its craft center. Museum historians explained the brewing process, so the event reflected the museum's brand focus on Early American handmades. The April 2015 event certainly tied in with the museum brand, and introduced small businesses to their neighbors and visitors. Museums can do another favor for local businesses: they can hold events, such as this one, during the shoulder travel season before summer tourism really kicks in.

The Autry National Center of the American West paid attention to several of its business neighbors in Los Angeles with an event that featured an evening of traditional and contemporary Western songs. The evening gave gigs to many museums, and it was hosted by the California Chapter of the Western Music Association. Pay attention to other not-for-profit businesses such as trade associations. They might not have a physical presence, but their influence is big and solid.

#3 CIVIC AND GOVERNMENTAL COMMUNITIES

Your museum has a hometown, a postal address, a neighborhood, and neighbors, and many aspects of the museum are based on that home: education programs; size of parking lot; volunteer pool; board composition; architectural distinction; climate control; media attention. Your community is in your DNA, and it will determine many of your decisions. Two Western museums highlight the role of community. The Steelworks Museum, in the Bessemer section of Pueblo, Colorado, positions itself as a museum of Western industry, its origins in the Bessemer steel works and a neighborhood that was practically a company town. The American National Cowboy and Western Heritage Museum in Oklahoma City, Oklahoma, ties its identity to the evolving nature of Western culture that started with cowboys; it invites visitors to "explore" and the word explore, as well as wide vistas and fearless horse-riders, pushes through every page. Oklahoma City was a cow town and then an oil town, and then a town whose citizens kept exploring new ways to flourish and grow. Every city and town, whatever its size, has many publics living there.

Another museum, miles to the east, speaks eloquently about its community: The Mint Museum, in Charlotte, North Carolina, notes that the Charlotte community "came together to transform a historic structure into a world-renowned museum," that it employed "its resources to service the area community," and that it deployed "that same sense of civic pride, philanthropy and entrepreneurial spirit . . . [to drive] . . . investment in the museum for the benefit of those around it."

Civic and government publics require a precise—as contrasted with warm and fuzzy—kind of relating. It's more of a negotiation: your halo, their laws; your social programs, their money; their culture policies, your visitors/members/voters; your low profile, their high profile. Make no mistake, beyond the dollars and sense lies an understanding of museums' value; however, the numbers people in government like facts to support your programs.

Relationships with governments mean understanding the goals of local officials—and then helping them understand how your goals mesh with theirs. This kind of engagement is a linking of arms in mutual advocacy: museums need government support and governments need the citizens that museums attract. In making a cogent argument for your needs, and each museum's is vividly different, there is one rule of thumb to remember: organize your talking points, so that they succinctly state your museum's advantages and abilities. Advantages and abilities must be distinctive, worded in a way that shows them to be clearly the product of your museum, distinct from other museums or cultural institutions, and relevant to the government's goals. Good branding tells the truth and uses specifics:

Tell local leaders how many school groups visited, how many members you have, the exact ZIP codes that your visitors list (pay attention that they are within local, county, or state border). Government publics are partners that like facts to support your effectiveness. For example:

"We provided after school programs to over 250 children from October 15 to May 15 last year."

"Our twelve-month visitor total in 2015 surpassed 50,000, a ten percent increase over 2014."

If you want the mayor to address your annual benefit, write:

"Our museum reaches over 50,000 people each year, over eighty percent of whom visit from the three ZIP codes surrounding our building."

Or:

"Our sponsors of this wonderful benefit represent the education and business communities in the city, and we are proud to partner with them."

The former president of the American Alliance of Museums (AAM), Dr. Ford Bell, showed his knowledge of the government public when he spoke to a science and technology education subcommittee of the U.S. House of Representatives in advocacy of museums' contribution to science and technology education. He started his presentation by saying that the AAM included museums such as "Manassas National Battlefield Park in Chairman Wolf's district, the AAM-accredited Academy of Natural Sciences in Ranking Member Fattah's district, and the AAM-accredited Houston Museum of Natural Science in Representative Culberson's district." And then, considering his audience, he specified that the museum community includes aquariums, zoos, science museums, and technology centers. Did he forget art, history, and heritage museums? No, Dr. Bell, a PR-savvy museum executive, was selectively relating to the science and technology public in front of him that day.

"We provide supplementary educational modules to over 250 home-schooled children every year." If that sounds generic, add "from October 15 to May 15." That's giving you an advantage.

#4 EDUCATORS

This is a big group, in size, reach, and influence. It looms large because children are such a big group, and school occupies so much of the calendar year, and education is so relentlessly covered by the media. Education issues affect other publics: your civic, governmental, and cultural publics look to museums to see how to reach the educator public. So it's interesting to see events that go beyond the stated purpose of exhibition and interpretation. Chapter 3 discusses the major role education plays in a museum's brand; this chapter looks at the wider public of educators that museums of any size can court.

Day camps and summer camps are not a new phenomenon, but they're worth a special look, because they have a lot of competition for the consumer's summer leisure budget. And their own budget is daunting, including the costs of facilities, employees, insurance, food, supplies, and marketing. Families are an obvious public for vacation camps. So are educators, who understand well the need to keep young minds connected through vacation breaks, and welcome help in this important task.

Glazer Children's Museum in Tampa, Florida, makes a persuasive case to its particular public for camps: "It may not snow in Florida, but we're ready to spark winter wonder! Why are the poles covered in ice and what kind of animals live at each one? Don't let your child's education cool down during winter break—keep them engaged in hands-on education at Camp Connect." Glazer Children's Museum in Tampa also brands itself nicely when it reminds potential campers, their parents, and their Snowbird grandparents of Tampa's unique climate attributes. Attention to all museums in any clime: when it comes to education publics, remember grandparents.

Another educator public is that large group of self educators, the public centered on continuing education. Every time your museum presents a multi-day course or conference, one that requires a time and money commitment, it reaches an education-focused public, though not specifically teachers.

Spelman College Museum of Fine Art addresses this category in its annual Toni Cade Bambara Scholar-Activism Conference: "Complete with creative, intellectual, and community-organizing opportunities, the 14th annual convening is meditation on the contemporary struggles Black women face." It's an excellent branding tool because it's specific to the mission of Spelman museum—"the only museum in the nation that emphasizes art by and about women of the African Diaspora"—and because it's annual—an anticipated, familiar, loyalty-perpetuating part of the museum.

A less intellectual public, but still education-oriented, was addressed by The Historical Society of New Mexico in its 2015 New Mexico History Conference. The two-day conference was open to "New Mexico history enthusiasts." Enthusiasts are an important public because enthusiasm is so catching. Enthusiasts spread information freely and sincerely, the bywords of our socially connected culture.

#5 SCHOLARS

When a museum program is more scholarly, clearly aimed at the PhD thesis-, journal-, and book-publishing cohort, it is also a brandable event. This part of the educator public is influential and far-reaching; scholars are part of a global consortium of researchers advising governments, industries, universities, and other museums. They are quoted and cited, invited to consult and advise. This seemingly arcane community is very much out there.

An example is the Lighthouse Archeological Maritime Project (LAMP) at St. Augustine Lighthouse and Museum. Through its researchers and curators it expands maritime history and science to college interns, scientists, and the segment of the general public looking for in-depth and scholarly programs. It offers professional (and for a fee) field schools, conservation workshops specializing in waterlogged artifacts, and scientific research diving. As the museum's programmatic needs are met, so is its branding. One public looks at the St. Augustine Lighthouse and Museum as a tourist attraction with science *bonafides*. Another public sees a deep maritime resource. With both components, the museum has built a flagship brand.

Many museums have scholar publics waiting to be found. If you have talented researchers, the ones with scholarly ambitions can be encouraged to stretch. A museum brand should always cultivate scholars—it's part of your mission—and they can add strength to your brand distinctiveness.

Presidential libraries and museums are quietly renowned gathering holes for scholars, but they need not be so silent. A good start is made by the Eisenhower Presidential Library, Museum, and Boyhood Home and its Brown Bag Lunch Lecture Series for visiting scholars. These get-togethers foster "an informal setting where writers, graduate students, historians and others can talk about their research projects." And, presumably, spread the word when they get back to their home institutions.

#6 INDUSTRY PRACTITIONERS

You need only skim the website of the International Museum of the Horse to realize that this is a professional's museum. In addition to being beautiful and thrilling, the horse is an integral part of man's life, and each screen-wide banner atop each web page tells that story. If a visitor were a saddle maker, a geneticist, a veterinarian, or a transportation historian, for example, he or she would feel at home with the photos of young horses in the corrals, elegant tack, carriage wheels, and leather-bound, gold-embossed books such as *The Journey to Nedj*.

And an expert could tell by the list of education resource packets—Bridle Anatomy Worksheet, Fox Hunting Explained, Horse Breeds Activity, The Genetics of Horse Coat Color, Transportation in Early America Activity—that the brand promise was being fulfilled and passed on.

Industry practitioners are important to museums for the business and management sensitivity they bring. They serve on museum boards. They attract other big names and donors. They support the museum with their knowledge, as well as their gravitas and philanthropy.

When the Chicago Botanic Garden wanted to stay current with a specific public who saw gardens as adjuncts to beautiful homes, it hired an industry professional. One lecturer during its spring event was Mario Buatta, a respected interior decorator. When the Plimoth Plantation wanted to validate the importance of crafts to early America, it brought in professional craft brewers. Brands are noticed when they actively pursue up-to-date events. And they gain respect and trust from all new audiences.

A good example is the Columbia River Maritime Museum, in Astoria, Oregon. It moved beyond merely telling about the River and addressed real concerns of North Coast residents—one of its publics—with its 2015 lecture "Beyond Geology: How to Deal with the Risks of Living on the North Coast." The event emphasized "how people on the north coast can grapple productively with the threat of a large earthquake and tsunamis." Maps of vulnerable areas were included with the lecture. Several branding opportunities were utilized. The lecture reinforced the maritime mission of the museum. It related the museum to its physical community and also its professional community. And the "inundation map" was a take-home reminder of the museum that could last for months or years after the actual visit. It dealt with facts and it was professional.

#7 MEDIA

PR has an inimitable value for branding because it earns attention. Unlike advertising, which is paid media, or your own website, which is owned media, PR is earned media, and it has always worked hard to merit the trust and commitment of the communities it reaches out to.

A museum can't control what the media writes, but today it can load the media with information and through facts clear away any misconceptions and strengthen the brand's authority. A good example is the media frenzy that surrounded the Barnes Foundation and its move from a cul-de-sac in a Philadelphia suburb to an easily accessible showplace on the main artery of the city. Many said the will-breaking move was treason; some said the artworks would suffer in the new space; some said they'd miss the old place. And then the Barnes Foundation, at its new location, initiated new exhibitions and programs, and public relations people sent releases, and then the story was retold and reposted and retweeted so often that the fresh air made everyone a little dozy. And then Facebook posts and Yelp comments made new connections to ever-expanding news and opinion. Until finally, within three years of its infamous change of location, the new-old museum shines with its own light. The story of the eccentric Dr. Barnes and his betrayal has been replaced by the founder legend of the visionary Dr. Barnes, who saw his museum as an art school, teaching new generations of visitors how to learn about art.

#8 INTERNAL MARKET

You communicate with staff all the time, and with volunteers regularly, so there are opportunities for strong branded messaging—and on-brand messages. Unless you're a large museum, you'll be recruiting from a local pool, and this is a distinct public. Remember that people who work with you—paid or unpaid—have options, and you want your brand to be option number one.

All written or published communications should carry a brand identification, starting with the sheet they're printed on. It should be letterhead, or at least carry the name of the museum. Formal announcements such as meeting agendas or notes should always be written on letterhead. Announcements of employee news, congratulations, or condolence are always written on formal letterhead. The whole point is not only to show that the museum cares, but also to reinforce the brand name. Even an informal note tacked on a bulletin board should say:

> "The Springfield Valley History Museum will be closed on December 25 and January 1. We wish you and your family happy holidays."

Not:

> "We will be closed on December 25 and January 1."

Never miss a chance to state your full brand name, especially to people who are already inside.

The attitude of the museum as family is consistent with good branding, which instills familiarity and loyalty. You know that about visitors and members, and the concept is just as important with volunteers and staff. The attitude of "Us" will pervade all operations. Docents will talk about our museum; store employees will relate items to exhibits; cafe servers will ask diners about their visit; student interns will relate their expertise to the museum exhibits rather than to their college major.

Local community spirit, often praised, is referenced and channeled into the thinking of the Mint Museum in Charlotte, North Carolina:

> The Mint Museum in the Community
>
> With over 75 years of history and nearly 35,000 works of art, The Mint Museum is widely recognized as an invaluable cultural and educational resource for the city, the region and the state. Ever since the Charlotte community came together to transform a historic structure into a world-renowned museum, that same sense of civic pride, philanthropy and entrepreneurial spirit has driven investment in the museum for the benefit of those around it. . . . The Mint aspires to ignite and connect the communities of the world, starting with the ones right in our own neighborhood.

#9 UNDER-REPRESENTED COMMUNITIES

A local museum or historical society may find that a large percentage of its community is an active and distinct minority, ethnic, or other under-represented group. Often, as is the case with the Arab American National Museum in Dearborn, Michigan, or Wing Luke Museum of the Asian Pacific American Experience in Seattle, the strength of the ethnic group commands a museum of its own. At the Burke Museum in Seattle, Washington, exhibits and events are created specifically for Native Americans.

> The Autry Museum has for over a dozen years devoted a specific event to its Native American constituents who, no doubt, now hail from a much wider area than the museum's physical reach. It's a film festival, with a two-day schedule. It is billed as America's largest Native American film festival, but that's beside the more important point. Its longevity proves its commitment to listening to its important stakeholders and to remaining relevant, something all great brands do.

Even museums with a community-specific mission have other publics they can reach out to for broader visitorship and credibility. The Museum of the Americas focuses on North, South, and Central American culture, but within that large geographical area lurk issues that speak to niche groups. A case in point is the 2015 exhibition on "Fordlandia," Henry Ford's utopian town in the Amazon River basin that never took root and ultimately decimated the surrounding rain forest. The story of ecosystem malpractice is told in photographs by British artist Dan Dubowitz, and summarized in an excellent webpage—"About the Exhibition"—that will reach a farther-flung publics. It's a mesmerizing horror story in itself, and a cautionary tale for others. The museum's core values revolve airing issues such as development, human rights, and justice—as well as culture, learning and innovation—and this direction leads toward many groups not usually covered by the "Arts" category.

The Wing Luke Museum in Seattle addressed similar boundary-crossing in its 2014 exhibition on immigrants and work, with its highlighting of the struggle for finding dignity and self-sufficiency in a job market shut tight to Asians.

#11 INTEREST GROUPS AND SOCIAL COMMUNITIES

Today's interest groups are frequently signified by hashtags, Pins, Friends, and Followers. Social media platforms such as kickstarter.com are based on groups with so much interest in a common topic that its adherents willingly send money. These groups are narrowly focused but global in reach, so they can be large and, thanks to technology, influential. For a museum, these virtual communities open new audiences and new supporters. PR departments—or communications staff—often designate community managers to interact with them. Museums need these concept-focused communities: They validate your brand.

One community gaining a strong hold on museums, no surprise here, is the science community. Scientists—demanded by education, corporations, research institutions, governments, philanthropy, and the news media—add value to any museum. And one area where museums can play a major role is STEAM—Science, Technology, Engineering, Arts, and Math. This curricular offshoot of the STEM courses can be addressed by any museum, large or small.

Conversely, science museums can broaden their audience reach by relating the STEMs to STEAM. An example was the Mutter Museum at the College of Physicians in Philadelphia that offered a lecture of interest to historians and sociologists as well as medical people—on Abraham Lincoln's lifelong secret depression and its effect on the Civil War and slavery.

Local history museums, as well as their larger cousins, have ample resources to mount exhibitions of interest to the science community. The Snyder County Historical Society museum in Middleburg, Pennsylvania, has exhibits devoted to early optometry, photography, telephones, and printing presses—the technology of the day.

The Anchorage Museum has art, history, and science intertwined in its brand personality, and sees science and the arts as partners in its mission of "bringing the world to Alaska."

Its Polar Lab combines the art of the North as depicted by Romantic painters with the science of the North as studied by multiple disciplines.

The Lake County Historical Society in Two Harbors, Minnesota, features its lighthouse on its home page, with a review of the building's rock foundation (engineering); rain water collection system and lens (technology); and its radio-beacon-fog-signal direction + distance finding device (science).

Homeschoolers are another community, a subgroup quite distinct from the larger education group or family group. It is discussed more thoroughly in chapter 3, but this group is well served by social media, and must be targeted as a discrete interest group that crosses many traditional borders.

Scientist communities come in all strengths, from practicing doctors and researchers to local environmental groups. What makes these publics important to museums is their accessibility; you don't have to mount an exhibition if you have a good blog. You don't have to present a lecture if you know how to tweet. Exhibitions and lectures attract hundreds, or thousands, if you're lucky. Social media reaches the world with the added advantage of retweets and comments. One kind of public doesn't cancel the other out; each enhances the other.

Science, of course, is only one community to address; you could as easily highlight sports, health, food, or Mother's Day. However, emerging science was key to the survival of early American settlements and innovation was in the pioneers' DNA. As museums in every American country prove, their citizens could not have emigrated to and developed a new nation without the daily life tools of cooking, clothing, agronomy, commerce, communication, technology, and transportation. The art of daily living pervades the American lexicon; the science of daily living is equally apt, and timely.

And there are other, just as intensive, interest groups: communities formed around global issues—those big ideas that cross borders and reach all markets, demographics, and psychographic groups—create instant publics. Some endure seemingly forever, such as healthcare and environmental sustainability. Some are new like the STEM advocates. Some are transitory but intensely meaningful and possibly significant as inflection points. When Gertrude Whitney in 1929 founded a museum whose mission was American Art, it was seen as whimsical at best, traitorous to her class at worst. But she had a public: people who admired American artists and felt equal to the task of taking on European culture. Not a big group then, but they started something. Even small publics should be heeded because they could be influential.

An example of a museum reaching out to interest groups for broader visitorship and awareness is The Museum of the Americas, which focuses on North, South, and Central American culture, but within that large geographical area lurk issues that speak to niche groups. In a 2015 exhibition titled "Fordlandia," Henry Ford's short-lived utopian town in the Amazon River basin, the museum addresses the decimation of the surrounding rain forest.

The story of ecosystem malpractice is told in photographs by British artist Dan Dubowitz, and summarized in an excellent webpage, "About the Exhibition." It's a mesmerizing cautionary tale that, thanks to digital and social media, can reach the global audience of rainforest advocates. The museum's core values encompass the airing of issues such as development, human rights, and justice, and this direction leads toward many groups included in the "Americas" category.

Even seemingly single-focus museums such as the Buffalo Bill Center of the West, which combines several separate entities, resonate with many distinct communities. So important are these communities that the museum refers readers to them and their blogs on the home page. A look at their standing blogs suggests the range:

The Draper Museum Raptor Experience
Fieldnotes from the Greater Yellowstone Ecosystem
Cody Firearms Museum
The Center of the West's Conservation Department
Plains Indian Museum

Blogs reach specific publics meaningfully, because they're written by people who care deeply about a subject and write easily and often about it. For small-staffed museums, the nice thing about a blog is that it needn't last longer than the tenure of an intern. It's a perfect assignment for a student looking to burnish his or her resume.

The Combat Air Museum in Topeka, Kansas, housed in a former air force hangar, also courts a wide range of communities within its scope of operable combat aircraft, and here we see an undersung advantage of Facebook. While the mega-connector has become the link to all people about all things, it is superb as a targeter of specific groups, as evidenced by some 2015 museum Facebook posts from, among others:

Airplane lovers
Families of young children
People who like flight simulation and other interactive experiences
Historians
The U.S. Navy
WWII
Women's History

Take a look at the posts from your visitors, and analyze them for the individual interests they reveal. Each of these groups can be addressed specifically with your own well-written posts, newsletter items, or events. It is the challenge of public relations to identify a promising publics and communicating meaningfully with them; this is how a good brand takes full advantage of its core values.

Even a small museum can expand its brand promise. When the Winnetka (Illinois) Historical Society mounted an exhibition on local travelers in the 1920s, it expanded its community to communities of people interested in adventure travel, business travel, geography, women's history, fashion history, and innovation in luggage. If visitors can't see the actual exhibition, they can visit the website. There was a time, the museum notes, when most people lived and died within twenty miles of where they were born, so travel was a museum-quality topic. Horizons are still out there, in the form of exciting new communities.

The brand challenge for small museums is to put their core values to work. All historical societies or local heritage museums have exhibits on subjects with a wide appeal, from underground railroad stations to local astronauts. Activate these from static items for physical visitors to branded events for virtual and potential visitors. Bring in new visitors on, say, the anniversary of the moon landing or the Civil Rights Bill, collect their e-mail addresses, and encourage these news publics to become members. The stair-step of visitor-member-donor thus begins and PR has done its job.

Chapter 12

Digital and Social Media

Figure 12.1 Fountain of the Righteous, Illinois Holocaust Museum & Education Center, Skokie, Illinois. The museum gets the best endorsement there is—unsolicited and in social media. *Source*: © David Seide/DefinedSpace.com.

Media—and that means all digital and social platforms—are not created equal and from the moment of their birth they are nurtured by distinctive communities.

Most museums place three to four social media icons at the bottom of their website home page, and some have elevated them to the beginning of the website.

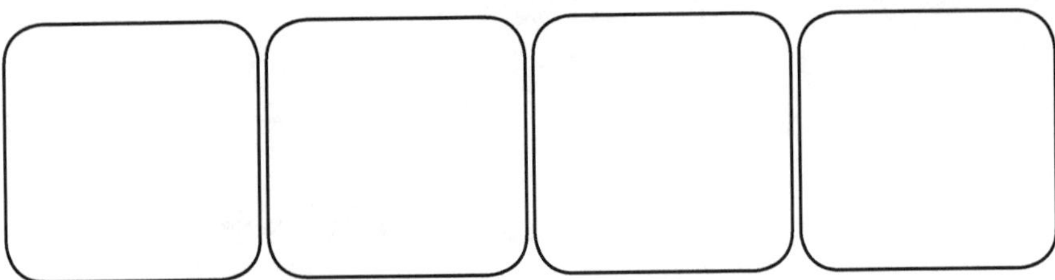

Figure 12.2 Four Squares.

You can probably guess which letter or symbol fills the first box in figure 12.2, and whether the Bluebird or the Camera icon is the second, but the choice and placement of social media are as varied as the museums that use them. Some museums, with good visitor reviews, put the Owl icon in a prominent position.

When you put their familiar icons on your website, you tacitly join the unique cultures of the various social media. Each is different from the others, with different benefits for museums. Each has strategic advantages for your brand.

SOCIAL MEDIA IS MESSY

Clutter and noise suffuse social media. Everyone with an opinion, from loyal neighborhood visitor to a pundit across the world, can alter the tone and thrust of your message. After just a few retweets, mostly what anyone sees is @s and #s. By comparison, the stolid, old-fashioned newsletter is an oasis of calm. This icon should always be as easily available as Facebook, Twitter, Instagram, Pinterest, and YouTube.

Figure 12.3 is the box that invites visitors to enter their e-mail addresses and receive the museum's newsletter. A newsletter, unlike social media, weights the discussion on the side of the museum, not the crowd. Newsletters provide spaces to comment and links to share, but that's not the purpose of a newsletter, whose singular voice tells your brand story unadulterated by streams of

Figure 12.3 Square.

tweets, sidebars of ads, or the vagaries of amateur photography. Chapter 13, "E-mail," covers the branding advantages of messages sent from one (your) to the many (everyone on social media). This chapter discusses how to control messages before they fly out of your hands and get re-sent many-to-many.

To avoid being beguiled by popularity, learn how each social media platform accomplishes different goals. For starters, look at two ways to categorize Facebook, Twitter, Instagram, Pinterest, YouTube, peer-review sites such as TripAdvisor and Yelp, and blogs.

One: categorize social media platforms by target audiences.

Facebook—Reaches everyone, although with some segmentation

Twitter—Targets people already loyal to or interested in a brand

Pinterest—Selects specific interest groups and communities, adeptly uses visuals as communication, and can be organized by the museum

Instagram—Reaches many different kinds of people, depending on photographer's choice; perfect example of citizen-generated, pure unmediated visuals

YouTube—Reaches interest groups, third-party endorsers (other media), and a wider cohort of video fans

Blogs—Targets museum loyalists and a broad segment of scholars

Peer-review sites—Narrowly targets prospective visitors

Website—Targets a lot of very interested people; mostly people are already aware of your museum or predisposed to visit

Two: categorize social media by how much maintenance is required.

Website—High maintenance but at discretionary times

Facebook—Unlimited amounts of regular posts

Pinterest—Regular maintenance, but curating more important that quantity

Twitter—Constant writing and curating of photos

Peer-review sites—Constant monitoring and response

Blogs—Regular output on a schedule of your choosing

YouTube—Lengthy production but no regular schedule

Instagram—The crowd does most of the work

Now, learn your own priorities. No museum has the time for more than two-four media, and you may want to reassess which ones you use. Of course, start with the one that makes sociability possible.

WEBSITE

Your website is the branded anchor that tethers all social media. It lists the icons that suggest what media to follow. Your website is the link that all media refer back to. Websites are owned media, as compared with social media that are shared media. Your museum authors and controls your message on your website. Here, you are the authority.

Home Page

It talks to all your constituents. It is the first thing they see when linking from social media such as Twitter or Pinterest. It's where tourists go to for trip planning. It's where devotees go to research their philanthropy. There are ten brand opportunities that the website accomplishes and each must reflect and reinforce your distinctive personality. Once a visitor starts down the path in a website, it's easy to lose track of the brand, so you have to leave branded signposts on every page. In *Writing for Museums*, the chapter on websites discusses in detail how to design and write a website. In this chapter, I highlight the branding opportunities in the various parts of your website. When time and budget allow, any one of these opportunities can be addressed:

Opportunity #1: Define your brand/collection/competitive place in the leisure marketplace

Opportunity #2: Provide basic information in a non-basic way

Opportunity #3: List exhibitions and collections that are your brand's DNA

Opportunity #4: Announce job and volunteer openings to people supportive of your brand

Opportunity #5: Solicit donations and other support from people who share your brand vision

Opportunity #6: Sell merchandise that reinforces brand memories

Opportunity #7: Describe the restaurant, where an enduring relationship is nurtured over food

Opportunity #8: Provide knowledge for researchers who respect your brand's authority

Opportunity #9: Explain your education program to new generations of brand loyalists

Opportunity #10: Announce brand-building programs and events

Opportunity #11: Anchor brand information disseminated through social media

Define Your Brand Position in the Competitive Culture Marketplace

Branding starts at the front door, with your home page—the first place to establish your brand identity, core values, and personality, visually and verbally. It sets the tone for every page that follows. The home page is not an advertisement for this weekend's event or what's on sale at the store. It is for defining your collection, mission, and competitive place in the leisure marketplace. As with any marketing decisions, you have to select the visuals, photos, text, and organization that best support your brand. The home page of Vesterheim National Norwegian-American Cultural Center regularly changes but always stays on brand. For example, classes are important to the mission of this heritage museum, and that aspect is always depicted front and center. For a quick, visual reminder of Norwegian culture, a rosemaling or knitwear pattern is usually within scrolling distance.

Provide Basic Information in a Non-Basic Way

If it comes from your museum, it is no longer basic. It is your information. A good example, worth repeating, is the one given in chapter 1, "Exhibitions" on the way Spencer Museum states the time of an event. On a printed invitation it states "Sundown." Most events give a time that says "6–8 p.m." It's so basic. But the Spencer is a brand that dares to show its personality.

List Exhibitions and the Collections That Are Your Brand DNA

Exhibitions are where you bring to 360-degree life the mission you embody, and where the website can plumb your brand and collection in depth. State that purpose on your website. Your website can also display objects in the collection that don't get viewed as often. The website gives you space to describe why they were acquired and how they relate to your brand. Chapter 1, "Exhibitions" lists exemplary exhibitions.

Announce Jobs and Volunteer Openings to People Supportive of Your Brand

Lavish the Job/Career/Employment page with the visuals and text that enhance your brand—the reason why people want to work with and for you. Your text must be factual and concise, but since job responsibilities tend toward the generic, highlight your distinctiveness with photos of your building, neighborhood, and objects, where appropriate. This web page can boast about your museum to a community that is already enthusiastic about a museum career—even an unpaid one. The Chicago Botanic Garden keeps its brand in sight in every photo, where something green and growing is always part of the volunteer shot.

Solicit Donations and Other Support from People Who Share Your Brand Vision

Your Support page has the tough job of raising money from people who, at this point, are conversing only with a screen. Welcome these highly desirable audiences with a page that exudes brand personality. Utilize photographs that are specific to your museum. Continue the same design elements that typify the rest of the website. You'd be surprised how many websites stint on charm at the one place that it's needed most. Remember that, for donors, giving money to a favored institution is a brand act—one set of individual values buying into your core values.

Sell Merchandise That Reinforces Brand Memories

The online store is more than a way to make money. It is also tasked with keeping your brand awareness front and center. The online store is a reason for people to revisit your site, even if they aren't planning a trip to the galleries. And if your museum is seasonal, or closed for construction, as San Francisco Museum of Modern Art was for several years, the online store is nonpareil in keeping your fans in touch. Their website does a thorough job of keeping the museum name top of mind. The connection to the museum brand is evident in their write-up for the toys section.

> Toys section: For Kids
>
> Our children's toys and books are specially selected to be both educational and fun, exposing youth to key concepts in modern and contemporary art with strong visuals, energetic color schemes, and engaging themes and shapes.

Describe the Restaurant Where an Enduring Relationship Is Nurtured over Food

The objective of this page is to help your café, restaurant, and catering facilities leverage the love of eating and the opportunity for reflection on your brand. It makes it easy for a visitor to plan to stop, refresh, relax, and ingest brand memories.

Provide Knowledge for Researchers Who Respect Your Brand's Authority

This part of your website addresses a special constituency that deserves more online attention. Researchers today include not only scholars but academics, authors, investigative journalists, autodidacts, precocious children, family genealogists, and the perennially curious. Be proud if they come to your museum for information; flaunt your brand. Your prestige is based on your brand distinctiveness, and that includes a distinctive web page.

Explain Your Education Program to a New Generation of Brand Loyalists

The student and adult programs have one important unintended consequence: branding. When people learn about your collection, then see it manifested in exhibits, then reinforce it with more involving activities, they are immersed in your brand. Make sure you follow up with e-mails and do your best to capture for the long term the addresses of those who have become engaged for a short term.

Announce Brand-Building Programs and Events

These expand your brand into new territory. Good brands are flexible, and their reputation eases the stretch into new markets. Innovative programs and challenging lectures carry some risks—not everyone will like them. However, the main risk is being too likeable, so that attendees remember the enrichment, and not the museum that made it possible: remember to stay on brand. Reach out to new market segments that will stay with you.

An example of a branded annual event that keeps members engaged is Plimoth Plantation's annual two-day conference on seventeenth-century "life-ways," dealing with material culture in topics such as the 2015 "Trimmings Conference: Adorning the Fashionable Figure in the Seventeenth Century." It appeals to many stakeholder segments and some may be new; the brand stays firmly rooted in seventeenth-century New England life.

Anchor Brand Information Disseminated through Social Media

Almost anything in your museum could also appear on your website, and many are the cost and benefit advantages. However you cut costs, don't cut corners. The Henry Ford does an admirable branding job of all the materials that now appear only online: its digital magazine, education curriculum guide, store merchandise holiday catalog, and annual report. Each, not just the magazine, is presented as an enhanced magazine with a dynamic cover design, Flipboard-style turnable pages, excellent and abundant four-color photography throughout, and well-written text. The annual report is titled "The Henry Ford Effect." The Educators Resource Guide is titled "OnLearning." The Magazine, "The Henry Ford," is subtitled, "Gain Perspective, Get Inspired, Make History." On each page is the tagline of The Henry Ford: "Take it forward."

Owned Media

In a world of shared media, where everyone is an author and all content is subject to citizen approval or rebuttal, your website stands distinct. It is owned media that you create and in which your authority is manifest. Others can comment, but they cannot redirect your brand image or identity. It represents your brand and must act appropriately.

FACEBOOK

Facebook is oxygen, all around us, all the time. Some people inhale it, some take shallow breaths, but everyone uses it. So, maintaining your Facebook page in a branded way is challenging. How do you stand apart when every other museum in the world is on Facebook? Once visitors visit your page, how do they feel connected to you?

- Get your name and logo up front and large.
- Post only photos that include a feature—object, architectural detail, scenery, building—from your museum.
- Select posts that are brand specific. Try to keep parties, though fun, to a minimum.
- Write brand-specific headlines.
- Post regularly (not necessarily every day), to build a branded presence among all the other posts.
- Curate your posts to represent a wide range of your collection; it's your brand DNA.
- Write text with authority that refers to your brand mission.

Avoid posting just for the sake of posting. It consumes everyone's time without saying anything about your brand: Here are some speed bump "Don'ts" to slow you down until you have some branding words written:

- Don't omit captions for photos.
- Don't forget to mention your name in captions.
- Don't start posts with generics such as "We're proud to be honored by a major . . ."
- If you've been honored, lead with the award and why it's appropriate for your brand. Don't give the awarder, which has its own brand name, priority.
- Don't speak to the masses. It's tempting to be general and friendly, but it's not necessary. Your choice of Facebook already signals that you want to reach out and be friended. Act yourself, and talk your own talk. Be a brand, not a commodity.
- Don't lose your enthusiasm, just curb it.

For a good example of brand-specific photos and text, look at the Facebook presence of Washington Heritage Museums, Fredericksburg, Virginia, which devotes its space to photographs of buildings associated with George Washington.

For a fine example of thoughtful branding, look at how the High Desert Museum in Bend, Oregon, fills its Facebook timeline. Provocative photos and text continuously set the tone for its natural science exhibits and programs: with subjects from feeding falcons to meteorology, its brand identity is also manifest in headlines such as these:

"Black bear, black bear, what do you see?"
"What do flashlight fish, vampire squid, and fireflies have in common?"

To capture the range of your museum, use photos and explanatory captions and headlines that reinforce your brand. Burke Museum, in Seattle, like many science museums, conducts research as a part of its brand mission, and its headlines tell the story as well as the images do.

"This is so neat! Suquamish weaver Betty Pasco studied a historic cedar sail in the Burke collections while working on this project."

The project—recreating a Suquamish expeditionary boat—was complex. The photo and caption were easy to understand.

The museum also wanted to make a statement about its science programs for girls, and the photo, though excellent, was too generic for good branding. The headline blasted the point:

"Girls in Science—Burke Museum"

Horses are like kittens to the paparazzi of horsedom, and the National Museum of the Morgan Horse, Shelburne, Vermont, does not lack for reader-sent photographs. The Facebook page ties them together with a branded standing headline: "Sharing Carrots." The leading photo on September 14,

2015, deserves special mention: a horse in a (human) hospital room, cheering up a prone (human) patient. That carrot was a special treat.

The National Museum of Mexican Art, in Chicago, also brings its brand to life with photos. Its timeline is full of relevant shots that feature Mexican art or Latino people.

Speaking of people, it's fine to post events on Facebook; your viewers see how your brand extends into programming, and your donors see how your brand attracts gala benefit support. But if these photos feature only people, they're generic. Make sure there's an object, prop, or sign in the shot that depicts the brand.

TWITTER

Twitter, with its followers, does part of your branding job for you. People who already follow you feel an affinity that you can strengthen with more concisely written, brand-specific messages. The main challenge is to write tweets that get to the point with twenty characters of your 140. You already have a thumbnail visual reminder with your logo. Here's the rest of the assignment:

- Name your museum at the outset.
- Only send a tweet if it has a brand-specific first sentence. It's better to send fewer tweets per day if it means more careful writing.

Of course, it's not what you tweet, but what gets retweeted. So your brand name or brand-focused message has to be stated upfront, before all the #s and @s get added. There are salient pitfalls to avoid, and good examples come from the National Science Museum, London.

Pitfalls

- Promoting IMAX without clarifying its relevance to the museum core values
- Promoting a speaker first, topic second, relevance only if characters are left
- Showing kittens without a pretty darn good reason
- Naming a program speaker before you name your museum
- Selfies

Examples of Pitfalls Navigated Smartly:

"Experience the sights and sounds of an Apollo mission with our Legend of Apollo 3D film"

"Are we alone in the Universe? Nathalie Cabrol's plan to find life on Mars"
"Explore this pawsome Japanese town through the eyes of a cat"
"Revelations @sciencemuseum reminds you that photography is an integral scientific tool—not just a medium for selfies kids!"

This last example is a retweet. You can see how quickly a neat tweet gets cluttered by retweeting. Science Museum avoids all the branding pitfalls of Twitter and never ignores the science perspective, which is its core value.

Jobs and Careers

Twitter can be used to pre-sort prospective employees. Job and internship hunters comprise a community of museum fans that Twitter reaches very efficiently. Many museums have omitted or hidden the Jobs section on their websites; often they simply post a terse "Not hiring now." There is seldom time or staff to handle unsolicited requests. However, when a museum does need to hire, Twitter works hard and smart.
Here's What the Nantucket Whaling Museum Tweets:

"Like history? Want to share your love of #Nantucket & work for a great cause? We're hiring!"

For seasonal museums such as the Whaling Museum of the Nantucket Historical Association, it's timely and doesn't remain viewable quite like a web page does.

Q & A Personal Responses

Use Twitter to collect Q & As, those involving after-the-talk sessions that bring the audience into the brand event. This is especially effective at reaching people who are too timid to speak up, and those that the intern-on-the-floor can't reach. An additional branding advantage: It's electronic and you can respond individually even after the session has ended. You can archive the questions and answers for future audiences. You can analyze the questions for insights on what's relevant for your supporters.

Don't Take Twitter for Granted

Twitter is not just another conduit for chit-chat. Treat it as a branding device, with a tagline or mission statement or your logo. Note that Twitter's format, with its tally of your followers, brandishes your brand credentials for you. Here's what a tweet from the Science Museum, London, looks like:

- Strong logo, even when reduced in size
- Name and address: Science Museum @sciencemuseum
- Tagline: "Welcome to the home of human ingenuity. We curate a world-renowned collection & organise exhibitions and events for 3m visitors a year."
- Street and URL address: Exhibition Road, London, sciencemuseum.org.uk
- Third party endorsement: 7,877 following 538K followers

PINTEREST

Pinterest is, of course, thoroughly visual, and that alone targets the audiences for many museums. Beyond the visuals themselves is the Pinterest's unique organization by themes and topics. Your current and potential constituents immerse themselves in Pinterest because it speaks directly to their interests. They commit to their pursuits—be they weddings, weaving, or travel—and you can maximize this devotion by adding your brand to every image.

Because Pinterest attracts niche audiences, not large ones, you won't necessarily reach people who already "like" you. You won't reach people who don't yet follow you. Pinterest reaches people who appreciate good visuals, and they come to Pinterest selectively, because they're following layer cakes or textiles or architecture. Exploring any of those pursuits, they might end up at your board. If this serendipity happens, be prepared with an excellent photograph. If it's not excellent, it won't get pinned or re-pinned, and you're wasting your time. Write a short line of text to help searches, and then hire a good photographer.

PHOTO APPS

Photo apps like Instagram are the media to use if you want some control over citizen photographers. The posing for snapshots in the museum might raise eyebrows and ire, but not yours! Be proud that your visitors are involved in your galleries, impressed by your architecture, and eager to share their memories with friends. The best way to control photo apps is with photo ops.

Place well-designed signage at selected points in your museum: points that you select for their brand identification. Place chairs next to iconic exhibits. At family events, produce life-size historic figures, representative of your museum, with holes where the face goes; they're irresistible for children and their rooting-shooting grandparents. For doubly smart branding, follow the lead of the Strong Museum of Play, in Rochester, New York, that lets visitors put their ZIP codes on a sign, share it on social media, and possibly win a prize. It's a photographic memory for the families and data collection for the museum. Good branding on both sides!

PEER-REVIEW APPS

Apps such as TripAdvisor and Yelp represent social media at its most social. Here, peers review museums for people like them who travel and ask for a lot of advice before they go. In consumer behavioral studies they would be called innovators and followers, or explorers and settlers—adventurous, but some more so than others. Innovators and explorers don't care much about brand image and reputation because they aren't afraid to explore and evaluate for themselves. Followers and settlers, on the other hand, revere brands. Moral: When you get a good TripAdvisor or Yelp review, respond with a brand-focused post of thanks. When you get a negative one, respond quickly with a positive counter-suggestion. Here's how the Science Museum responded to one person's weep-tweet:

"We try our best. Have you seen our #Cosmonauts videos?"

You would expect a museum of conscience to attract passionate visitors, and that some of them would post comments. But you can't count on them writing well. When they do, respond. And if the review slips off brand, you can reinforce your brand in the response. Here's a brand-affirming review on the Illinois Holocaust Museum, Skokie, Illinois, written by citizen-brander Bob R.:

> I have been to a few Holocaust museums around the world. And, while I've not been to the one in Washington (which is *[sic]* hear is fabulous), I do think this one rivals any I've seen.

A museum that gets a five-star brand-specific review like that can reply with words such as:

> Thanks for your comments. Next time you visit [name of museum], be sure to see our new exhibition on . . . [provide a brand-focused description here]

TripAdvisor

TripAdvisor comments are utilized all the time by your potential visitors, but although they contain authenticity—that attribute beloved by social commentators—they lack the authority of your brand voice and expertise. An example is Mt. Moriah Cemetery in Deadwood, South Dakota, whose TripAdvisor comments run into the hundreds. They're all glowing and visitors rank it #4 among competitive culture sights, but they don't tell the story. The City of Deadwood website must be visited to find out what to expect. For museums whose website is part of a comprehensive municipal or historical association's website, make sure your comment page on social media apps links to a brand-perfect web page. Mt. Moriah Cemetery's does.

Many museums now put the owl with the red and green eyes—yes, the icon incorporates a stop and go light—up on its home page with other social media. It's daring but powerful reinforcement for their brand integrity.

YOUTUBE AND BLOGS

Take ownership of your intellectual property—your collection, interpretation, preservation, education programs, and employee knowledge—and write blogs and YouTube videos.

Personal and Familiar

YouTube and blogs are ideal branding tools. They favor a personal approach—two real persons, talking one-to-one about a subject they both find important, usually a museum employee and a museum fan. YouTube is contemporary, and shows that your brand, whatever its collection and mission, is in touch. YouTube focuses on a brand-worthy topic for four to six minutes, time for the brand and the familiarity to take hold. Blogs are also brand immersive, and utilize photos rather than video. YouTube videos and blogs are designed to a theme, so it's easy to add content with some regularity. This frequency also reinforces your brand.

About frequency: daily blogs are a luxury, but if you don't have time, staff, and budget, weekly or monthly is all right. Regular appearances will seem frequent if they are interesting and consistent.

An excellent example of YouTube consistency is the First Division Museum's "Staff Picks: Favorite War Movies." So simple, so distinctive, and so memorable! This feature is perfectly on brand, and so interesting that any movie lover will return often. Notice "movie lover." The First Division Museum has just stretched its brand to a new niche audience.

Blogs, which of course frequently are produced in video format, let your staff stretch their intellectual muscles. Individual people can relate to different stakeholder groups. The Walker Art Center, Minneapolis, opens its collection to a variety of engaging speakers through "The voices of the

Walker Art Center: what we're thinking about, who we are, and how you can connect."

Science and Natural History Museums

For science and natural history museums, YouTube and blogs fulfill the branding requisites of distinctive expertise. Each, in its own way, provides the long-form journalism and the in-depth information that reinforce its brand core values. Each is authored by real people who represent both the museum's core values and the viewer's interests. Either can be as conversational or serious as your brand requires. YouTube obviously takes more time to create, as does long-form journalism. YouTube and blogs serve a lot of information, well-documented examples, and news. They are engaging media that enhance your brand by their expansiveness.

YouTube has the advantage of being shared by third-party endorsers, frequently mainstream media, as well as by members of like-minded communities. Blogs have a little more shelf life than a video with a real person; they can be repurposed in papers and digital archives. YouTube looks of-the-minute, which is good for a brand. Blogs look expert, which also enhances a brand.

For more scholarly expert knowledge, look at Science Museum's written blogs, which link the museum's experts to a current exhibition.

"In their research for our *Cosmonauts* exhibition, Science Museum curators traced the origins of the first great leap into space by Yuri Gagarin in 1961 to events that took place well before the turn of the twentieth century." The blog connects brand core values and brand relevance.

It's a long article, and not everyone will read the whole thing, but the point of brand authority has been made. The Science Museum's blog reinforces its authority in two lines of text that head every blog:

"Inside the Science Museum"
"Welcome to the home of human ingenuity . . ."

Repetition of headings—consistency—is another way to signal brand distinctiveness. The page also lists other categories of blogs, insider information on everything from Alan Turing to Gaming to Punk Science.

Here's another insider piece from the Science Museum. It reads quickly, deals with material culture, and still reveals the same authority. This blog ends with a question to the reader:

"Do you think your favourite hobbies will stand the test of time?"

One-to-one talk and engagement, You Tube and blogs are branding classics.

Your Message, Your Media

Media is a mediator. It facilitates the communication between the speaker and those who want to listen. Choose your middleman carefully, because the message is all yours.

Chapter 13

E-mail

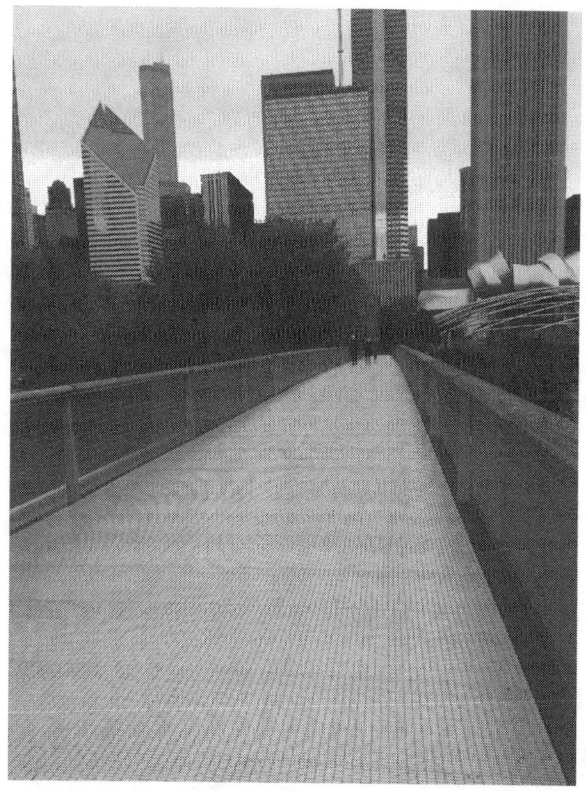

Figure 13.1 Renzo Piano-designed Bridgeway connects the Modern Wing of the Art Institute of Chicago to the city and the world beyond. The museum uses e-mail masterfully to bridge the distance between its collection and programs and the people who enjoy them. *Source*: © 2014 Margot Wallace.

Old yet newsy. Ordinary but proven. Common but universal. Low-tech, but wait until you start hitting the links. E-mail continues to be an essential tool for communicating with your public.

Consumers like e-mail. According to a study by Forrester Research, "Take Advantage of Positive E-mail Attitudes," summarized by MarketingCharts, although forty-two percent of U.S. online adults delete most e-mail advertising without reading it, the number is down from forty-four percent in 2012 and fifty-nine percent in 2010. Though the percentage of consumers agreeing that most e-mail ads they receive don't offer anything that interests is thirty-eight percent, that number then fell by three percent from 2012.

There appears to be a clear trend toward improved attitudes, says the report, as more consumers agree that e-mail offers are a great way to find out about new products or promotions and fewer complain of receiving too many e-mail offers and promotions. Sure, many people don't read e-mail; the challenge is to appeal ever more meaningfully to those who do.

Ninety-two percent of marketers agree that to maximize social media, they need e-mail as the ignition switch. Let's give the original interactive breakthrough its due. E-mail was the first marketing tool that gave viewers the option of how much to read, what to read, or to opt out of reading anything at all. When e-mail included a link to open in the browser, or the website, it gave viewers a tempting promise of limitless content. E-mail remains a singularly useful marketing tool because it is totally under your control. Unlike a post, which can be forwarded with non-authorized opinion, you control the message; if viewers want to comment on it, they have to Reply or Forward and your original message is always there. You control the Subject Line. You decide when to send the message, down to the minute of the day, and you also designate exactly who receives the message, down to an individual mailbox. Nobody has to search for your message, it's in their e-mail. Love it or hate it, e-mail is one thing everybody sees.

This chapter will show how a generic strip in a cascade of e-mail, a message that was the same size and shape and color as every other message, can blossom into a glorious piece of brand marketing. The format consists of eight elements:

1. From line
2. To line
3. Subject line
4. First linked page or message
5. Visual
6. Date
7. Banner
8. Tagline

1 FROM LINE

This is your identity, as important as your logo. It's like the name on your letterhead stationery and invoices, or the sign outside your building. The From line is the first information the reader gets about the credibility of the e-mail, it authorizes the whole communication. Readers will be intrigued, one hopes, by the message the Subject line promises, but the From line reassures them into clicking on it. The e-mail becomes more urgent if the reader recognizes the sender.

The "From" box of an e-mail carries more weight than some names can bear. Museums that are called galleries, institutions, societies, or foundations may not be recognized as a museum the e-mail recipient would love to read about. Museums named after people, especially names that start with "John A. and Susan B," don't mean anything to recipients accustomed to calling it the Smith Museum. Sometimes excessively long names in the From box are truncated in e-mail transit. Some museums, as discussed in a thread from the Association of Academic Museums and Galleries, even consider changing their names to better accommodate the formats of the electronic age.

Museums that are part of a college or university may have names that start with the college; the admirable Faulconer Gallery at Grinnell College, which offered seven programs and two temporary exhibitions during the short month of February, 2015, has, as its From address, not Faulconer, but Grinnell.edu. On the other hand, at the Hammer museum, part of the mighty University of California, Los Angeles, e-mails comes from Hammer.ucla.edu. The relationship between academic museums and their parent have many balances to strike (to be discussed more thoroughly in chapter 18, "Academic Museums") and some appear in e-mail addresses. The main branding point is that brand names have the authority and trust that encourages people to halt an endless scroll of e-mails to actually open them.

#2 TO LINE

The marketing advantage of e-mails is their pinpoint targets; they go to people who have either indicated an interest in your museum—through ticket, store, restaurant, event or membership purchases—or have otherwise been identified as museum-likely. The advantage of e-mails as brand tools is repetition and reminder; when a brand is in the mailbox, it's in the mind. A recipient may not open the mail, but the sender's name is in his or her field of vision. Depending on how sophisticated your database is, or how intensively you want to mine it, you can target recipients by the following:

General interest consumers
Recent visitors
Recent attendees at programs or events
Educators
Members
Scholars and researchers

The Burke Museum has a special e-mailing for the education audience, which could include teachers and homeschoolers, as well as the general public of parents; the Burke has a special logo on its website. Sent by "Burke Museum: Education Department" and titled "Burke Museum Education Department E-News," it even looks different from e-mails sent to other constituents. This site features a frieze of ten images—flora, bird eggs, fossils—and looks encyclopedic, promising that the Burke's education programs will range far and explore wide.

And this is before you get to the detailed messages about the programs.

Regardless of what audiences you target, e-mails remind them of your brand's distinct place on their agenda.

#3 SUBJECT LINE

Imagine a person reading the current spate of e-mail huddled over a device waiting for a meeting to start; or another person scrolling while waiting in line. Best scenario: Imagine one of your loyal members sitting leisurely at a desktop perusing the last hour's inbox. Which of these Subject lines would merit a click?

April calendar
Update
This month at the Smith-Jones
News

All too often, museums subject their e-mail readers to Subject lines that are so generic, it could be any museum that has an April calendar. It takes longer to write a Subject line with personality, but your brand has a personality, and here's the place to show it. You no longer have the kind of mail that puts your logo in the upper left hand corner.

If your name is distinctive, then a Subject line announcing "News from the Battleship New Jersey Museum—April 2015" works fine. It takes only fourteen characters to get to the distinctive part. And then the "Sent From" line also lists "Battleship New Jersey Museum." That museum has identified itself.

Specific, Specific, Specific

No, you can't be too specific in marketing. Viewers read with their egos—looking specifically for what interests them. If the specifics are on brand, you will capture eyeballs and engage readers before they even open the e-mail. Here's a Subject line from South Dakota Heritage:

"Pioneer Girl, Easter Cards, and Land in Her Own Name Exhibit"

It targets and engages all in one long line. Length need not be a problem. Send a trial e-mail to yourself; you'd be surprised how much worthwhile information you can pack into a line.

Teaser

Don't be afraid of teaser lines. It's standard advertising and it works. Teaser mail such as "One Day in Pompeii," from the Franklin Institute in Philadelphia, motivates the click that opens mail.

Here's a semi-teasing subject that doesn't cross over into the generic:

"Check out what's in bloom this April at Telfair Museums!"

If you're on the Telfair list, you know that it's in Savannah, Georgia, and the April blooming distinguishes it from other organizations that don't have floral connotations.

Relevance

E-mails should be relevant; good branding dictates that announcements be meaningful, not just splashy. The more ingenious the theme, the higher the bar for linkage to the real world and your museum's role. Plimoth Plantation found just the theme and language to tie its fundraising event to its own mission and the local community:

"Join us April 23rd for Living Proof: Celebrating the Makers Craft Spirits Tasting!"

The Subject line alludes to the tradition of craftsmanship, which is part of the museum's identity. And then it opens to a wonderful page praising "the artisans of New England's booming craft distilling industry" and linking them to the centuries' old tradition of craft distilleries.

Broad Range of Programs

It's hard to stage new exhibitions every few months, and relatively easy to offer a changing schedule of programs. The Tenement Museum, for example, whose exhibits are apartments unchanged since the late nineteenth and early twentieth centuries, can't change their exhibitions much at all. They can change their smorgasbord of lectures, classes, and programs, and display their unique collection: stories of immigrant life. Here's a sampling of the Tenement Museum's offerings, as described in the Subject line of "Notes from the Tenement" e-mails, for just a few months in January to March 2015:

"The search for General Tso"
"Irish Luck"
"Walk This Way"
"Talk the Talk"
"Get Your Goat"
"A Queen of New York"

There's something for everybody, and after a few months recipients understand how much learning they can find in this museum. All these good ideas, and the inside of the museum never changes.

Lazy Language Lines

New for Mother's Day. Season opening next week. September programs. In addition to being shallow and uninformative, generic Subject lines provide a weak structure for bold thinking. Updating, filling in calendar spaces, and making lists—these notices depict a museum in maintenance mode rather than full speed ahead. If you've got a brewpub party coming up or a conversation with a famous actress, say so in the Subject line. You can list all the other events and calendar items on the first page readers see when they open the e-mail. But first, intrigue them so they want to open it. If your understaffed museum is struggling just to keep up with its digital communications, don't e-mail as often. Unlike social media, which viewers voluntarily open every few hours, e-mail can be opened by those who aren't following you so closely. They won't notice if you contact them less often if each time offers a treat.

#4 FIRST LINKED PAGE OR MESSAGE

This is becoming the most important part of the e-mail. Now that museums send so many e-mail messages, there may not be time to craft specific Subject lines. So when a viewer decides to open an e-mail from your museum, that first opening page must explain everything. It shouts the news, in visuals and words. If your Subject line promised no more than an Update or Calendar, your Opening page fulfills that promise with facts.

Your Opening page message may have the same content as a post, but in an e-mail it carries the weight of a one-to-one message, and it must be delivered with the immediacy of a "hello". E-mails aren't the result of a mystic algorithm; they aren't just sitting there when a reader opens his Facebook page. Readers are in your e-mail database because they bought a store item, museum program ticket, or membership. When they entered their name and e-mail address, they said, in effect, "Call me sometime."

Explaining a Teaser Subject Line

Teaser lines attract those people on your mailing list who are regular visitors or members; they might not attend every exhibition or event, but they consider the option.

The Autry, in a follow-up to its good teaser Subject line, has a wonderful opening page to explain its "Last Week of a Floral Journey." Readers on The Autry list know the brand's values are rooted in the American west, so "floral" is an easy imagination-leap, right over to the page with flower motifs on its beaded vests, moccasins, and bags. The North American Indian floral beadwork explains the brand at the same time it describes a very alluring exhibition.

When a reader lands on a page with the unmistakable face of Winston Churchill, the "What's Blooming" Subject line is paid off. The Telfair Museum's message opens to a photo of the WWII British prime minister at his easel; the page is wisely designed so that the famous visage is the first thing seen, even though the page scrolls down to a lot of additional text.

Context and the So-What Factor

Not all e-mail announcements seem relevant to the viewer. Unless the recipient is already a loyal member or a committed museum-goer, you'll need to explain quickly why the subject of your e-mail matters to them.

The Anchorage Museum calls upon the director of the museum to provide the rationale for its exhibition, *Arctic Ambitions: Captain Cook and the Northwest Passage*. The opening page text reads: "Cook's voyage North is increasingly relevant; with melting sea ice, now we see cruise ships in the Arctic." With this statement, the director encompasses global melting plus a new market segment to target.

Because e-mails are harbingers of your brand, both the Subject line and Opening page will ideally be brand-appropriate. Such an ideal was reached by The Smart Museum of Art, University of Chicago. The Subject line said simply, "The Technology Question." The Opening page visual was a detail of a richly colored classical painting almost totally obscured by a black and white QR symbol and text that announced "Technology and the Museum." It was a brand-appropriate event introduced by a well-branded e-mail. When you have an exhibition or event that meshes perfectly with your brand identity, headline it in your Subject line and expound it on the Opening page.

#5 VISUAL

The visual is the first thing a reader sees when the e-mail is opened—not the headline and certainly not the text. The visual is like your lobby, an impression of what lies ahead. So pore over visuals and select the one—not just Sir Winston but the photo with him at a painter's easel—that best matches your brand's mission. The visual helps sell the event, but also reinforces the personality of your brand. Mr. Churchill is shown at his easel because the Telfair is an art museum. The flower beadwork is shown on moccasins because the Autry is a museum of the American West. The Lower East Side Tenement Museum in New York pictures archival photos of early-twentieth-century immigrant life. Frankly, some of these old photos are blurry, or show careworn people; but that's what tenement life often was. All the Opening Page images illustrate the story that is told in the accompanying text, like a storybook. That's because the soul of this museum is stories. Don't be lured by just pretty pictures; be tough and literal and pick the picture that communicates your brand.

All museums should stockpile photographs of their objects and events. It's better to have too many, and select the right ones as you need them. The same rule applies for these as for the photos used in publications; as described in chapter 17, "Publications," select them for brand aptness, and crop them to eliminate unnecessary visual information. It's amazing how good they'll look because, viewed with the backlit light of digital screens, e-mail photos look newsy and vibrant.

#6 DATE

Timeliness is everything. Digital culture demands no less than right-now and on-time. That doesn't mean you have to e-mail every day—in fact, that just encourages readers to delete and wait for the next one. You do, however, have to communicate regularly. When your audience does a search for an old e-mail, you want them to see a record of steady communications. Remember the genesis of e-mail announcements: newsletters. Wait until you have something fresh and timely to talk about, and no reader will notice or care if he or she receives an e-mail from you every third, seventh, or fourteenth day.

#7 BANNER

Sometimes, the first linked page is all type, informational but not visual. That's where your standing banner is essential. This broad strip across the top of the screen is like a logo, but bigger. It's specific to your museum as a first-page photo, but not specific to an individual e-mail's content. Here are some excellent banners from a variety of museums.

Vesterheim Norwegian American Museum

The banner of the newsletter e-mailed from the Vesterheim never fails to joyously celebrate all things Norwegian. The museum's archive of photographs is admirable and each is selected to work as a long horizontal; whether it's a line of red-vested marchers or a rosemaling design, each depicts the brand in relatable ways that month after month freshly illustrate the breadth of the culture.

National Postal Museum

This wonderful American history museum has a shot of its impressive Washington, D.C., façade, shot from the heroic angle so that the image portrays soaring strength and permanency. It also has an excellent newsletter name—"Postmark."

Burke Museum

When viewers first open a Burke Museum's e-mail, right at the top they see the striking screen-wide signature visual of northwest fauna silhouetted against a blue sky, and the tagline: "Discover the life before you." If your e-mail readers recognize and like your brand enough to accept the e-mail and decide to visit its contents, welcome them with a visual as obvious as a name on the front door; let them know they've come to the right place.

The Burke goes even farther for the education audience, with a special e-mail with the Subject line: "Burke Museum Education E-News." It features a header that's a frieze of ten images such as flora, bird eggs, and fossils. Colorful and encyclopedic, it promises that the Burke's education programs will range far and explore wide.

#8 TAGLINE

Not all e-mails contain "content." Some are just business letters, delivered digitally. If you have a tagline, even if you change it often, use it as a signature at the end of e-mail communications below your contact information. Remind vendors, partners, colleagues, and other stakeholders of what you stand for. Contact information identifies the writer; a signature tagline identifies the museum. Use your logo as a visual tagline. Or use the tagline seen on the first linked page of the National Postal Museum:

"Thank you for your interest in the National Postal Museum!"

Whoever you are, it always improves your image when you thank the people who read your letters.

Chapter 14

Lobby

Figure 14.1 Cité de l'Automobile, Mulhouse, France. The auto museum's façade announces its mission from a block away. The reinforcement continues through a long welcoming ramp in the lobby, which features mounted screens showing cars scenes from vintage movies. *Source*: © 2014 Margot Wallace.

Finally, the journey ends, the visitor parks the car, exits the bus, ends a long walk, or gets to the head of the line. The doorway is breached; the goal is in sight. At this point, your museum will either convince visitors it was worth the trip, or it will look like a chore. The lobby is the visitors' first impression and everything they think about the subsequent exhibitions will be built on the preview.

The lobby is also a transition zone; most visitors, being neither scholars nor regulars, use the lobby to acclimate and prepare. Consider the meaning of museums to visitors. For some it commands respect and awe. For others it leads to exploration. Many use museums as meeting places, or places of leisure. College students speak quite sincerely of museums as places of learning, challenge, and achievement. Whatever exceptional role museums play, their lobbies are on-ramps that ease the timid into the main galleries.

These staging areas couldn't be more different. The High Museum of Art in Atlanta has a huge lobby, brightly lit and contemporary in its spare lines; visitors understand they're in for a new and big experience. Of course, when it comes to big, nobody outsizes the Metropolitan of Art in New York or the Art Institute of Chicago, but their main lobbies are cozy by comparison; objectively visitors know they could spend days inside, but the lobbies welcome them gently.

Across the country, the Wing Luke Museum of The Asian Pacific American Experience in Seattle positions itself, in its lobby, in a much different light. In an old building, entered from a Chinatown sidewalk, it's kind of cluttered, very unpretentious. At the desk, an engaging staffer gives a brief history of the museum and its mission while fastening your wrist ID. You know exactly what's coming.

This prelude is necessary for branding, because it lets visitors—including all those casual customers who are there for a lecture, wedding, meeting, or as part of a sightseeing tour—understand the museum's relevance to their lives. As they find other visitors they relate to, see what's on exhibit today and what's coming, locate the café and the bathrooms, they begin to feel comfortable, and the museum becomes a friend, not a challenge.

There are seven features of lobbies that impress the brand on the visitor:

1. Signature visual
2. Information
3. Signage
4. Staff
5. Museum store
6. Seating
7. Dining area

Each plays a different role, and even if one or more is impossible to implement in your museum, you'll know how other features can fill in for them.

#1 SIGNATURE VISUAL

As branding tools, lobbies are powerful signature visuals. Marble pillars and monumental stairs convey one image. Bright lights and colors convey another. A large information desk, populated with well-dressed volunteers sends a message, as does a plain counter staffed by college kids. Some reception counters practically block the entrance, while others are a football-field's length away. What impression do they give? Or, more to the point, what impression is perceived? Whatever experiences unfold beyond, they are launched by the lobby experience. Ideally, the lead-in will perfectly presage the experiences to come.

Following are some foyer features that all museums should consider when making a first—or last—impression. You can implement some of them. Some are locked into the architecture, but you can borrow or adapt ideas.

When all museums were marble, the communication was clear. This was a place for the elite, whether in net worth or brains, a cathedral with a direct line to culture.

Some museums still look that way. If the entry is glass, the message is transparent. "Welcome, welcome! Take a look around. Go to the rooms that interest you." These are museums that meet their guests at the door, with no butler intervening. Most twenty-first century museums, holdovers from the other century, but having to expand, now compromise. The old lobbies remain grand and awe-inspiring, and that's appropriate. The new wings are brighter and more people-friendly, and that also defines museums. Small museum lobbies also have a look, one that's easier to achieve with just a prop, sign, or poster. LUMA, Loyola University Museum of Art, in Chicago, sends all the right messages. The small lobby has an information counter staffed by knowledgeable people, and a large space for bookshelves, tables, lots of books, and a few tasteful souvenir objects. A recent exhibition, Shaker Life, was a surprising subject for a Jesuit university, so one's initial reaction could be "Interesting, but why?" The books in the lobby explain why. And the exploring, broad view of this excellent museum makes its brand clear. If you're a small museum with a grand lobby, you give the wrong impression and you're probably wasting space.

Internal Vistas

Lobbies should be more than collection areas for entrance fees and bag checking. They should be vantage points. From the high and mighty spiraling lobby of the Guggenheim in New York comes this eternal lesson: Show your stuff quickly. There's no point in keeping your guests waiting.

The lobby of the Field Museum of Natural History in Chicago does that. The first exhibit seen is the iconic Sue, the dinosaur that is now almost the logo of the museum. Enter this museum and you know it's about natural history. The Field never lets a visitor wander long without seeing an object. In the long lower level with its meeting rooms and off-the-beaten-path exhibition galleries, the long corridors are lined with objects along the way. Many museums have the problem of old, repurposed buildings and no new budgets. However, awkward layouts can be ameliorated: Provide a view by placing artifacts in the corridors, by the stairs or elevators, or in the stairwells.

The promise of exhibits to come would seem to be no problem for a botanic garden, and the Chicago Botanic Garden does, indeed, greet visitors with lush vistas. However, until the visitor physically traverses great distances to a wetland, a Japanese Garden, a lily pond, or a prairie, it's just a pretty panorama. To explain what's out there, the Garden places a surprisingly small exhibit at the entrance to its lobby: a table with five glass vases, each with a stalk of flora, and a simple white card to describe the plant, grass, or flower. This human-scale exhibit is part of the brand of this celebrated museum.

Scope

The greatest viewing lobby belongs to the old San Francisco Museum of Modern Art. Right at the doorway one could see across the lobby to the upper floors, to a colorful glimpse of the art ahead. In fact, from the sidewalk, passersby can look through a large window and see the museum within. Off the lobby is the restaurant, a reassurance of sustenance at the end of the tour. The lobby has been compared to an older-era marketplace, a place to find everything.

Even small museums have scope that is belied by the size of their small lobbies, so it's especially important to give a sense of the exhibitions ahead and the collection in storage. Whet the appetite for what's inside. All it takes is a display case that highlights an artifact of the month. One better understands the mission and the vision of the museum.

Technology, because of its interactivity, personally welcomes each individual to the lobby. The seductiveness of a computer can steal the limelight, so you might want to set aside a special place. There are limitless ways to enhance the museum, beginning with a short "About Us" movie. Visitors can select their routes, explore a given exhibit in detail, leave comments, and send e-postcards to friends. It's a private way, in a public space, to collect visitor study exit interviews and other kinds of research. Instant memberships, offered at the moment when visitors are most involved, can be handled without any sales pressure by a screen and a keyboard.

Donor Walls

Donor walls are an integral part of lobbies, and they should reflect the brand as carefully as does the rest of the décor. The names on the brass plaques—or customized shapes—are objectively important, and they will be scrutinized by many. But the space they occupy is also important for its look. Some are near the entrance/exit, a silent welcoming committee. At the Chicago Botanic Garden, in Glencoe, Illinois, there's a bench across the aisle from the names, for more leisurely scrutiny. Some are arranged chronically, which gives the impression of endurance and stability. At the Strasbourg Museum of Contemporary Art, the names are on a wall, readable when one descends the steep stairs from the second level; the possible explanation for this is modern thinking.

The point of flaunting donors is proving loyalty, offline corroboration that many people also liked this museum. You may find the same corroboration on Yelp or TripAdvisor, but donor walls are visible visuals of respect.

#2 INFORMATION

At the Brooklyn Museum, information is central to the lobby experience. It's a huge circular counter in the middle of the large lobby. Around the cornice of the structure is a running LED display giving wait times and other information. Because there are so many stations around the counter, no one line seems long. Even on a weekend of one of the most popular recent shows—the Fashion World of Jean Paul Gaultier, From the Sidewalk to the Catwalk, October 25, 2013, through February 23, 2014—the unusually long lines didn't fill the large lobby. It's a big space, well managed, and it was those electronic messages, giving information, that made you love the museum anyway. The Franklin Institute in Philadelphia accomplishes a similar goal with its large video screens above the long ticket counter. These are short documentaries on the exhibits and exhibitions, very consistent with the brand of a science museum that echoes its namesake in its love of science, even in a wait line.

Even small museum information desks accomplish branding by informing. When handing out a ticket, they can hand out a sheet of paper with information on the exhibits ahead. Some people read the advance lecture, some fold it up and pocket it; the brand message is stated, and it can be read later. This kind of written explanation is important in our visually unconfident culture. We don't trust our eyes to "read" art, sculpture, or objects of any kind. Labels inform, but they don't always reinforce the museum brand at the same time. A handout, on a sheet of paper with your logo at the top, comforts the visitor, humanizes the museum, and augments its brand.

#3 SIGNAGE

Here's where visitors learn why they came, where to go, and when to return for future exhibitions. Signs tell where the restaurants and restrooms are, because people need to be comfortable before they can learn. Signage, because it is visual, also reinforces the museum brand. Large posters of the current and future exhibitions telegraph the mission; they're large and creative, so they give another insight into the museum's personality, and large enough to flaunt the museum logo, again reminding all who enter whose house they are now visiting.

One of the best branding signs was spotted in that large lobby of the High Museum, and it said simply:

> "Donate Today. Help us continue to make Atlanta the Cultural capital of the Southeast."
>
> The High believes in community. A panel on the history of the new building is titled:
>
> "A Village for the Arts"

The museum's walkways have floor-to-ceiling windows, which look out on Atlanta. Its urban location is easily accessed by public transport, which is right at the entrance/exit to a subway stop.

A sign is easy for any museum to make. A floor stand holding an "8.5' 11 Height . . . Portrait Orientation" sheet of letterhead can be had at Amazon. com for $35. There are several messages to write on that sign, together or one at a time:

- Museum mission
- Brief summary, perhaps from a panel, of the exhibits on display
- Bio of the town, the personality of which frequently informs a local museum
- Bio of the museum founder or the founding legend
- Special hours
- Special events
- The story of your museum

Many lobbies miss opportunities by not filling ungainly spaces with clues about what goes on within.

#4 STAFF

Employees play many roles in a museum, none more important than at the threshold. Uniformed or t-shirted, standing or seated, information staff represent the brand in ways human visitors can readily relate to. Conversely, sometimes these janissaries don't represent the museum well at all. At one elegant mansion-style museum, the ticket-takers sat at a folding 8-foot table, crossed legs visible, conversing almost without pauses. One receptionist was a senior, well-dressed and coiffed. The other was a youthful arty type in baggy black and wild locks. It was hard to tell what the museum stood for. At another mansion, the guardian at the gate was an elderly man, standing at a podium, overwhelmed by incoming crowds and looking unnecessarily hapless when ticket stubs started falling. One got the impression of a falling-down museum, when, in fact, it is an effectively delightful one. At a contemporary art museum in a large city, the ticket squad at the entrance counter was a group of young people in diverse dress, presenting a well-trained yet creative face that perfectly prefaced the exhibits beyond. At many small museums, the store clerks double as the cashiers. These people are so knowledgeable and involved, they perform the introductions perfectly.

Living museums get it. Being greeted by a costumed, trained actor with a script tells the visitor exactly what to expect. Frequently, these welcoming committees will guide the time travelers to the next exhibition and answer questions at the end of the trip. If the aim of the museum is to show how earlier societies interacted with each other and their environment, the "lobby" experience establishes the mood at the beginning and reinforces it at the end. The greeters at the Portland Museum of Art also put a human face on the institution's content. Wearing sashes, or medals, or headgear appropriate to the featured exhibition, they transformed a temporary exhibition into the museum's own. This is no small feat in the museum industry, when several brand name institutions may share the same traveling content.

Staff on a Screen can be called up quickly to substitute for a missing person. At the Brooklyn Museum, a laptop on a pedestal occupied the center of the "Connecting Cultures" gallery when it was undergoing construction in 2013. On it ran a thirty-second video of a curator explaining the renovation. When you get into digital tools, you have people, information, and conversation at your disposal. In Brooklyn, visitor response was encouraged, which was like having fellow museum-goers help you understand the situation. It's a smart way to listen to on-the-spot visitor comments, and an easy way to respond.

It goes without saying that the best lobbies are staffed by impeccably informed staffers who understand that information is the raison-d'être of a museum. The people at the lobby desks are the first link in a long chain of interpretive experiences, and, in most cases, the most sensitive link. They interact when the visitor is most confused, when they must, in a few moments, convey the mission and persona of the whole experience.

#5 MUSEUM STORE

Most museum stores are located, wisely, in the lobby. At the beginning of a visit, their wide selection of books and postcards provide a preview to the works inside. At the end of a visit, they summarize the experience, giving the mind-overloaded visitor a place to review and make sense of what was seen. Most museums, mindful of the profits from stores, locate them near the front doors, so customers can shop without paying a museum admission.

In case of renovation and reinstallations, the store serves as proxy. Online stores, of course, keep the brand and its collection vivid and dynamic through closings, as well as after hours. The actual store at the Milwaukee Art Museum is open for business as usual. As the website says, "Under construction for renovation and reinstallation, the Museum's Collection Galleries are currently off view. While we prepare our next exhibition, Van Gogh to Pollock: Modern Rebels, opening June 18, please enjoy the architecture of the Santiago Calatrava . . . shop at the Museum Store, or relax in The Coffee Shop."

Often, the first person a visitor talks to is the museum store assistant, and these staffers are invaluable in propounding the brand image at the outset of the visit. Their helpfulness at the end of the visit, when purchasers are collecting memories, puts the final bow on the brand experience. Make sure your store personnel understand the merchandise and its tie-in to the exhibits; they're brand ambassadors, and good ones.

For museums where the store staffer also sells tickets and conveys information, add counter cards with information about selected items in the store. Every kernel of information gives a clue to the structure of your exhibitions and the mission of the whole museum.

Where space allows, museums place satellite stores or kiosks near the galleries. Some see this as commercialism, the better to sell more stuff. Look at them, rather, as interim lobbies, places where people can pause, rest the mind muscles, and perceive the exhibits in a different way. Museums need more space for people to think and share, not just view. Visitors don't need their cameras to share; sometimes it's effective just to chat. You read a lot about the imperative to "experience a brand." No expensive interfaces are needed in a museum store; just let visitors point, touch, and talk.

#6 SEATING

Chairs are relatively new in the history of sit-down man. Before the nineteenth century, agrarian men and women worked all day, came home for dinner, and went to bed. Children, with luck, got to sit on school benches for a while. Rich people enjoyed parlors, and everyman had Sundays when one could sit down in church. The concept of take-a-load-off-your-feet must have been a revelation: suddenly, people had physiological permission to think.

All lobbies need chairs, preferably comfortable ones; and galleries in larger museums need sitting spots, if only for people over fifty. Chairs allow visitors to reflect, look around, and make solid connections between exhibits and the museum itself. There are many spaces where a brand message, logo, or signature visual can be placed. Chairs are the only place where visitors can put themselves in the picture.

One memorable sit-down was at the Norton Museum of Art in West Palm Beach, Florida, back in the aughts. Here, body-length benches encouraged visitors to lie down and gaze up at the gorgeous glasswork ceiling by glass artist Dale Chihuly. The couches were filled, all the time, and what was more remarkable was how strangers talked to each other from this position. Perhaps proneness explains the popularity of pajama parties and overnights at museum.

Another chair situation that stands out in memory was at the Menil Collection in Houston, where simple chairs were set out on the arcaded deck that surrounded the museum. One could relax with a view of the neighborhood. It's an unpretentious neighborhood, with none of the elegance of the museum. How bold of the Menil, it of the plain white walls and simple design, to trust that its brand would stand out in any setting!

The Figge Art Museum in Davenport, Iowa, holds a place of pride overlooking the Mississippi River, and from inside one can sit on a bench and watch the activity on and beyond the great water; one can connect the museum with a vision, as well as a view. The Pulitzer Foundation, in St. Louis, Missouri, offers just one seat, carved out of a large stone, which overlooks a reflecting pond and thence offers a view of the skyline of the city.

Chairs of all description are landing in museums of every type and size; some are sleekly part of the interior design, and some seem brought in from the attic. All chances to sit are commendable; it's how people feel comfortable with their museum.

The places with the most seats are the tables of restaurants and cafés. Since they serve to refresh the body, as well as the soul, they deserve a special mention.

#7 DINING AREA

Minds don't function for long without nourishment, and restaurant chairs and tables provide an extended time to reflect and bond with the museum. Crystal Bridges Museum of American Art, in Bentonville, Arkansas, goes a step further with a menu created explicitly to match its brand mission. Serving regional food in a room with grand views of its natural setting, the museum states its culinary philosophy on its website:

> The robust cuisine of Eleven not only nourishes, but tells a story—a story of the American spirit, inspired by the artworks, natural surroundings, and fascinating regional history connected to our Museum.

Not all museums can tie their menu to their brand as neatly as Crystal Bridges does. The Museum of Glass in Tacoma connects in another unique way that highlights the brand. The most distinctive feature of the Museum of Glass is its Hot Shop, the place where glass is made, and in this museum is a large stage filled with huge ovens, where visitors can sit in amphitheatre seats to observe skilled artisans at work. On Fridays, visitors can also buy a box lunch to eat while they're following this molten process. The Hot Shop is key to this museum's brand; its high dome is visible from outside and its entrance is right off the lobby. Giving visitors a chance to take it all in over a lunch hour is very smart branding.

Tables with chairs are essential if the museum covers large distances—such as a garden or zoo—or is far from town centers, because the visit lasts longer. They're also necessary when the visitors are children. And while everyone is happily refueling, they can see the museum, just beyond the restaurant doors, a reminder that lasts throughout the meal.

GOOD-BYE

One day at the Art Institute of Chicago, I observed the many visitors who had been waiting in frigid weather for the doors to open; arriving at the lobby ticket-taking stand, ninety-nine out of hundred smiled and actually thanked the staffer. Your visitors come in with high expectations and excellent spirit. "Thank you!" When they leave your lobby, you hope it's with the same goodwill. What exactly does your farewell comprise? It's time to look at the lobby from the exit viewpoint. On this Exit Checklist, please note:

Visitor body language
How they talk to their companions

Where the museum's exit paths lead
View from the museum exit—street scene, nature's scenery, a building corridor, parking garage, and so on
What staffer says "Thank you" to them?

There are many ways to enhance the end of the visit, to treat your guests just as cordially as when they entered. Think like a host or hostess and put those words into action in the lobby.

Chapter 15

Store

Figure 15.1 The Vesterheim National Norwegian-American Museum & Heritage Center takes its store—and brand heritage—into a broader marketplace. *Source*: Embroidered church gloves from the Vesterheim collection, courtesy Vesterheim Norwegian-American Museum.

"Welcome" and "Thank you for your visit."

Only the store is so perfectly positioned to greet new visitors and acclimate them to your unique mission. Only the store is in just the right place to close the visit with a positive, come-back-soon reminder. Making first impressions and last impressions, the store is a powerful branding tool, for a wide, wide audience. Your online store stands at the threshold all day, every day, for people who may never have set foot in your galleries. Your actual store, in the lobby and near the functional coat check and audio device return counter, reminds visitors of the objects and learning that distinguish you as a brand.

Look who visits the store: it's not just visitors but also their bring-along friends—those people who didn't plan the trip, but are accompanying your loyal visitor: members; donors; community partners; event guests; scholars and lunch-hour shoppers. They also see your brand through the portal of the store.

Throughout this chapter, the lobby store and the online store will appear as twins: similar but with different strengths, often overlapping and sometimes heading down their own paths. The digital aspect of retail, as in so many areas of life, is so enveloping that today we usually just say "retail," and employ digital or actual techniques as budgets and goals dictate.

It's a similar experience online, where "Store" or "Shop" or "Shopping" have always held pride of place on the menu bar. Which comes first in the twenty-first-century visitor's mind—the actual lobby store or the store landing page—is a chicken and egg question; they reinforce each other seamlessly and each has advantages for strengthening your brand with a wider range of stakeholders.

This chapter will show how to leverage the power of the store in reinforcing your brand to current visitors, return visitors, influencers, the multi-literate, members and prospects, donors, community partners, internal market, and seasonal visitors. Your store is a major touchpoint that communicates your brand through:

The space
Rotate your merchandise
Bookshelves
Bags and tags
Store staff
Seasonal visitors
Niche segments
Dangers in the online store
Consumer insights

Getting insights into your visitors and shoppers and following up on them is an essential part of retailing, and this chapter will touch on that.

THE SPACE—PREVIEW AND SUMMARY FOR CURRENT VISITORS

Please touch.

Amidst the shining glass paperweights in the store vitrine of the Museum of Glass, a sign says, "Please feel free to pick up . . . and take a closer look."

This is a smart move, because branding is all about keeping visitors in touch with the museum, emotionally and practically, and over time. Actual touch is one sense that's usually lacking in a museum. There are many ways your store touches visitors: The store is the one space in a museum where visitors can talk out loud, and they can stroll aimlessly without people bumping into them; it's a familiar space where, no matter how stimulating or intimidating or tiring the rest of the museum is, they can relax. Here, they can reflect, a necessary step to internalizing the experience and bonding with the museum. Big museums have visitor reception areas, lobbies, and restaurants where this sharing can begin. Small museums always have the gift counter.

Located right in or off the lobby, stores are in the visitor's path: On entering, the visitor sees the familiar sign of shopping and recognizes a haven; on exiting, the visitor gets a lasting impression in the form of a tangible memory. Here's the spacc to acclimate to a strange building; it's also the space to unwind after the formality of the galleries. To help visitors reflect, the store is the space where a real person who knows the museum will talk to them, say "Hello" as a welcome and then, as they're leaving, say "Thank you for visiting us." That's quite a lot of branding from a touchpoint that also produces revenue.

Make this area as welcoming as size and budget allow. Keep the aisles wide enough so two people can congregate.

Where possible, situate the store within sight of the exhibits. Visitors will be reminded of the connection between the two. If they visit the store at the beginning of the visit—and many do just to get their bearings—they'll be prepped to better appreciate what lies ahead. If they stop at the end of their visit, it will serve as a decompression chamber, a summary of what's been seen. Even if nothing is bought, the store sends visitors away better educated and satisfied.

Many people drop in on a store before they take the time to visit the exhibits, a good reason to locate it near the entrance. Don't make the mistake of several big city museums that forget the store is an educational extension of the museum and hide it in distant corners or, worse, in the basement.

In small museums, the merchandise counter might be the first place visitors meet a person with the museum-wide knowledge to answer your questions. And in a store, you can talk out loud to your friends, rehashing the experience and prompting your memory with visual cues.

ROTATE YOUR MERCHANDISE

Local patrons can stop in your store frequently, as they would in any store they like. We think of visitors as tourists, but shouldn't forget the locals whose ongoing loyalty is paramount to your success. Rotating merchandise frequently keeps the museum fresh and robust. Gallery exhibits can't change at will, but your store can. Give local patrons reason to return, and reward them with a few changes. When the museum's exhibits do change, you're poised to change with them. Even the smallest museum can stay relevant to changing exhibits with signage that says:

"Take a piece of [name of exhibition] home"

You can make change happen without special items, but, rather, with just a special sign:

"Enjoy holiday shopping at [name of museum]"

or

"This month we're open until 6 p.m. to join the festivities of [local summer festival]"

Experiences

Another way to cement relationships with local customers is with in-store experiences. Other retail stores might entice customers with climbing walls, tastings, or massage chairs; museums can offer book signings. A wonderful example comes from the exemplary Crystal Bridges Museum of American Art in Bentonville, Arkansas, where an Arkansas artist was in the store to meet visitors and sign copies of his book. This 2014 experience was On Brand for the Museum and good business for the store.

Online Space

Just as the lobby store provides a branding space, so does the landing page of the online store. And it's even more important here that this first impression be on brand. Visitors can't see the rest of the museum once they've entered the online store, and with most links it's not that easy to link back. The store is on its own representing the museum. Make the first impression a strong one. It's tempting to simply line up a row of books and other items on the screen and call it your museum store, but these thumbnail-size images—art directors call them flyspecks—don't represent anything very attractively. There are several ways to solve this serious problem:

A screen-wide photograph of the store, replete with merchandise, looks like a place anyone would love to visit, virtually or otherwise. The Delaware Art Museum has a charming panoramic shot of its story. The Museum Shop of the Nantucket Historical Association beautifully integrates its online museum with its actual New England cottage home. The photographs on the home page show both the inviting inside of the well-stocked store and the white frame exterior with its red door and hanging shop sign, so symbolic of its heritage brand. And the Arab American National Museum, in Dearborn, Michigan, shows only brand-specific products. Link to the Apparel page and you'll see a close-up of a stack of colorful keffiyah, with a caption that says they were made in Palestine.

Your store, online as well as off, is even more important when repinned or grammed. When proper names such as Instagram—like Google and Xerox before—become verbs, you know they're important. Now your interesting spaces are publicized for you. Although amateur photographers are allowed, with restrictions, in most parts of the museum, the store is an easier place for them to compose and get a good shot. Make your store photogenic with these simple adjustments:

Place reproduction objects on the bookshelves, between the books.
Provide a few wearable items that can be put on for poses. Include signs that say, "Please try on this colonial bonnet"
Prompt children to use some reproduction items. Write signs that say, "Kids, please try this lute and serenade your friends"
Provide a charging station with a sign that says: "We love cameras"

Merchandise

The Adler Planetarium, Chicago, stocks a lot of celestial items. The Museum of Music in Phoenix offers thumb bells, and talking drums. Obvious, you might say, and that's the point. Store items are obvious touchpoints because they're tangible memories that can be taken home and used and shared.

It's harder than ever to find just the right things to express your collection. The available pool of merchandise is finite, whereas museums have infinite possibilities. Stocking one shelf or an entire store is a branding challenge that, like everything else in the business of museums, takes stamina. You need to make hard decisions. When given a choice of yet another mug, or t-shirt, or generic learning toy, learn to say "That's Off Brand." Then you can add On Brand merchandise to your inventory. Just as you'd demand that your vendors tell you their prices and discounts and shipping schedules, also demand that they show you items that have competitive advantage and relevance. Ask what's trendy, by all means. Also ask what other museums are buying. Then ask your vendors what else they have. For support, link up with the excellent Museum Store Association whose mission is to help individual nonprofit retailers do their individual customer-satisfying best. The smaller you are, the easier it is to pinpoint the right items, and ignore the rest. You don't need quantity and you can think like a boutique. If your merchandise is distinctive, you can charge a little more and your vendors will be able to find what you need.

In addition to vendors, talk to your curators so that you understand an upcoming exhibition, and can get suggestions about what items might supplement it: and start your talking early, so you have plenty of time to coordinate merchandise with shows.

Think food. Jars, bags, and tins of regional foods please almost every visitor and recipient, and it should be easy to source local specialties. Their colorful labels and packaging continue the conversation on your shelves back home. Food from a museum makes an especially good gift for adults, a market segment you should woo whenever possible. After all, these are the people who plan trips, do the driving, and carry the wallets. What's more, adults become members, donate, and form partnerships.

Logo Ware and Dullness

Use caution when plunking your logo on mugs, caps, or bookmarks: It won't make it special and there might be situations where a generic product runs counter to your mission; baseball caps were not part of colonial wardrobes, and the clever science slogans on t-shirts may not suit the research focus of your museum. Generic items can creep into more shelf space than you realize; suddenly your shelves say "mall" rather than "museum." Dull items are, of course, to be avoided, because your museum stands for vitality and scintillation, and those are some of the treasures that you send visitors home with.

Of course, you can stock many more items online. And there is space to write longer captions that make the connection between items and collection. The challenge is to balance brand-specific items with big sellers that are more generic. The Steelworks Center of the West is a heritage museum that nimbly balances selling with branding. Its mission is telling the story of industry in the American West, and just in case all the merchandise doesn't perfectly fit this mission, here's how the museum store web page handles that branding dilemma: it shows a photograph of an early 1900s Colorado Fuel & Iron Company store in a small western town, with a heading that says, "In the tradition of the CF&I Supply Company Store we offer a variety of goods for visitors."

Merchandising

Museum stores have practiced good branding longer than any other part of the museum. With education the stated purpose of tax-exempt stores, they have a template for their buyers to follow: The merchandise must reflect the museum mission and further the education started in the galleries. With those guidelines, store buyers can focus on items that help visitors understand Shaker life, the whaling industry, or wetland science. In providing shoppers with such in-depth information, they're also providing brand memories not to be found just anywhere. The items can be as curious and expensive as the leather race car driver's helmet at the Museum of the Automobile in Mulhouse, France; at over $100 when translated from euros, it's definitely a conversation piece. At the other end of the wallet is the handful of plastic animals that can be had for $5, and scattered like business cards among grandchildren. Only the creativity of buyers limits the range of memories.

Once you select the merchandise, let merchandising make the brand connections. One of the most charming museum stores I ever threaded my way through was at Asia Society in New York City: a small museum store with small tables and small items. The table coverings, walls, and shelves were dark and rich in color, and the lighting was suggestive rather than highlighting. "Asia" covers a lot of territory, on the map and in the mind, and the store didn't try to find an item from each culture, or even the current exhibitions. The store decided to represent a mysterious bazaar, and it made a point. It didn't try to be all things to all people; no brand can do that.

Hang Tags and Counter Cards

Many items can be made more appropriate, to more people, if you verbalize the connection. That's where a researched, well-written hang tag or counter card works wonders.

If it's a learning toy, write a card that explains, as the Museum of Music in Phoenix does:

> "This bird whistle teaches children to listen for nature's sounds."

Actually, in this case the "card" is an online store caption. It is recommended that the online and actual store stay consistent with their messages. If this bird whistle is available in the store, the card should be there as well.

With food products, merchandising is fun because everybody loves eating, recipes, and making other people happy with food. A generic jelly or sauce becomes your museum's jelly or sauce when you add a booklet or counter card with lore about local meals. Most museums won't be making fudge on the premises, as Plimoth Plantation does, but if your product comes from a local kitchen or furniture maker or weaver, flaunt it.

If you're not lucky enough to achieve the interior designer look of the Asia Society store, use simple props that can reinforce the theme of an exhibit or the whole museum. The American Museum of Natural History in New York has a hodge-podge museum space that sprawls over several floors. Look up, gaze down, and squint toward the far corners—there's a tree or a bird on a wire to remind you of nature.

And then, remember once again the comfort zone that characterizes a store. Use the store space to show a five-minute video about an exhibit or project of the museum. Perhaps you can use a video created for a blog or presentation. Use the intimacy of your space to simply give shoppers a different aspect of your brand. It achieves an important branding goal of reinforcing the museum in an informal space where there's space to stop, reflect, and discuss the experience with a friend. Add a chair and you've got a learning activity for restless husbands or children accompanying the shopper. Companions of shoppers usually don't connect to a museum through the store, but through more information.

If your museum has produced an exhibition poster, or a poster of the museum itself, place it in several spaces around the store. If you stock one book whose cover photograph captures your brand—a book on covered wagons or colorful fish or colonial furniture—use it like a poster and place several copies around the store.

Online merchandising mimics in-store table tents, hang tags, and handouts, and then goes so much further. On the website, the depth of information is limitless, and each further insight strengthens the core values of the museum. An example of online merchandising that deepens knowledge comes from the Musical Instrument Museum of Phoenix. The store page for instruments states:

> Pincullo Flute
>
> Our colorful *Pincullo* flutes let you make the music of the mountains! Played by indigenous people of the Andes Mountains in Peru, Bolivia, and Ecuador, the *Pincullo* is used both in group performance and as a solo instrument.

The Anchorage Museum of Art emphasizes its exhibitions, and its history, by harking back to a 1990s exhibition in this caption for a book sold online:

> The 1994 Pioneer Family Exhibit in the Anchorage Museum of History and Art was the inspiration for this book.

Even in inexpensive items, there's a connection to the museum brand:

> This fun pen celebrates the Anchorage Museum exhibit 'Mammoths and Mastodons.' A background scene full of mammoths sets the stage as two foreground mammoths float across the pen barrel when the pen is tilted from side to side.

The MIM online store takes a further step that is rare, if not unique, in online selling: It posts its distinct online store philosophy:

> Welcome to the MIM Online Store
>
> Thank you for shopping at the online store of the Musical Instrument Museum. We offer a selection of items from around the world that educate,

inspire, and entertain. Providing these quality products and exceptional service to our customers is our priority. Best of all, your purchase supports MIM and its programs.

Shopping can't be underestimated; people shop to own, and ownership brings with it pride and commitment. With just a small souvenir, visitors are showing their allegiance.

Let there be no mistake that although online stores can expand sales, they must also stay on brand.

BOOKSHELVES—FOR THE MULTI-LITERATES

To benefit from visitors' love of the learning in your museum, connect all the architecture, gardens, history, and photography books to your mission. The people who come to a museum store to read are serious about building on what they've seen in the galleries; they're the multi-literates who engage in all the arts, and find echoes of theater and architecture in your museum's exhibits. Many museums are now bringing music into the galleries and, during the years of new construction, a theater has become de rigueur. These multi-literate activities have been linked in museum bookstores forever.

One way to emphasize the link is by pasting a bookplate on the inside cover with your logo and the words: "A gift of knowledge from the [name of museum.]" Less permanent, but equally effective, is a well-designed bookmark with the same message, and your address, telephone number, and website, as well.

At the New York Historical Society, header cards above the shelves, and rail cards at eye level, divided the books by less generic categories: the heading "Roosevelt" instantly gave New York history a face.

If you have the manpower to research the books, write some copy for a table tent or shelf talker that can be displayed next to it, explaining why the museum has chosen these titles. At the Chicago Botanic Garden, in Glencoe, Illinois, white pre-printed cards in holders prompt buyers with recommendations such as:

"Our staff recommends …"

Small slate boards are used for special mentions, such as this hand-chalked announcement:

"Our Japanese Garden is featured in 'Quiet Beauty' pages 114–120. Enjoy!"

The educational component of a store reaches full flower when an expert shares personal suggestions. This kind of insider tips works with items from books to toys to jewelry, deftly combining salesmanship with branding.

Observational research I conducted at many museums around the country demonstrated the importance of table tops. People like to look at items at a slightly downward angle; they don't like to squat or reach up too far. Merchandise on a table gets scrutinized and enjoyed. Books, particularly, benefit because their covers are fully visible; other items can be safely rotated, lifted, and touched when they're displayed on a table. On a table top, two people can stand side by side and discuss an item, good reinforcement of their significance.

Obviously, mass-market visitors aren't the only audience your website reaches. An advantage the online store has over the store in the lobby is the huge potential of readers, and you can provide books for so many different multi-literate tastes. If prospective donors, scholars, job seekers, civic leaders, and facilities renters are visiting your site for one reason, there's a chance they might click on the store. Categorize books online as you would on the shelf and let visitors virtually wander to the section that interests them. It's a powerful way to show the range of your mission.

On the other hand, don't allow the unlimited space to load bookshelves to bulging. Restrict yourself to relevant categories and let your brand inform your suggested reading. Book buying is difficult when there are so few publishers' reps to talk to. But they are available, and it is their job to help you find the right titles for your brand's mission and personality. Make sure these vendors, like all your business partners, understand your brand.

BAGS AND TAGS

Once your merchandise leaves the store, other people besides the purchasers will see them. The potential for increased awareness is exciting, so invest in merchandise tags and shopping bags; it's a sensible branding expense. A colorful tag with your logo immediately communicates a relationship between the merchandise and the mission of the museum. A tag gives credibility to the least expensive of items, or those with tenuous relevance. If you don't have too large a stock, write comments on the tags, as antique stores do, telling how the item relates to an exhibition, how it is used, or the materials it is made of. Another way to connect merchandise to the museum is with a line on the tag that says something like: "This product was selected by [name of museum] because it reflects the [mission] to which we are committed." Affix easily removable price stickers so that tags remain on gift items.

Shopping bags with your logo, and colors, are essential. They can be the flat paper variety used for small items, or the handled variety. They can be paper or plastic, clear or opaque. This is the cheapest advertising you can buy, because everyone who walks out your door will be a mobile billboard. Bags get used over and over, long after the visit, so this advertising has frequency as well as reach. The bag should have your name as well as logo, and possibly address, telephone number, and website. Like tags, shopping bags lend authority to your museum. More important, they make the purchaser feel proud: a member of a special club. Shoppers wear their purchases like a badge of honor. One visitor commented, "I shop at a museum store because I know—or believe—I'll get something special. It makes me feel proud to give a gift from a museum store. When I carry a shopping bag from a museum, I feel like it's enhancing my brand image." As a brand manager, you couldn't ask for a better loyalty builder.

There's no online equivalent for a shopping bag swinging from your hand, but there's something better: "Look what I just bought" photographs. That sentiment, with picture, can be shared with dozens of friends on social media and should be encouraged. Again, remind online shoppers of their purchases with follow-up e-mails. You want more than comments; you want their satisfaction and you can guarantee this if you keep in touch.

STORE STAFF

Quietly, and behind the scenes, the store sales assistants are your frontline branding agents, impressing your brand on every purchase. In fact, in small museums, they might be the only information desk. Volunteer or paid, they should be good salespeople for the museum, as well as the merchandise, and you might have to train them for this double-barreled selling job. Remind your salespeople how important they are as familiar types: For many shoppers, museums are an unaccustomed treat, and even after the visit they might feel overwhelmed. Don't let people leave feeling that way. Encourage your staff to make shoppers feel comfortable by imparting friendly insights into the museum they've just visited. Assure them that they can use their own words in explaining what the item means and that they don't have to talk like a wall label panel. Docents put your brand into the mind of the visitor; store staffers put it in their hands.

A visitor through the door is a member in the making, and there's a good opportunity to nurture them in the store. If the experience is good, visitors will return, and a habit can start to form. Your goal should always be repeat visits. And that can happen often in the store. Repeat visits then should be ratcheted up to membership, and that, too can be encouraged in the store. If your store offers member discounts, make sure there's a stack of membership forms at the checkout counter.

If store business is booming, sales clerks might not have much time to chat with the customers, but attitude counts a lot. I watched two cash registers ringing away at the Brooklyn Museum, and two staff members loading item after item into bulging shopping bags. One staffer was silently efficient. I checked out at the counter with the smiling, ebullient young lady who had just sent a customer off with $400 worth of coffee table books. "Those books are really popular," I commented. "Oh, that's because they're so beautiful," she volunteered. Staff who know and like the merchandise are a big asset; they're also a touchpoint in your brand.

I don't know any details about the online course, "Retail Store Management for Small Museums," offered by Northern States Conservation Center, but I did note that the course lists seven specific topics, and the first is "Museum Store Staffing and Training." One thing about a course you can replicate is a group dynamic; gather your staff together and discuss how to talk to customers.

Feedback from the Sales Floor

The people who work in your stores are in the best position to provide you with customer feedback, since they're the ones who interact daily with the consumer. Tour guides are also invaluable information collectors, but not everyone takes a tour. Everyone shops! What is heard and observed inside the store is CIA-quality intelligence for curators, docents, directors, and trustees. People who sell learn to relate to the customer. They ask thoughtful questions, and get revealing answers. Imagine the insights you could share by asking the question a sales assistant at the Terra Museum of American Art (whose collection now partially resides in the Art Institute of Chicago) once posed to a purchaser: "And what memory of the Terra Museum are you taking home with you today?" This simple research technique is the beginning of visitor studies. You don't need expensive, time-consuming, professional research to get information. Start by simply urging your staff to talk to customers and listen carefully.

SEASONAL VISITORS

Botanic gardens, zoos, living museums, and many heritage museums are closed during the winter. That's two to five months when visitors don't think to visit, and members learn to live without you. Keep them in the loop by encouraging them to shop. The online store is always open.

The Great Lakes Shipwreck Museum, located in the icy extremes of Michigan's Upper Peninsula, handles the store winter availability in a particularly customer-friendly way:

"Online shoppers and Members, please note that all 'Winter Season' orders will be processed on Mondays and Thursdays. Your order may be delayed when I cannot get to the office during blizzards, sleeting ice, or really-super-bad UP weather. Thanks for your understanding!"

Museums that are closed for renovation or expansion face a similar closing problem. The Museum of Contemporary Art, San Francisco, uses this language on its website to keep visitors informed during its temporary relocations around the Bay Area:

"SFMoma is on the go"
"Closed for construction yet more open than ever"
"Take a virtual tour of our future museum"
"We've temporarily moved . . . everywhere"

This is excellent language to keep the brand top of mind while it's physically absent from its building. However, these are words that do not appear on the store website. They're not necessary. Online, it's business as usual.

Six different shops may be a lot of physical travel for visitors to Plimoth Plantation in Plymouth, Massachusetts, but off-season, from November to March, online excursions bring visitors back to the premises.

Each museum is delineated, such as Children's Shop, Native Shop, so that online visitors have an itinerary to follow to keep them glued to the site. Along the way they will find brand-specific items such as a seventeenth-century thumb-controlled watering pot that doesn't look anything like its contemporary descendants. The $40 carved-wood bird bank is a worthy, memory builder, and for enduring memories, there is the seriously engaging book titled "MaMake a Joint Stool from a Tree: An Introduction to 17th-century Joinery." It's targeted to people who really appreciate the culture at the heart of Plimoth Plantation, and for those who actually construct a hand-hewn joined wood stool, an item that will last for years. As a constant reminder of Plymoth Plantation, it's a branding tool without peer.

The detailed description of the book's content, as well as other merchandise descriptions in the online catalog, is great for reading during the between-season gap. This is where online presence trumps the actual store: it's open throughout the season when the museum is hibernating, and keeps awareness alive.

NICHE SEGMENTS

So far, this chapter has mostly talked about the museum. However, as with all marketing, it's time once again to talk about the visitors. Because the store is such a microcosm, it's a good place to get a handle of who visitors are. No broad strokes here, but niche segmentation.

The people in your store are not just visitors. Other people who are already inside your museum include field trip teachers and chaperones, donors, board members, business people in your community, facilities guests, speakers, staff, and volunteers. Each of these groups has a stake in the brand promise; to each of them, the brand must be reinforced and vitalized.

All your shoppers fall in several other niche categories: Some shop for their own use, some for their family back home, and some for gifts. Some expect to find knowledge gifts and some want prestige, one-of-a-kind purchases. Some have already spent a lot of money on tickets, food, and transportation. Some are at an event and can't carry a lot of bags. Some are men, not there as spouses but as meeting attendees. Offer many price points appealing not only to demographics but also to psychographics. Many people have the money to buy expensive items, but may not want to do so at the end of a tiring tour. Conversely, shoppers of modest means will often pay a premium in a store they perceive as special and prestigious.

Be aware of the wide range of demographics among the consuming museum-goer. Some are children given a spending stipend. Some are grandparents with generous wallets. Some are visitors on vacation from distant ZIP codes. Some are locals showing them around. More and more, your shoppers will be foreigners, buying with an eye to cultural differences. While it's early in the century to suggest that all museums have translation services, it's wise to be alert to the longer range of museum-goers and the potential language opportunities ahead.

The store is a way to give a tangible part of yourself, an actual mnemonic device, to your supporters. Here are some of the niche segments in your store, and how to brand to them:

- Return visitors. These are usually members. Mention what's new in the store and what's coming in. I overheard, in the Museum of Contemporary Art Chicago, a customer commenting on the compliments she got on the store's one-of-a-kind jewelry. "Yes," said the elegantly dressed woman behind the counter, who mentioned by name the store buyer saying, "She has a wonderful eye." It was insider talk that positively encouraged repeat purchases.
- Volunteers. Items they can't find anywhere else except at their own museum's store.

- Interns—see above
- Educators. With every field trip comes a teacher and chaperones. They are shoppers, too. They won't have time to shop, so hand them an entrance pass, or coupon, to encourage them to return on their own time.
- Members and donors. Remind them that the store is a great source for their own personal gift lists by sending targeted e-mails announcing special items.
- Corporate sponsors. Promote the store to your corporate partners to give them an additional perspective of the museum and its mission.
- Local businesses. In your community, suggest that your merchants join the local Chamber of Commerce, Rotary, or civic business groups; get the brand message out to non-visiting local people who are potential visitors and partners.
- Guest speakers, civic partners. Use your logo items for gifts to guest speakers or government officials.
- Community. Put up signage that gives your store a presence on the street so that the community can see you, especially if you're in an area with sidewalk traffic. Stores are so user-friendly that many people will just drop in, where they might think twice about "dropping in" on a museum.
- Local merchants. They might want to borrow your space as a venue to sample their products, for example, a local nursery displaying plants or heritage seeds. It's a meaningful, real-world way to reinforce your mission to preserve the cultural character of your environs.

The museum store can reach out to niche segments in ways that are different from news of exhibitions and programs. Stores and shopping are part of daily life and an e-mail message or web page statement about the store is more immediate than a future event.

The South Dakota Agricultural Heritage Museum used Valentine's Day at the store to market to consumers. A charming Valentine's Day e-mail announced a free gift at the museum store: a workshop for making paper flowers for Valentine's Day. The image of an antique Valentine card was beautiful; the photograph of colorful paper flowers was enticing; and the workshop offered a good deal for the member or visitor and a growth event for the museum. But the museum didn't stop there. Under the big photos and compelling text was another message:

> "About the South Dakota Agricultural Heritage Museum
> Founded in 1884, the South Dakota Agricultural Heritage Museum is dedicated to preserving the history of agriculture and the heritage of rural life in South Dakota."

This museum understands that the store is more than a revenue source, and uses its popular store page to help remind shoppers of the mission at the core of your brand.

DANGERS IN THE ONLINE STORE

You never know who's coming through the door. Your store is open 24/7, all over the world, and for starters, you have to be dressed and ready. There are real chances that people you never dreamed of will get the wrong impression of you, your brand, and your very identity. The flip side of this exposure is all the new people who will swarm into your galleries through your portal.

The main danger is veering off brand and distorting your brand mission; that is not acceptable with not-for-profit organizations filing under a 501(c)(3). Major donors are sophisticated philanthropists who study not-for-profit mission statements carefully. They want a museum's goals and activities to mesh with their own, and often must defend their choices with their boards.

Civic leaders, too, watch the mission of their arts partners. They have constituents to answer to, and budgets to keep. Scholars visiting your site may stray over to the store; they'll be reassured of your brand bonafides if they see reinforcements in the books. As online stores carry more saleable and less brand-appropriate merchandise, they need to watch the balance of generic to branded carefully. Nobody objects to designing websites with the Shopping or Store link on the main menu bar, but the first image one links to should be spot on: On Brand. Cultural consumerism is here to stay, and the importance of the store to the bottom line is well known, but there remains a difference between telling about your brand and selling it. It's a fine but drawable line.

Some examples of online stores that tell and sell the brand:

The High Museum of Art sets a good first impression on its landing page with a photo of rows of books on bookshelves. It's a good omen, a fine introduction, to the High's attitude.

Even the page that starts with a mug has a brand message of particular interest to donors:

> the famed Roy Lichtenstein house design . . . *House III* (13 × 17½ feet) . . . Donated by John Wieland Homes and Neighborhoods, in honor of its company members . . . [part of] the High's growing contemporary art collection and figures prominently in the Museum's planned outdoor sculpture program.
>
> A High Museum of Art exclusive!

Mug shoppers learn about the High's collection, its collecting philosophy, its planned capital expansion, and, by the way, the philanthropic strategy of a key donor (it's like having a mini donor wall on the website). This mug is shouldering heavy brand responsibilities.

Another museum that remembers its brand roots is the Japanese American National Museum, which coordinated its online store with the rest of the museum by using Japanese item names throughout. Socks are "Maneki Neko Socks." Totes are "Yancha Tote Chrysanthemum (Kiku)."

As you develop your online store site, and add to it, keep these pointers in mind:

1. Feature one lead item large enough to have impact. Layout artists call the small visuals flyspecks, and that's what you see with lots of little photographs on one page. They're not big enough to help the visitor make a purchase decision, so sweep them away and open your store site with one item that makes a statement for the store and the museum, as the Arab American National Museum did with the Kaffiyeh. It could be a book cover, toy, houseware item, or reproduction. And, of course, you can change these as you would any store display.
2. Put your logo on every page, including the store pages. This section should not look different, even though there are technical exigencies of the shopping cart icon and multiple images and links.
3. Picture merchandise that is relevant to your mission. Call a meeting of your staff to select items that best express the museum's personality. If you want to offer more items, organize them in categories that can be linked to.
4. Organize your merchandise by product categories to highlight your mission. Instead of merely displaying children's toys, reproduction ceramics, and books, lay them out under the headings "History for Kids," "Historic Hostess Gifts," or, obvious but effective, "History Books."
5. Tell stories about the merchandise that relate to your mission. Don't just post pictures and prices; use the infinite space of the Internet to delve into the lore of the items.
6. Show a photograph of your bricks-and-mortar store, to emphasize the fact that the online store isn't just a catalog, but a part of the museum. A photograph that has a good concept will show a familiar detail of the store, or a portion of the space, not the whole store. Frankly, retail spaces are famously non-photogenic. The photo of the Nantucket Historical Association focuses on its clapboard façade surrounding the red door.
7. Merchandise the items in the online store by color. If your site has a color scheme, one that echoes the image of the museum, select merchandise in that color. Pick three or four items and feature them large on the online store's home page. It will give the pages a consistent look that will help

reinforce your identity as a museum, not just a store. Color establishes a feeling and an image, and with the Web, you have a large surface to work with.

8. Include a message card, with your logo, on all purchases, whether they're gifts, or not. On the Web, it's simple to pre-print the choice of cards with "For your new home," or "Happy Graduation to the future scientist," or "This is what I'm reading this summer, thought you'd enjoy it, too." Get the staff together and invent occasions for visitors to send gifts and relate to the museum. It doesn't take much to remind store visitors what museum site they're visiting, and it's a fun way to reinforce the brand.
9. Keep the scholarly books section separate, with appropriate data collection questions such as academic affiliation, year in school, name of library. The academic-educational audience is quite different from the visitor or donor audience and needs different appeals. Not only can scholars and teachers look at your site academically, but potential hires can also check your bona fides online. One way to demonstrate your research and curatorial strengths is through the books you offer. When you write the description of the book, relate the subject to the mission of the museum. If it's a book people associated with the museum wrote, edited, or illustrated, credit them fully.
10. Offer a museum membership through the store, as an alternative to a reproduction or book. For example, "If you don't see anything you'd like, we'll be happy to send a gift membership to the recipient of your choice." What might be an awkward solicitation at the actual store, one that the store personnel are untrained to handle, is an easy appeal online. Because so many website visitors click to the store, it's an excellent place to suggest membership, and to once again reiterate the mission of the museum.
11. Reach out to community partners by linking to tickets for their events: concerts, performances, walk-a-thons, and street festivals are all candidates for cross-promotion on your site or Facebook page. Choose your partners carefully and tie-in with a group whose mission complements yours because the link will be seen as an endorsement. For an especially apt tie-in, connect to local college or university programs that augment your mission.
12. Another way to curry favor with influential people is to sell their books or copies of articles they've written online; and, with apologies for the repetition, offer only material that fits with the museum's mission.

CONSUMER INSIGHTS

For deeper insights, you can start conducting market research in the store. Give your staff a checklist of behaviors to watch for. Have them jot down comments they find significant.

It's amazing how much you can learn about visitors from seeing their shopping behavior. In research I conducted in 2008–2010, I observed different shoppers:

- Holding hands as they wandered through the store, much as they did through the galleries
- Studying each object for five minutes
- Always moving counterclockwise through the store
- Consulting with their friends
- Jumping up and down with glee as they exited the store
- Dozing in chairs (husbands)
- Crawling on the floor (children)

Observational research isn't as thorough or fact-producing as focus groups or surveys, but it's inexpensive and easy to conduct. The clues you pick up will direct you not only to better ways to buy and display merchandise; they'll also indicate how well the museum is engaging its visitors. Here's a checklist of behaviors to note:

☐ Length of time in the store
☐ Length of time with any one item
☐ Repeat visits to any section of the store item in the store
☐ First area or item visitors head for
☐ Picking up or handling the item
☐ Reading or skimming of a book
☐ Showing or talking about items to companions
☐ What items get a smile, and which ones cause puzzlement
☐ Body language
☐ What visitors say to the sales clerk
☐ What they do when they leave the store
☐ Other (describe) ____________________________

This is a lot of research, and any part of it will give you insights on visitors that you didn't have before. It is not expected that you take up store staff time in collecting and managing quantities of information. This is simply a start. More complete database information is covered in chapter 19, "Database of Supporters."

Online Feedback

Online information gathering, so prevalent with restaurants, hotels, and Amazon, is still underused in museums. Some of the standard techniques include

- Comments. Ask for them with a follow-up e-mail and print them on the web pages or Facebook page.
- Pop-up message after purchase. The British Museum has a multiple-choice screen pop up during long browsing sections; it asks shoppers to grade the visit one to five on merchandise, navigation, and checkout process.
- Endorsements. Monitor your social media posts, tweets, and pins and utilize wording such as "fifty-one shoppers liked this product" or "this scarf was pinned twenty times."
- Popular trends. Use your information management system to identify best sellers of the month and announce them on the store pages or in Facebook posts
- Shoppers' blogs. Be proactive and ask permission of store shoppers to briefly interview them on their favorite store items. Then write a shoppers' blog. Although research is considered intrusive and must be handled extremely sensitively in a store setting, journalistic interviews are commonplace, and usually indulged. Just tell the shopper exactly what the blog is about, and never use full names or other identifiers.

Here's how the Science Museum, London, announced its shoppers' preferences in a post-holiday e-mail. The Subject line of the e-mail said:

> "Find out our customers' favourite products." It opened to a page that said:
> "See our customers' favourites . . . What's yours?"

Simple Data Collection

Even if you have scant resources for visitor management systems, there is a way to collect and analyze data from store sales. Credit card information is one. Recording a purchaser's ZIP code is another.

A verbal questionnaire is an offline way to collect data; it's called getting information. Keep a checklist at the checkout counter so that the sales associate can ask easy questions like:

> Where are you from?
> Who is this pretty bracelet for?
> Did you find what you want?

Don't obviously write down answers. Don't worry if you forget some details. This is extra information that adds surprising amounts of depth to your knowledge about visitors. One small history museum I consulted with (anonymity must prevail here) said it was amazed how many visitors came from outside its immediate area; they had assumed for years that their visitor base was local. With this kind of knowledge you can start to reinforce your mission more effectively. In the store you can augment the neighborly "Thanks for visiting us today" with the more brand-specific "Thank you for traveling out here to learn more about our unique history."

Another people-to-people data collection involves "hiring" an intern to do what young people do so well. Have a roving intern watch out for undecided or lost-looking customers and ask: "Can I help you find something?" This is a lesson learned from the Highland Park Public Library, Illinois, where a roving librarian asked visitors if they needed help finding something. One doesn't expect this kind of personalized service at an arts institution and it is greatly appreciated. Also, pleased customers almost all talk and you can get some shrewd insights into their wants and needs.

Another intern job, this time at the Magritte exhibition at the Art Institute of Chicago, placed a young man with a tablet at the perimeter of the store; he hung out and casually asked anyone not obviously in the throes of shopping how they liked the exhibition. Surprisingly, the questioner asked about the exhibition design, and if there was anything confusing. Turns out this astounding blockbuster had generated confused comments, and this was ostensibly a method of discovering just how confused visitors were. It was also a good way to defuse any bad impressions and encourage verbalization of positive impressions. Again, the comfortable informality of the store makes information gathering possible.

More labor intensive, but worth the effort, is the response card. The Cleveland Museum of Art has a version in a gallery near the Conservation Studio, a gathering area for field trips. Visitors are encouraged to leave post-it notes with questions that will be answered later at that site.

Here's a slightly more sophisticated visitor management system: a laptop with a questionnaire; it's possibly more effective in the store than at the information desk where visitors are in a hurry to get in and which they ignore when leaving. In the store, where people are relaxed and chatty, it's non-threatening for them to stop for a few minutes and respond to an online questionnaire like this:

Please help the [Your Museum] provide a better experience.
What was your favorite purchase?
What would you buy if it were less expensive?
Who is shopping with you today and what did he/she like?
Add your name to our online store mailing list.

At the store, visitors are converted into loyalists, because they have invested time, thought, and money into a tangible reminder that becomes part of their daily life, or entrusted to a friend. Your brand now resides in their life. At the lowest level of information gathering, you have connected to a stranger. With each additional outreach, the stranger becomes family.

THE EXIT

This chapter has spent a lot of time inside your stores. But all good things come to an end and eventually the shoppers leave. You have one chance to touch them. On the checkout page or on a floor stand, post your logo and these words:

"Thank you for visiting us."

Chapter 16

Café

Figure 16.1 The Asia Society in New York offers an enticing, brand-consistent menu.
Source: © 2013 Margot Wallace.

An eight-year-old boy blew up my thinking about branding and the museum café. He enlarged my perspective and shook loose a lot of preconceived notions. The boy, working on a game of some sort, was with two parents, and they stayed longer at the table than any other group having lunch that day. I started looking at all the niche market segments who took the opportunity of eating in a museum to enjoy it a little longer: young parents with a few moments alone together; friends talking with each other by mouth, not e-mail; out-of-town tourists reading brochures for the museum and the rest of the city; grown men with their aging fathers having a meaningful get-together and teenagers feeling comfortable in a palace of learning.

There is no doubt that museum restaurants offer a pause to reflect and refresh. For many, it will be their introduction to the museum, a planning lunch before hitting the galleries. For others, it will be the exit interview, hearing what others thought about the museum before they take their leave. Many will use it as a rest stop with more exploration ahead. In each case, there's a comfortable orientation, and a chance for your brand to state its unique position.

Other segments that shook me to attention were businesspeople who were able to order, eat, talk, and leave in thirty minutes; proud paterfamilias types, heading up a "culture" trip with their families; clubwomen fresh from a morning lecture; and a young server struggling heroically to articulate why the menu was so perfectly suited to her museum.

Sharing information at mealtime connects people to the museum and its experiences. It gives them time off their feet so that their heads can think. In many museums, the restaurants possess the only chairs in sight.

Restaurants aren't for every museum. They require space, licenses, professional managers, and staffing from a labor pool notorious for its turnover. They may compete with restaurants in town or, worse, not be competitive at all. Branding opportunities are academic if the business operation doesn't run smoothly.

If, however, a museum restaurant or café operates comfortably, looking at it from a branding perspective will reap many rewards: familiarization, loyalty, repeat visits, membership, community partnerships, employee solidarity, and good standing in the scholarly universe.

To reap these rewards, this chapter will offer suggestions for using:

Locator signs
Chairs and tables
Menu
Staff training
Catering and facilities rental
Feeding the staff

Feeding the community
Name

Whether you have a vending operation in the corner or in a fine dining destination, your café is a strategic branding tool. For many market segments, current and prospective stakeholders, the table is the place where the personality of the museum starts to exude its pull.

LOCATOR SIGNS

Like the lobby, and similar to the store, the restaurant provides a space to check out the surroundings, to see how other museum-goers look, and to start to feel familiar with the process of museum-visiting. As Elaine Heumann Gurian, an early expert in visitor studies, pointed out, many visitors don't feel they belong in a museum; for many, it's a first-time, intimidating event. If anything, this problem is only intensifying as the world becomes more multicultural and the economy continues to squeeze the leisure budget; museums are not familiar places. Your museum can smooth this first step; you can turn a doubter into an advocate. Start by making sure everyone know where the restaurant is.

Put up signs, even if they're just photocopy sheets in sign holders, showing the way to the food. If the restaurant isn't in a convenient place, and visitors have to go outside, downstairs, or back through the galleries, place signs at the entrance, exit, and throughout the exhibition spaces, so that it can be easily found the minute there's a need for a break. If there are laptops in study rooms, or at the information desk, designate a page for the menu. If your museum has LED displays flashing information in the lobby, throw in a mention of the restaurant. Train your reception area staff to pay special attention to visitors who enter at 11:55 a.m., and encourage them to mention the lunch room. Signs will make the food stop an extension of the visit, a part of the experience. To give you an idea of the importance of signs, think of any large supermarket or drugstore; every aisle is clearly marked. Museums are retail spaces, too, the old-fashioned kind where walking is required to get what you need.

If you have a choice, placing a small café near the entrance has distinct advantages. It reassures visitors they can stay as long as they want and that there will be a place to rest at the end. Locating the café by the museum store makes for a refreshed shopping excursion at the end of the visit. When the eating area presents sight lines to the lobby, galleries, or store, it promotes additional activity. But it's not the smallness or remoteness of the café that's harmful; it's the diminishing of it. Flaunt the food.

CHAIRS AND TABLES

You can't expect visitors to stop and reflect if you don't provide comfortable chairs. Spend time and money on this feature, even if you have to cut back on other places. Spend some time in other restaurants and notice how people sit and talk. Do they lean in, relax back, talk head to head, pass around the mobile photos; spread out brochures; take group shots? Try to fit your tables and chairs to how people really eat a meal. On the subject of photos, have your servers offer to snap a shot of the whole group. As a final touch, tell them to provide a menu to use as a prop, "so you'll always remember where you had this great lunch."

MENU

That menu should be ample enough to fill at least a thirty-minute hiatus. Give visitors a time to relax, read the marketing literature, and talk. Give them a menu with a choice, and food good enough to think about, even if it's just a selection of teas and pastries. If the menu isn't physically long on items, add text about the museum and the exhibits.

The cafeteria menu at Philadelphia's Franklin Institute is posted above the counter and is, frankly, meager. But on the overhead wall are scientific nutrition tips and that makes for wonderful, brand-appropriate reading at this science museum.

Menu Creativity

Most of your menu items will go on the list, or get kicked off, based on cost, and that's how a professional restaurant should be run. But there's every reason to start the process with dishes that reflect your brand, including regional specialties or historic dishes. If you plan early, the costly dishes can be balanced out. Food is such a major leisure activity for your audience that the restaurant's offerings should be as creative and provocative as the exhibits. Even a small operation can offer novelty teas, salads, sandwiches, or cookies.

Design the menu itself to be graphically pleasing and, of course, consistent with the image of the museum. Use the space to tell the history of the museum, or the story behind an exhibit. If you have had pro bono work done for the restaurant, such as the interior design, menu development, and printing of the menu itself, you can credit the donors on the menu. Menu credits are also a wonderful way to amass free wall hangings, music, and wine, and to thank your local businesses like food vendors, linen suppliers, print shops, and cleaning services. Don't forget to put your name, address, telephone number, and website on the menu.

Restaurant dining, of course, is the one area of commerce that isn't transacted more easily online. But that's one place to build up prospective visitors' appetites. Luscious photos and well-written text will schedule your lunch on tourists' agenda, and encourage them not to plan their day around lunch elsewhere. Oklahoma City's National Cowboy & Western Heritage Museum beguiles visitors with this restaurant text:

"The Museum's restaurant, Dining on Persimmon Hill, is decorated in an early prairie motif of yellow sunflowers and is rich with Western tradition."

And sure enough, the photo shows sunflowers and traditional western table tops, and, by the way, a restaurant layout that looks new and able to produce quality meals.

STAFF TRAINING

Remember the first rule of food establishments and be gracious. Hire your staff for their politeness, and train them in diplomacy. In many museum visits, the wait staff will be among the only humans beings that visitors actually talk to. Their tone might be chipper, motherly, or solicitous, depending on the museum's personality; it should always be friendly. Encourage your staff to ask guests if they enjoyed the museum; it helps frame the experience and establish the concept of reflection. If you think your staff is able to answer questions, encourage them. But be sure they know to say: "I don't know the answer to that, but I'll find out." Have a supervisor available who can answer questions, or give an "info@" e-mail address that diners can write to. Remember that (whether they have their mobile devices out or not) visitors can be on social media or Google in an instant to get answers. Your answers have the authority of the brand behind them. Better yet, ask your staff about the most common questions, or overheard comments, and have Q & A material at the table. It's a good way to brand the museum and make mission-specific points in an informal way.

CATERING AND FACILITIES RENTAL

Catered events, along with generating profits, generate brand familiarity. At weddings and meetings, people who never set foot in your museum are now walking through your lobby to get to the dining room, and spending hours inside your environment with hosts who know and appreciate its distinctiveness. There are many ways to leverage this foot in the door:

Literature at the Name Tag Table

Ask the event organizer if you can set out one stack of tasteful brochures. It's their table, so it's a valuable opportunity to explain your brand to a new audience. Use only your most professional materials.

Meeting Room Walls

Conference and meeting rooms should be branded up. If the walls are bare, hang exhibits or a photograph of the museum on them. Since meetings frequently include decision makers and prospective donors from the community, have a stack of your magazines or Annual Reports available. Subtly place a card rack holding business cards of the director. If you're just starting to build a meeting room, give it a name, like hotels do—one that reflects your identity, and design the logo into a wall plaque that keeps your identity visible when the doors are closed.

Name Tags

Everyone expects name tags, so make sure they aren't generic. The museum logo should appear on all name tags or badges of wait staff and other personnel assisting with the meal and the event. If any of your staff are also present—tour guides, volunteers manning the store, the director stopping by to say "Hello"—they should also wear branded name tags. Have both the lanyard and pin tags available; it's astonishing how many organizations still design tags for men's suit jacket lapels.

Signature Dish

The menu, of course, even when customized for a particular group, carries the museum logo and tagline, address, and website. Dishes for catered events will, of course, be selected heavily on price, but this is the time to bring out the regional, historic, or conceptual dishes that connect the meal to the museum. It's wise to develop at least one signature dish that will become a permanent part of your special events menu, a branded item that sets the museum apart from the event.

Inclusion of a Museum Visit

Sounds like a perk, but actually it is a smart branding strategy to indoctrinate guests who may not know the museum. The New Bedford Whaling Museum positions the whole museum as one of its event spaces:

"The museum proper [is] a spectacular salute to New Bedford's rich history. The guests are allowed to wander the museum for an hour at the start of the event."

This reference to the city is smart for attracting weddings and conferences, and nurtures the museum's relationship with its civic stakeholders.

The Abraham Lincoln Presidential Library and Museum in Springfield, Illinois, is the granddaddy of Lincoln museums, in his hometown and his final resting place. The charming tea offered by the museum's facilities rental department has subtle ties to the brand and a few resounding reminders:

"After tea, your guests will be welcomed by a Museum representative into the Presidential Museum, which tells the inspiring Great American Story of Lincoln's life, and be provided with brief information about Foundation membership. Each guest will then depart the Museum with a souvenir of their visit."

Branded Area of Room Designed for Photos

The New Bedford (Massachusetts) Whaling Museum has a designated photo op space, and announces it on its website:

"This room has a panoramic view of New Bedford Harbor. . . . The view as a backdrop is great for wedding photos."

Museum-Branded Events

With catered events being such significant revenue sources, consider developing your own that reflect the museum's brand, such as Mother's Day brunches, holiday teas, and children's parties. Take your message to new groups, in an appetizing way.

Children's parties reach out to the local community in a way that school trips can't. This event focuses on the individual child, not a lesson plan. It involves parents and relatives. It introduces other parents to the museum. The Omaha Children's Museum also includes the whole museum:

"Omaha Children's Museum . . . offers . . . hours of play in its interactive exhibits . . .."

And as for trumpeting its brand loud and far, it promotes this extra:

"Birthday child's name announced in the museum (optional)," http://www.ocm.org/visit/birthday-parties/

Wi-Fi

It's a given in most fast-food restaurants, and certainly makes sense for your café. Brand it well on the log on page; you're paying for the internet connection, so users expect to see this technicality. Make sure your web developer has a graphic sense, so your brand identity is represented tastefully.

Ironically, the nicer you make your rental facility, the more important branding becomes. If the meeting—or wedding, or charity lunch—participants agree that the facility is beautiful, the food excellent, and the chairs comfortable, they'll remember their event for a long time. You want them to remember the museum! Lest the museum's image should get lost in the general event glow, museums are well advised to follow the example of the Art Institute of Chicago, which attaches a mandatory gallery tour to every event.

Name

Not all museum restaurants have brand-appropriate names, but many do, and it's effective, both on-site and online. "Restaurant" and "Café" are generic categories that don't begin to associate the dining-reflecting experience with your identity. Names are a place to tie in with your museum's personality.

"The North & Clark Café" emphasizes the Chicago History Museum's location in the city that gives it its brand direction. It helps pinpoint a restaurant that's open for breakfast, lunch, and dinner, and welcomes local visitors, the community, scholars, and others who are resident for a while in the city.

Penguins Café™—note the trademark—at the Mystic Aquarium in Mystic, CN, emphasizes its marine identity, invokes a beloved icon, and is wonderfully visual.

La Piste is the French word for track and as the name of the Museum of the Automobile, in Mulhouse, France, it is very appropriate. One of three public dining spaces, La Piste overlooks the oval track of the Autodrome. Even when there's no activity at the track, the concept is compelling and a perfect brand reminder.

And for the Sharpest Museum Restaurant Name, my award goes to the snack café located near the dinosaur exhibits at Minnesota Science Museum:

"Chomp"

You'll read more about this museum's brainily branded website in chapter 12.

Brand Name Partners

It's good for professionalism and good for branding to contract food service with a local firm. There is genuine neighborliness and goodwill involved in partnering with a known name, and you'll get expanded awareness as you put your literature at their regular location, borrow their mailing list, and solicit the owner for donations. You may want the owner or manager for your board. Any co-op effort will, of course, compete with your brand, and may bring its own brand baggage.

As an objective observer, I loved the old name of the restaurant at the Museum of Glass in Tacoma: Prizm. The new name, Chorpian, isn't as glassy. But there are strong justifications, as the web page makes clear, for a museum to use the catering service's name. The operator is also the exclusive purveyor at catering events and it's advantageous for visitors to know that the same good food enjoyed at lunch can also be provided at meetings and weddings. Event food and regular lunch food—the two work together: at events, guests learn about the museum; over lunch, visitors learn about renting the facility for parties.

FEEDING THE STAFF

One important community that always needs mission reinforcement is also the one that tends to be taken for granted: your staff and volunteers. Administrators, curators, volunteers and interns—like employees everywhere—attack their tasks more vigorously when the mission is fresh. These are already dedicated stakeholders, so it doesn't take much to reaffirm why their museum is special. Though they may not use the café often, the lunchroom is a place where they can get in touch with each other and their institution. Certainly they should be familiar with the menu and environment, so they can answer any visitor questions about the restaurant and talk knowledgeably about it to their family and friends. It can't be repeated too often, and will be in this book: Employees and volunteers are ambassadors who wield a lot of authority in spreading your brand story.

FEEDING THE COMMUNITY

Museums fit comfortably into every segment of the community. Your education programs, adult programs, social services, and other innovations have made your institution more accessible than ever—more a part of daily life. Continue to occupy that prized position with the community by providing meals. The Milwaukee Art Museum is temptingly close to downtown offices and workers, but across a multilane highway. The dazzling new building, which opened in 2001, included a pedestrian footbridge to connect the town with its new museum. A way for other museums to prove that you're within reach is to invite your neighbors to lunch. Whether this is a promotional offer, or just an announcement, make sure that the business lunch- and the bag lunch-workers all know about your lunch. It's a fact of marketing that people who visit museums with their families on weekends are a different consumer from those who stop by during the work week. Your brand is likely known to everyone, and its values and identity will connect with theirs when they break bread there. Think of the realtors and beauticians who come to museums at noon, and return later with their families. Think of the hotel manager and the coach who don't usually spend their leisure time on the arts, but always spend some leisure time on food.

Branding Opportunities

1. Art or reproductions in the dining area remind diners where they are and what they saw. The National Gallery in Washington, D.C., has wall murals in the casual dining rooms, and an original mural in the white-tablecloth restaurant. The maitre d' has printed material describing the mural; the visiting diner is made to understand the commitment of the museum.
2. Service staff trained with a simple, "Thank you, I hope you are enjoying your visit to the Museum of . . .."
3. Cash register receipt with the logo or tagline of the museum included.
4. Menu with the logo or tagline of the museum.
5. Maps of the museum on the tables or checkout counter, making it easy for visitors to return for another look.
6. Signage throughout the museum announcing the location and hours of the dining facilities.
7. Small specialty food items, with the museum logo affixed, for sale, to keep the memory alive in the kitchen cabinet.
8. Napkins or placemats with children's games, to kindle young people's memories and, incidentally, give the whole family more quality time at the museum.
9. Crayons on the table are a staple for families with children; you could add some coloring book-style pages depicting items from your collection.
10. Table tents announcing future exhibitions.
11. Menu copy that describes selected exhibits.
12. Discreet brochures announcing catering possibilities for private or business groups.

Upon Reflection . . .

The restaurant is a place to integrate a visitor's new experience into his or her daily life. As the Science Museum of Minnesota says, "Exploring can be hard work," and the restaurant is where diligent explorers can relax, reflect, and refuel.

Chapter 17

Publications

Annual Report, Magazine, and Exhibition Catalog

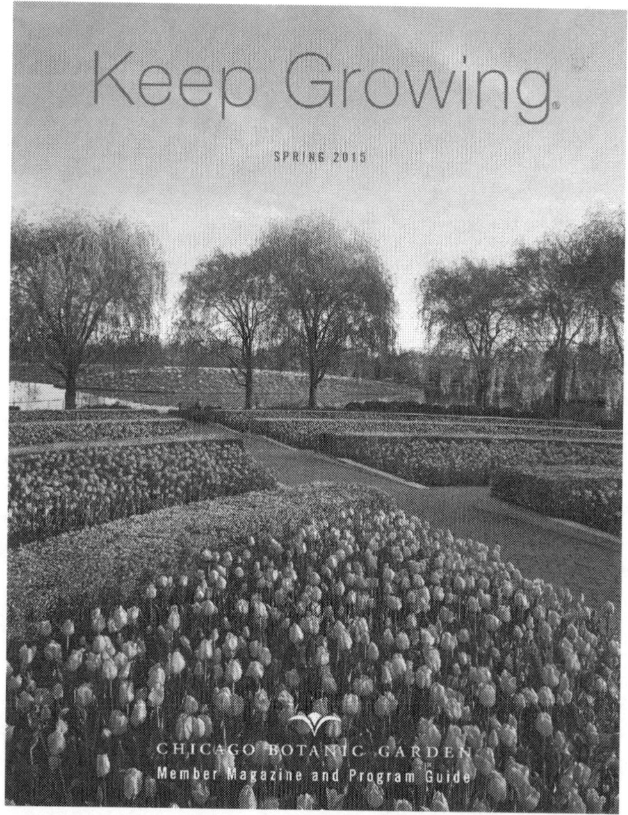

Figure 17.1 The Chicago Botanic Garden sprawls over acres of real estate and branded material. It never loses sight of its brand: growing things. This members' magazine is a flourishing example. *Source*: Tom Harris © Hedrich Blessing.

Publications are your way to tell the public your news, discoveries, learning, and vision, writ large. Printed or online, publications in this chapter are defined as bigger news, longer articles, better visuals, and stronger impact. The most important publications are magazines, annual reports, exhibition catalogs, and program catalogs. Many are still printed on paper and distributed the expensive way to more selected audiences' actual mailboxes. Many have gone online to save money and reach more people, and include video, all with shorter deadlines. In either or both formats, publications are big deals that aggrandize your brand. If they don't reinforce your brand at every step, they fail big time.

Annual reports, magazines, course catalogs, and exhibition catalogs set out to be expensive. In print, their high-gloss look and immaculate reporting look rich and special. It is money well spent because all these publications stick around. On the coffee table or online, publications are worth reading slowly, and savored on other days. When they are distributed electronically, they cost less and last a little longer each time they're forwarded to a friend.

This chapter emphasizes how visuals and text, in publications that allow time for careful planning and assembling, reinforce your brand in eight ways:

1. Magazines
2. Annual report
3. Program and course catalogs
4. Exhibition catalogs, including letter from director
5. Description line
6. Photographs and captions
7. Essay titles, articles, and quotes
8. People

MAGAZINES

Magazines are wonderful marketing tools for retaining members and donors. Even though they are often available as a museum handout, a way to tell the whole museum story to visitors who have allotted only two hours to learn all about you, magazines sent through the mail to your database reinforce the bond between visits. They remind members why they donated in the first place. They reinforce why the reader has volunteered free time, renewed membership, and sent store items to friends. As discussed in chapter 8 on marketing, like all marketing materials, are an important strategic tool, and must stay on brand. It's easy to forget the brand when the subject matter is so interesting: beautiful photographs, carefully selected and cropped; well-researched articles; professional design of each magazine page; and depth and intellectualism inherent in a good magazine. Here's how to keep content on brand:

- Mention the department or gallery in which the pictured item appears
- Give context to a new acquisition
- Reference curators, educators, and lectures that add to the subject of an article
- Take photographs of donors at a gala with a prop or backdrop that identifies the museum, not just the party venue
- Relate store items back to the exhibition that motivated their purchase
- Never photograph a cute child without including a recognizable museum object in the shot
- Forgo several small photographs for one large photo that tells a better story

ANNUAL REPORT

The purpose is federal tax laws and IRS regulations, but the annual report fulfills a much broader brand mission: accountability. Donors, sponsors, partners, vendors, trustees, and many other stakeholders want to know that you're accountable to them and your mission. Along with accountability, another big "A" concept devolves from the annual report: authenticity. Here is where you demonstrate your museum's unique knowledge, insights, and expertise. Suddenly, the once narrowly targeted report on financials expands to fill a world of museum interest.

The annual report of Eastman House in Rochester, New York, is one such enlarged document. Like most statements, it is now online, easily accessible on the museum's website, and its right on brand from "exhibitions" and "programming" to "conservation" and "fundraising." Every single page is headed with a large photograph of a museum activity, and except for the page on trustees, advisors and staff, and financials, all photographs are of photography and film. Each page's image adds to the breadth and conservation of the disciplines George Eastman fostered, a historical overview essential to this museum's mission of heritage, discovery, preservation, and legacy. There are images of an old camera, a lightbox, filmstrip, 1930s trick photography [before the Photoshop Era], and a poster for D. W. Griffith's film, "Hearts of the World." These annual report communications were part of a selection process—with limitless possibilities—and they all support the brand. It seems so obvious, but this kind of brand consistency is hard to accomplish.

Annual report covers don't act like covers anymore. Think of the opening shot of a movie, where a detail or singular concept is shown and then slowly revealed to be emblematic of the entire film. So it is with an annual report. They set the stage—to switch to another form of entertainment—for what's to come. Two good examples come from the Burke Museum at the University of Washington, in Seattle. In both 2012–14 and 2013–14, they opened with a "Huh?" page, and you had to wonder what it meant; then you got it and happily started reading the rest. One cover was bright magenta, with words such as Cele**B**rate, Val**U**e, Explo**R**e, See**K**, and Notic**E**. The highlighted letters spelled "Burke." So, of course, you kept reading to find the "m-u-s-e-u-m" words. They are all discover-imagine verbs, the guiding vision of the museum. The next year the cover was a simple handwritten card that said:

First name: ____________

What I collect: __________

My collection is special because: ________________________

This is what was handwritten in the space provided:
_______ Burke Museum of Natural History and Culture
_______ 16 million objects
_______ Every object has ~~stories~~ a story to tell

Stories behind the object is a hallmark of the Burke. Words and numbers are printed in black and white, but the stories behind them are always in full color. Annual reports have long been written for the general public, as well as financial audiences. The Burke goes a step farther by writing with pictures, and writing very well.

The Chicago Botanic Garden adds value to its annual report with a page of videos featuring thirteen people—visitors, volunteers, and staff—talking about the value of the Garden. Each of the thirteen scripts is perfectly crafted to let the speakers talk naturally and convincingly about specific advantages of this particular nonprofit museum. It's not just beautiful flowers and the glory of nature but photographic documentation, development of focused funded projects, and the role of a living laboratory. Tribute to fascinating writing and casting: I would have loved to hear more from the plant doctor who switched from engineering to working outside with the built environment.

Magazine-style annual reports aren't new, but the financial environment is ever-changing, and it's not just foundations and mega-donors who have a savvier sense of your museum's positioning in the competitive world of philanthropies. Well-selected photos and well-written text help them align your core values with their own.

Print versus Online

At this point, it's time to confront the issue of print versus online. It's a discussion worth having, because a printed piece is tangible and authoritative, and it used to be traditional for end-of-year financial reports. But print is expensive, and no longer the convention, judging by all the museums that produce beautiful annual reports online. When it comes to an expression of everything a museum stands for, all the things that stakeholders pay for, there's no question that digital rules. Save money for collectible pieces that should be printed, such as exhibition catalogs, member magazines, and time-sensitive brochures. Use your interactive ingenuity on the nine benefits of an online report; they reaffirm your brand at every click.

All the News, All Year Long

Online reports let you tell the full year's accomplishments. Acquisitions are one bit of news whose backstory far outbalances what visitors see and most stakeholders are told. Why is the piece important to the vision of the museum? What gap does it fill, or thread reinforce, in the museum's story? What efforts were shouldered to make the contacts and the purchase? Online stories, with their ability to "click here for more information," are ideal for long paragraphs. The museum needs to document their branded thinking on acquisitions, and many people want to learn it. The sum total is impressive for your brand.

Up-to-the-Minute Accuracy

It's every designer nightmare that last-minute figures will come in that have to be changed at press time. Now, changes are easily made.

Glossy Photographs

Frankly, full-color photos look better on the screen than the page.

Interactive Graphics

Viewers are used to dashboards in their apps. Show your public that you're current.

Stakeholder Bios

As you list the people who contribute to your financial and programming success, give them full credit with brief bios. It's important to show how their talents and expertise—their background—enhance your brand.

New Initiatives

Museum supporters want to see what's new, and how it builds on what the museum did last year. The added space of online reports allows you to sing the praises of even small initiatives. If you make these little stories interesting enough, they may motivate more giving.

Partnerships

Laud your corporate, community, and education partners. You now have the space to explain their goals, as well as your own. Even small partnerships will show other potential supporters how they might work with you.

Community Immersion

You can never venture too far into your community. With the space and photo opportunities of online publications, you can explore the nooks and crannies and show your supporters how a museum can effect social well-being. It's part of being a strong brand.

CD Version

You're already digital, so it's a shorter step to produce and mail a digital gift. This return to more traditional distribution—to an actual mailbox—reinforces your brand message to specific supporters.

PROGRAM AND COURSE CATALOGS

Take a class! Unlike schoolchildren, for whom classes—even at a museum—are the norm, adults who take museum courses are leaving their comfort zone to learn something new. Newness for adults is more than just discovery; it's new associations and new pride, and branding fosters those goals. Branding depends on consumers trusting your museum to broaden their world. The course catalog, as well as the learning it describes, is nonpareil in immersing visitors in your brand's learning values.

On the first pages of its bountiful course catalog, Longwood Gardens relates its extensive list of professional and lay courses to its brand mission of teaching the art and science of horticulture to "students and others." It's not just that the founder, Pierre S. du Pont, believed in new horizons; the extent of the course list delivers a strong message of the limitlessness of learning. The number of stakeholders identified by the courses—professional gardener program, master's degree, domestic and international internships, and continuing education—also reinforce the plenitude of learning just ahead.

The course catalog can go even further in using education to reinforce its brand so much further than title, time, date, and cost:

- Create course titles that evoke your brand personality
- Outdoor painting at the Art Institute of Chicago becomes "Painting in the Park: Plein Air."
- Landscapers will learn about "Vibrant Viburnums" and home gardeners about "Made in the Shade" baskets at the Chicago Botanic Garden.
- Add context to the course description
- Students don't just learn to observe color and capture the changing light outdoors, but "along Chicago's lakefront and Grant and Millennium Parks."
- Describe whom the course is designed for
- Embellish with one sentence describing the instructor
- Personalize with a nicely worded quote from a student
- Use brand-appropriate photography
- Even precisely described certificate programs at the Chicago Botanic Garden benefit from being on a page with four-color photographs of *Hydrangea macrophylla*

The old saying about education has new meaning for brands: Get people while they're young, and keep them until they're old enough to become members.

Many culture organizations share an important identity issue with museums: a nondistinctive brand name.

The Chicago Symphony Orchestra has a branding challenge that many museums face: its name is almost generic. Like Louisville, Omaha, Springfield—name your city—more than one culture organization shares the same first name. The name identifies and lends validity to the brand, but it doesn't quickly distinguish it from the pack. In Chicago, the Symphony Orchestra did something distinguishable that any arts organization could do—in its 2015 program, it owned "Chicago." Page after page of the twenty-eight-page publication showed individual musicians and their renowned maestro, Ricardo Muti, photographed against the backdrop of Chicago landmarks. The photos were beautiful: photogenic city landmarks as backdrops for a cellist sitting outside Soldier Field with her cello, the Concertmaster smiling at the railing of a Chicago River bridge.

A caption on the page opposite Music Director Muti's welcome letter, says, in part, "We celebrate our unparalleled musicians and wonderful city with a series of portraits captured in iconic locations in Chicago . . . throughout the year." This publication is so flattering to the city and the orchestra, and so fascinating to its stakeholders, that it extends the brand incomparably.

In a publication, with the time to plan and space to accomplish it, you can visualize your written brand name to strengthen its distinctiveness.

EXHIBITION CATALOGS

Exhibition catalogs are big deals: big in size, number of color images, scholarly articles, and price. They are coffee table books with gravitas. Don't let that intimidate you. These catalogs document your mission and brand; they give weight to your words and proof to your claims of distinction. They are visible proof of brand loyalty on the part of the purchaser; on a coffee table, they shout the owner's interests.

There are three good reasons to embark on an exhibition catalog and one unexpected consequence:

1. Donor, patrons, and major gifts
2. Top-tier awareness
3. Global partnerships
4. Signage in the museum store

The seriousness of effort reinforces your brand core values and promise; major supporters need to appreciate what makes your museum and its programs unique, because they have many options of where to invest their hearts and funds.

Awareness comes in a variety of levels, from the casual tourist with a day to fill to the destination tourist, to the larger world of opinion disseminators and makers. The third, top tier of awareness needs more attention than it's been getting.

Global partnerships are more than prestigious. They pay the bills. Global partners loan you works, and ask to borrow yours. They share the production of marketing materials such as catalogs, videos, brochures, media kits, and photographs. They share the research and insights of curators. If, additionally, they introduce your museum to the wider world of museum professionals and ideas, that's frosting on the cake and between the layers.

Information about an exhibition in the museum store can be achieved, of course, with simple signs and table toppers. The exhibition catalog directs visitors and links the information to the special effort of the museum, giving credibility to the effort, crowds, and extra ticket price of the featured show. Big books, additionally, allow visitors to take all that information—and memories—home. In research conducted by this author with museum-goers of all levels of experience, a common refrain was: "I wanted to share my visit with people who weren't lucky enough to be there themselves."

Letters and Forewords

Whatever the size of the catalog, the first and most important feature is the letter or foreword from the director or directors of the museums hosting the exhibition. There must be a link between this book of wonderful pictures and the wonderful museum itself. The director can make that branding association.

Here are some simple, effective ways to brand your museum right at the beginning:

- The Smith-Jones Museum has been deeply involved in this exhibition for four years because . . .
- When the Smith-Jones Museum had the opportunity to be one of two American museums to feature this exhibition, we were delighted because . . .
- This is a first-of-its-kind exhibition for the Smith-Jones because we wanted to . . .
- As our curators note in their essays, this exhibition allows the Smith-Jones Museum to . . .
- Working closely with [creator, artist] on this exhibition, the Smith-Jones Museum developed exciting new perspectives on its mission to bring . . .

The New York Historical Society finessed the connection like this:

"The NYHS is in a unique position to revisit this pivotal event in the history of both the city and the nation, and while the. . . .It is also a natural continuation of N-YHS's [sic] mission to document and interpret watershed moments that resonate not just in New York but throughout the nation and the world."

DESCRIPTION LINE

The more generous space and time frame of a publication give you another way to reinforce your brand name: the description line. The new Guggenheim Abu Dhabi, scheduled to open in 2016, is calling itself a transnational museum instead of a global one, because the curators say the latter "connotes money rather than art." Richard Armstrong, director of the Guggenheim, says this museum represents "the rich fabric of information being shared among cultures in the Middle East." That's a pretty good description line, too. In a publication, you can expand on the description line with a short paragraph. As mentioned in chapter 8, "Marketing," The Steelworks Museum of the

West does a good job of emphasizing the industrial nature of the "entire Western United States" on every website page. It also states its mission at the bottom of every page. If your name has changed, or no longer uniquely defines your position in the cultural world of your community, utilize every publication you have to explain yourself fully with a description line.

PHOTOGRAPHS AND CAPTIONS

Click open up the Cleveland Museum of Art Annual Report and be immersed in the bigger-than-life world of a museum: captivating objects and behind-the-scenes professionalism, full-color in profusion. Like so many annual reports now, the digital version allows for many photographs, so you can show objects such as mummy cases and native American masks, and also the way items such as these are cared for before the actual visitor sees them. The two-man handling of a mummy case gives a sense of its size and weight, in addition to its beauty and history. The large, floor-mounted X-ray equipment gives new insight into the research behind even the smallest detail of a Monet lily painting. With such knowledge are museum visitors rewarded and enfolded.

Photographs in print publications, magazines, and annual reports lack the spontaneity of video. To substitute human activity in print: crop. Select the main idea of the photo and zoom in. If you haven't used the zoom when actually not clicking the camera, zoom now with the cropping tool. Tighten the frame and lose all the extraneous visual information above the heads. Crop down to hairlines. Eliminate elbows. Never ever show a floor. Then reconsider what you can slowly add back into the frame. Perhaps it's a sign on the wall saying "Kids Space." Or a tall décor item next to the gala chairperson. You may have to stage a shot with the guest lecturer holding his book, or the major donors on their site tour with hard hats. An advertising writer called close cropping dynamic cropping; it focuses so closely on one point of the photo that a still shot gives the impression of action. The best advice I got was from a college photojournalism professor who scolded: shoot with your feet, don't zoom, get close. The more narrowly focused your photo, the less generic it looks, and the better it represents your museum's brand.

Captions Complete the Picture

Photography of art works, paintings, sculpture, decorative arts, and video always appeals and, as some might say, "grabs your attention." But even with the most dynamic photos, grabbing is never enough; captions convert attraction to engagement.

Photographs tell good stories because contemporary readers like lots of pictures, and just enough words to explain what they're seeing. That's where captions come in. These short sentences—no more than two or three—let you interpret the picture to include your brand values. The Cleveland Museum's captions on conservation shots explained how the conservator achieved the desired goals by continuous interaction with the museum curators.

In its annual report, the George Eastman House Museum, Rochester, New York, scrolls a series of film series and programming photos that tell about the venues, sponsors, dates, and audiences for each photo. Here there are facts, and in abundance, which is important because the total effect reinforces the brand of the museum: an expanding universe of photography that all began with the vision of George Eastman and the Eastman Kodak company.

For artistry with captions, read *Indian*, the National Museum of the American Indian/Smithsonian magazine. Its articles are deeply researched and richly illustrated, and the photograph captions add frosting to the layers of cake. Readers accustomed to scanning the photos and captions will be rewarded with good stories, and most will want to slow down and appreciate the full story and the museum that publishes it for us.

Most photos don't have captions. They assume the reader will know what the person at the computer, or the podium, or the benefit dinner table is doing. The caption tells what he or she is doing to fulfill your museum's mission. Don't stop there. Consider your captions as mini articles that tell about the pictures.

ESSAY TITLES, ARTICLES, AND QUOTES

One of the reasons to publish anything, online or in an elegantly produced book, is to explore ideas in depth. This is the place to be scholarly, and reach a wider audience than just scholars. Museums need to reach out, in as many ways they can, to that silent segment of autodidacts who swoop in and gobble up all the information they can find. It's on your walls, of course, and it's also in serious books. You demonstrate the extent of your knowledge, and also the personality and mission of the museum, with essay titles such as these in the exhibition catalog from the *The Armory Show in the Provincial City* at the New York Historical Society. Some of their smartly branded essay titles:

Max Page, The Armory Show in the Provincial City, p. 99
Leon Botstein, Echoes of the Armory Show: Modern Music in New York, p. 127
Susan Hegeman, A "Wordminded People" Encounters the Armory Show, p. 155
Charles Musser, 1913: A Feminist Moment in the Arts, p. 169
Carol Troyen, "Unwept, unhonored, and unsung": The Armory Show in Boston, p. 379

Artist quotes

Exhibition catalogs have a lot of pages to fill to justify their price, and many use the space for artist comments. This is appropriate and interesting, but overemphasis on the artist detracts from the connection to the museum. Good editing suggests that every artist quotation be followed by a line from the writer of the article that draws a connection to the museum that is bringing the show to the public. It doesn't hurt to edit the quote itself. Visual artists, with notable exceptions, are not so talented verbally. Here's an example of artist-museum connectivity, found on a sign in the museum store at the Guggenheim Museum in New York. An *8.5 × 11* sheet of paper on a lucite stand shows the cover of a Robert Motherwell Collages exhibition catalog, with two brief paragraphs telling what's inside, and why it matters for $45:

> . . . four essays that delve into the artist's engagement with collage in the first half of the twentieth century, his early career with patron Peggy Guggenheim, underlying humanitarian themes during World War II, and the artist's materials.

In the foreword to the exhibition catalog for *Magritte: The Mystery of the Ordinary, 1926–1938,* the directors of the three museums that participated in this major exhibition each wrote excellent pieces that gave the relationship between Magritte and the three presenting museums. You can see that these connections need not be long:

From the Museum of Modern Art, New York, ". . . first Magritte retrospective in US . . ."
From the Menil, Houston, ". . . [the] Menils, Dominique and husband, were great collectors and friends of Magritte . . ."
From the Art Institute of Chicago, ". . . [the] Art Institute holds important Magrittes . . ."

PEOPLE

Faces swarm all over the pages of magazines and annual reports. There are so many people a museum wants to thank: large donors, new and eager members, hard-working employees, and time-generous volunteers. A published document seems the appropriate place to record the contributions of people. But, there's a big problem when you elevate people to "people." Before you pour pictures of people into the People pages, take their proper measure. Zero in on the exact nature of their contribution. Underlying the thousands of dollars and man hours are motivations, and it's worth your time to figure them out. They add up to your brand values.

Some motivations to look for:

- Loves the arts
- Admires scientists
- Flunked history and has been making up for it ever since
- New to town and the museum was the first place they discovered
- Talks to animals
- Lives in city, dreams of a garden

Not insignificantly, the motivations of these people will motivate others!

Chapter 18

Academic Museums

Figure 18.1 The Michael C. Carlos Museum at Emory University, a brand within a brand. *Source*: © 2015 Margot Wallace.

Museums on campuses are sleeper brands, full of distinctive objects not enough people know about. Students and professors don't know their full collection and insightful exhibitions. Outside visitors, both local and tourist, may not realize the academic museum's value. Yet, the focus of academic museums is everything a good brand needs. Like all good brands, an academic museum has loyal stakeholders who come in contact with it at many touchpoints. Alumni are important stakeholders who read newsletters and attend football games and events, and are predisposed to donate. Scholars are brand stakeholders, attracted by their brand reputation, to conduct research there. Because of a splendid reputation, an academic museum already has a brand; and it's well earned, the best possible way to be branded. The challenge is to make the brand manifest. No fight songs need be sung; there are equally stirring ways to bring the brand out from under the ivy shadow.

The number of academic museums is large and growing—over 650 in the United States, about fifteen percent of the total 4,400 colleges and universities—and this chapter will talk to them specifically. However, several other kinds of museums fall under the aegis of a bigger entity. Two examples, albeit large ones, are museums in arts centers such as the Baker Art museum, part of Artis-Naples, or museums with locations apart from the parent, such as The Cloisters, which is a branch of the Museum of Metropolitan Art in New York located in northern Manhattan. Many of the concepts discussed here will apply to the smaller museums in this category.

In thinking of your museum as a brand unto itself, not just an annex to the parent college or university, you'll have to reexamine the parts. Here are six branding goals any academic museum, of any size, can accomplish:

1. Think of teaching modules as brand touchpoints.
2. Review your website and logo for brand distinctiveness.
3. Think of your building as a brand logo and heighten its visibility.
4. Write a blog, the most brandable marketing piece a museum can have.
5. Look at existing or new target audiences as stakeholders.
6. Flaunt the difference between the museum's brand and the college's.

RETHINK YOUR TEACHING MODULES

Before you change anything, take inventory of what your brand has to offer college classes: visuals, relevance, provocative issues, interpretive skills, experience in guest lecturing, and a novel venue. Then blast some e-mails to the faculty of your college or university. To restate Eric Segal, Director of Education at the Harn Museum of Art, University of Florida, from the 2015 annual meeting of the Association of Academic Museums and Galleries, community outreach is everyone's responsibility; no staffer has that title. When you reach out, talk as a museum with a name and identity of its own, not as a department of the academic parent.

Here are some advantages your museum might emphasize, and some examples from the academic partnerships between the Harn Museum and Museum of Contemporary Photography and their respective academic partners, the University of Florida. and Columbia College, Chicago:

Visuals

Your exhibits are visual, tangible, dimensional, and, sometimes, touchable. They're more interesting than a textbook or a slide presentation. They can be "read" standing up and moving around. Don't try to give a lecture; illustrate a talk the professor has already given. At the Harn Museum, doctoral students in "Tropical Ecology" conducted a research project based on identifying birds depicted in nineteenth-century prints. Their research addressed, among other things, ". . . questions of biological validity, accuracy of initial identifications, and habitat appropriateness."

Relevance

Good brands are current and respond to constituents' interests. Your exhibitions are timely. You do a great job of getting ideas off the drawing board and into the galleries, quickly, where a broader audience can learn about them. In addition to mounting exhibitions, you run a business. The Harn invited engineering faculty and students to study its HVAC system as a real-world project.

Provocative Issues

Your faculty may not be able to address some of the sensitive issues museums are accustomed to tackling in the course of dealing with art, creativity, and innovation. Risk-taking exhibitions are part of an academic museum's DNA.

For a course in the University of Florida's nursing program, "Restoration of Wellness," museum curators talked about subjects such as maternity and lactation, and death and grieving, using art works to start discussions on these challenges.

Interpretive Skills

Analysis is what all higher education wants and what museums have provided for 100 years of interpreting their objects.

The Museum of Contemporary Photography adapts its Observation module for teaching marketing students how to analyze the market segments in a photograph. Who's in the photograph? What are they doing? What market segment do they represent? Are they, perhaps, a niche segment you haven't thought about? Students learn not just to observe but also to analyze, discuss, and develop new ideas.

Experience in Guest Lecturing

For the "Geography of Alcohol" course, whose subject was the material culture of different societies, items from the Harn's collections illustrated the range of consumer production and usage throughout history. It was a matter of curating them for the course, and building a talk around them. A guest lecturer might be able to accomplish this feat of presentation, but most guests lecture: they talk about their field, their job, or their book. They *talk at* the students; museum educators *discuss with* theirs.

Take pride in your museum's guest lecturing talent. Museums know how to communicate with a group of students they've never met before and to connect.

Novel Venue

Students learning Spanish went to the Harn Museum of Art for their semester-long course, "Spanish at the Museum," which was developed by the museum. What a delightful way to visit another culture—by visiting another cultural institution.

Although the museum on campus often gets taken for granted—or taken for another building where the student doesn't have a class—the fact is, you're a change of place, and that's before students have walked in the door. Inside, there's a classroom like no other, one that allows wandering, exploration, and talking to classmates usually on the other side of the room. To point out the effectiveness of movement, consider the example of Megan Zylstra's teaching effectiveness workshop at Columbia College: It warms up with the faculty participants going to points of the compass to represent their hometowns. The 2-hour workshop has adults of all ages moving around several times. Is motion effective or simply fun? It is quite possibly a broader version of the gesturing-motion theory that helps speakers more clearly articulate the thoughts they want to communicate.

Your museum has a lot to offer the academic folks on the other side of the campus, just as they have a lot to offer you. As Scott Bishop, Curator of Education, Jule Collins Smith Museum of Fine Art, Auburn University, Alabama, said "We have the map; they have the wheel."

REVIEW YOUR WEBSITE AND LOGO

Websites are critical in helping you stand on your own four walls. You may not have an expensively designed website, but you do have a mission statement, exhibits, programs, and photos. Review your website with an eye to editing it and, perhaps, advocating for an update. Locate students on campus who can help you tweak it. One reason websites don't get changed is that the university webmaster is overworked. Show your administration some proposed changes and start the bargaining process. It's worth fighting for a website that will become your invaluable marketing and managing tool. More important, it will establish your brand for all to see. Make no mistake, people look carefully at websites.

Website

Critique your home page first. Check the visuals, layout, typeface, and color palette. Do they represent the DNA of your museum? Be ruthlessly objective and ask staff and volunteers for their honest opinion. Check the websites of other academic museums you know and admire. Ask the same questions of them: Are the visuals, layout, typeface, and color palette reflective of those museums' mission and personality?

For example, the website of Snite Museum of Art at Notre Dame University features different artworks as wide and deep banners across each web page. The art occupies fifty percent of the screen, and the camera pans across it. The Notre Dame name is prominent, but the Snite name is dominant.

The Logan Museum of Anthropology at Beloit (Wisconsin) College is very much a part of the college's website, but its brand identity is firmly established in the strong earth-toned visual of a pharaoh and pieces of pottery that banner across the top of its home page.

Blanton Museum of Art leads off with a work from a current exhibition. It has its own URL. And although the "University of Texas at Austin" is integrated into the Blanton letterform logo, there is blatant independence in the call for donations: "Support Blanton" is equal in size to "The Calendar of Events."

Then, again:

Some museum websites identify themselves first as the university, at the top of the screen, then, reading down, as the museum, and then, reading down just a little further, an artwork or object from a current exhibition appears.

Some academic museums have excellent web pages, which can be easily found by googling; yet, they are still buried so deeply within the website that even an internal search doesn't locate them.

Regardless of the space you get within your institution's website, there are several ways to stand apart.

- Tell the story of your museum. You will find a singular identity that connects you to the college without being subsumed by it. The Logan Museum of Anthropology has a short but cogent creation story:

  "The museums of Beloit College were born in 1848, when Rev. Stephen Peet, one of the founders of the College, donated his mineral collection, which became the nucleus of the College's 'Cabinet.' It was common practice in the 1840s for Eastern Colleges to develop geology and natural history cabinets of specimens to augment textbooks."
- Ask for a tab on the home page. Don't make visitors to the college's website have to hunt and click to find the museum.
- Use social media a lot; you can easily own your content by including your name in #s and @s.
- Talk to the college's webmaster and search marketing consultants, and use language that will get you found on search engines.
- Read the language of your website out loud. This is a basic good-writing technique, because you'll hear all the unnecessary verbiage. You'll also hear the tone of voice. Don't try to "find your voice," as the writing teachers suggest. But if you hear a style that appeals, hire the writer to write the entire site.
- Select photographs for their brand support, not their content. A group of students in front of a display is generic; an object that represents your collection, placed on the table in front of them, is good branding. A shot of a gallery is common; include in the photo an architectural element that distinguishes yours. If the photos are wanting, write captions that identify the photographic subject's significance to the museum. A few words next to the photo will do just fine:

  "Smith-Jones Museum Docent"
  "Sculpture Garden at the Smith-Jones"
  "Look what the Smith-Jones acquired"

Consistency counts in your website. It's the glue that holds your identity together, wherever you're placed within the parent website. Although all museums observe the branding basics of a consistent look, typeface, color palette, tagline, message, and tone of voice, it is more important when another, better-known brand shares the nearby space. Small brands appear bigger when they speak consistently. All materials—from letterhead and business cards to brochures, signs and website—should have the same look.

Logo

You may not have a symbol logo, but you do have a letterform logo (logo that uses the name to create a mnemonic picture). These logos may look simple, but they're instantly recognizable. You may not have a tagline, but you do have a mission. If you can paraphrase your mission in a few words, position it near the logo. While you probably won't have the opportunity to change your logo, you will have some freedom of size and placement.

These visual and verbal symbols of your brand carry a heavier burden than nonacademic museums because they appear right next to the college or university logo. It's confusing to everyone. First, viewers will wonder what the relationship is between your museum and the academic institution—partner, budget line within an academic department, independent. If there's one thing you, as a marketer, don't want, it is a product that bewilders people.

The first thing to consider is the spatial and size ratio of your logo/name to the parent's. The letterform logo of the Hammer Gallery at UCLA takes up one hundred percent of the logo; UCLA is not included. The college is identified only in the domain name, not on the website.

Another museum that owns its logo is Allen Memorial Museum of Art at Oberlin College. The Allen name and logo—yes, the museum displays its own visual symbol—occupies about eighty percent of the logo space, with "Oberlin College" appearing much smaller.

Newcomb Art Gallery at Tulane University also owns one hundred percent of its logo space. "Newcomb Art Gallery" in letterform logo stands alone. On each spare, uncluttered page of the website, however, "Tulane University" appears prominently at the bottom.

Nora Eccles Harrison Museum of Art at Utah State University leads in with a large museum letterform logo, followed by a slightly smaller university letterform logo.

The Ringling, in Sarasota, Florida, is termed "the State Art Museum of Florida" and is administered by Florida State University. The Ringling comprises four separate museums—art museum, historic mansion, circus museum, and historic theater—and the university's identity wisely does not intrude on the already busy banner at the top of the web pages. As a matter of governance, the relationship is spelled out on the governance page.

At the National Churchill Museum, the fulcrum is much nearer the museum's side. Churchill is arguably a much bigger identity than the identity of its parent, Westminster College in Fulton, Missouri. And the fact that this college was the venue for Churchill's "Iron Curtain Speech" is no small detail. The museum has its own URL, a rarity, although the college is named immediately in the opening paragraph of the website, and as the address at the bottom of each page.

From the college's perspective, the Churchill legacy is transformational. The college's tagline includes the words, "Educated to lead . . ." and the concept of leadership weaves throughout the website.

A prominent logo cuts through a lot of competition, and it doesn't have to be big or in color. One way to check if the mark or typeface is distinctive in a clutter is to see how readable it is when reduced, photocopied several times, or sent by fax. When the logo appears with the university, corporate, or foundation logo, it will hold its own if placed higher up on the page, or if it's surrounded by white space. Another way to stand out is to appear in multiple places; just as you place your logo on all print materials, place it on every page of your website.

The jockeying for position, even in something as small as a logo, is ongoing, as all academic institutions reconsider their own priorities. The symbiotic relationship between museum and parent is important, and both parties know it.

BUILDING AS BRAND LOGO

You want to be connected to the campus, not buried in it, and you have an advantage in your building. As logos go, this is as big as they get.

Abraham Lincoln Library & Museum, Harrogate, Tennessee, on the rolling hill campus of Abraham Lincoln College, has a prime location, on a rise, near the highway, at the entrance to the university. There's an unmistakable, large image of its brand namesake travelers can't miss.

The Snite Museum of Art, at Notre Dame University, is pretty much dwarfed by Knute Rockne Stadium and a soaring brand of global sports fame. It's about fifty yards away. Yet, counterintuitively, it is connected to the stadium by a brick walk and proudly announces its brand on a sign above the entrance that is visible from Gate E:

"Inspiration for a lifetime is seconds away."

Here's how Rose Museum at Brandeis College addresses the brand challenge of location within a larger footprint: with a large sculptural gateway and a permanent installation of antique streetlights outside the museum commissioned by the university. The lantern lights shine at night and provide gathering and performance spaces during the day. It is, in the words of the museum director, a social sculpture.

Loyola University Museum of Art, LUMA, in Chicago, announces its urban presence with banners hanging from lampposts throughout its tourist-oriented North Michigan Avenue neighborhood.

Directional signs are needed to show the way, all the way up to the front door. And the confusion doesn't end there. Some academic museums don't assert themselves, even when the mobile GPS says you have arrived at your destination. Make sure your lobby shines from within; signal your brand.

Lobby

Once the visitor is inside a hard-to-find museum, welcome them prodigiously. This is especially important if your premises look like an academic building. The lobby is a staging area, where visitors acclimate to the experience ahead. This sometimes seems like a luxury in an academic environment, but there are academic ways to make the entrance more welcoming. Provide an information desk, not a guard station, and stock it with informative—and well-branded—brochures.

Staff the front desk with well-informed, well-trained attendants. They will probably be students; use your discretion whether you'll allow them to study during their tour of duty. At the very least, they must be friendly. This is not a trivial demand: many college students are socially unskilled and as likely as anyone in the population to be introverted. A recent book by Susan Cain places the percentage of American introverts as high as 50%. Your staff has a unique opportunity to appeal to this loyal segment of the academic market.

Part of the lack of brand visibility in a college museum is attributable to the lack of staff. So make the most of the staff your budget allows. Supply all docents, guards, museum store assistants, and information desk personnel with badges and name tags that bear the museum's name and logo.

In addition to staff, build a few high-impact displays that quickly communicate your brand mission. Stock a small store with educational items that reinforce your mission. For a 2015 exhibition on Shakers, Loyola University Art Museum offered several books, as well as Shaker-style souvenirs, Furnish the lobby with chairs or banquettes, so visitors can relax and reflect as they would in a stand-alone museum, and then provide some visuals to give them more to reflect on. Posters on the wall are inexpensive ways to build in a contemporary look, and also seed some ideas.

Inside the museum, blazon your brand name or logo on every sign, wall label, and panel. These are constant reminders to visitors that they are in the museum, not the university. Mount video screens with a docent giving information or curators working on an exhibit, some branded content to reinforce your identity. With universities getting huge amounts of money to upgrade technology, they likely will have video signage all over campus. Ask to have a few screens of your own added to this budget line.

BLOGS

Of all the platforms for sharing information, which are discussed specifically in chapter 12, "Digital and Social Media," the one that maximizes the museum brand is the time-honored blog. With their sharp focus, blogs support branding elegantly. The blogger has time to select brand-appropriate topics and space to incorporate the brand perspective. Cantor Arts Center at Stanford University publishes "Cross-Currents," a student-written blog that follows the activities in the Conservation Lab. In a July 2015 edition, for example, the blog covered everything from a student's current notebook to a "top post" on attic vase silhouettes to an article on non-intrusive light technology.

There are many advantages that an academic museum has in writing a blog, and they all support the museum's distinctive place within the larger entity. Look what a blog can do:

- Address topical issues immediately—issues a university curriculum can't address as quickly.
- Appear frequently—you've already done the research.
- Speak with a range of ideas from different bloggers, encouraging a range of respondents to your brand.
- Give itself a descriptive name, such as "Beyond the Gallery Walls," the blog of Penn Museum at the University of Pennsylvania.
- Focus on one aspect of the museum at a time, building a complete picture of the brand.
- Utilize many visuals that depict your characteristic way of approaching a subject.

BROADEN TARGET AUDIENCES

Your audiences help define your brand identity. Students and faculty help explain your core values. And even beyond the college campus, there are communities that help establish your brand bona fides. Reexamine the market segment you call "faculty" for instance, it can be divided into niches by their interests. The segment termed "visitors" ranges farther afield. Social media brings just about anyone into your sphere. With the same creativity you've applied to your exhibitions, envision your brand appealing to a wider audience of people who are brand-appropriate. Here are some new ways to look at:

Visitors
Town
Faculty—on campus and off
Alumni
Scholars
Interns
Donors
Students

Visitors

Basic visitorship is easy to overlook when you're surrounded by campus people. The author was reminded of this fact one day, at the entrance of the Museum of Contemporary Photography on the campus of Columbia College Chicago. The museum was closed for installation, and two visitors at the door were disappointed. They weren't students or faculty who could return the next week, but photography enthusiasts from France who were leaving the next day. As you reach out to new markets, it helps you realize that you are a brand in your own right that people come some distance to see.

Town

If you redefine and broaden your definition of audience from the core college community, you'll find other ways to enhance your distinct brand. The town-gown axis includes the citizenry of the town and the businesses, the families and the employers, educators at all levels, and the social services. You already serve these groups, but when you recognize them as market segments, you'll be seen as a museum, not a campus resource.

Along the town end of the town-gown axis, you'll discover citizens and businesses, both of which can be reached with traditional and social media. Don't overlook the wait staff at local restaurants, the social service staff at local agencies, public safety officers and high school coaches, and retirees who may work and live in town without any prior connections to the college.

Faculty—on campus and off

Academic museums, of course, have always functioned as learning annexes for art, history, and science courses. But more is possible. At Columbia College Chicago, a class in leadership has developed a module with the Museum of Contemporary Photography on campus; it discusses, among other things, the viewpoint of the photographer, and subjects not seen on first glance. When you show how adaptable your collection is, you strengthen its brand.

A subset of faculty includes teachers of other education levels. A guest book at the Lucille Ball Museum in Jamestown, NY, included a greeting from an eighth grade teacher in the area; she praised two famous "I Love Lucy" episodes as teaching aids for her business classes: "Chocolate" for teaching job switching and "Aunt Martha's Salad Dressing" for teaching entrepreneurship. Lucille Ball the businesswoman and innovator is part of her brand and the museum's. Academic museums used to talking to college faculty may not realize the appeal of college-level material to other faculties.

Off campus, faculty members become a whole new market segment; they have a life of their own with families, hobbies, and, frequently, other jobs. Their interests are not just their courses, but these interests may well be aligned with an academic museum's programs. Take a look at the programs you offer, how they might appeal to all teachers, and you'll find new ways to express your brand distinctiveness.

Alumni

Alumni may live too far away to visit or attend events, but they still read newsletters and blogs. They contribute to social conversations of Facebook and Twitter. And they share a common community: They lived in your environment. Since they already love the school, they're ambassadors—walking marketing materials—for your brand. That makes them important touchpoints, as well as stakeholders.

Scholars

Researchers are also ambassadors for your brand. The research they conduct will frequently be cited in academic publications. They know your distinctiveness as a resource, and you can leverage that. A scaled-up example is the Science Museum in London, which publishes a huge blog that includes articles by researchers. If your mission is scholarly, this touchpoint is evidence for your positioning.

Interns

Interns are a little blurry as a group, because they're usually students. However, these are distinct students who are following you as a distinct brand, not a campus resource. They're budding professionals who want a career in your field. They are already loyal to museums, and are prime targets for continuing engagement, if not with you, then with your museum colleagues worldwide. Don't confuse interns with work study students, who are paid by the college or university to work at a job somewhere in the college; and don't ignore work study students. Like everyone who walks through your door, they are now familiar with your brand and are prospects for longer term loyalty.

Donors

Museums are seen as part of a well-rounded education, and that hasn't diminished with the current attention to academic museums' returns on investment. Big donors, especially, love museums, according to a 2014 New York Times article; and the creation of a donor class starts with students, faculty, visitors, alumni, scholars, and workers. Think of your brand, with this segment, as an asset to your college, not an adjunct.

Students

Students are, of course, your natural market, and such a good one that it's logical to look beyond art students if you're an art museum; history students if you're a history museum; and science students if you create science-related exhibits. As you look beyond the expected departments as partners, you'll have to change your own teaching modules. "Arts will always fight the 'alphanumeric bias," according to Thomas Lentz in a *New York Times* article. "If it is not text and not a number it is not considered knowledge." However, museums have something to offer every department: exhibits and ways of thinking that are based in their individual brand.

FLAUNT THE DIFFERENCE

There's a personality difference between museums and academic classrooms. Realize it and you can own it. This is especially important when seeking donors, partners, and other supporters. Donors will rightly connect the museum to the college and that's good. However, as a distinct brand, your branding task is to

- Point out that you're a distinct building on campus.
- Emphasize that you deliver many separate shows each year versus a curriculum that repeats.
- Highlight that your learning features no tests and no books.
- Brag about the low-to-no-cost of credit hours at your classes.
- Point out your different layout: no rows of chairs, keypad-locked labs, or whiteboards.
- Demonstrate your learning resources, which are visual and tangible.
- Explain all the learning that comes from labels and panels, as opposed to textbooks.
- Emphasize how your learning comes from guides rather than teachers.

Academic museums need to establish their credentials in the museum community. They may be accredited in their own right by the American Alliance of Museums and the Association of Academic Museums and Galleries. They loan and borrow objects for exhibitions. Scholars count on them for research. Tourists expect a museum, not a school. It's even more problematic in the community, where your old dusty image can last a long time, or worse, might be that of just another building on campus. The server at a local restaurant near a university once applauded a traveler's upcoming visit to a nearby museum, which had a name similar to its parent university. "It's great, we're so proud of it," the server said, and then went on to talk proudly about the university's new medical school.

PRESTIGE FOR THE COLLEGE OR UNIVERSITY

All the qualities that combine to make a great academic museum brand also enhance the parent college or university. Over and over, in museum after museum, their excellence benefits major higher education goals. Remember all the things you do.

Attract Visitors

Academic museums can attract visitors who might never otherwise know about the college or university. Some are sights along the interstates. Some are culture interludes for hikers and cyclists. Some are destinations for scholars, history buffs, or relatives visiting family in the area. Some have programs that complement community leisure and culture activity. And don't downplay happy hours, which are *de rigueur* for stand-alone museums but not customary for academic institutions. Lowe Art Museum of University of Miami has a branded name for its party: "LoweDown." Your membership-building events have broad appeal that your parent can only envy.

Earn Nationwide Prestige

Just as the broad geographic reach of conferences earn prestige for your college, so loans enhance your museum's credentials. Spencer Museum of Art, the University of Kansas in Lawrence, proves its own mettle in its loans. In its Fall 2014 newsletter, the museum lists fourteen different museums that were recipients of on loan works; three were academic museums, and the others were museums in Kansas City, Missouri; Savannah, Georgia; San Jose, California; Salem, Oregon; Tacoma, Wisconsin; New York; Indianapolis, Indiana; Corpus Christi, Texas; Colorado Springs, Colorado; and Phoenix, Arizona. This broad demand for items demonstrates the distinctiveness of its collection and its position in the world of museums. Its brand is widely known and respected. It does its academic parent proud; it stands apart.

Enhance Resumes and CVs of Faculty and Students

Involvement in a museum carries cachet; it adds to the resumes of student interns and CVs of faculty who collaborate with curricular modules.

Flaunting isn't in the nature of museums, but showing your brand carries weight where money is concerned. Financial people who have a stake in your success—donors, partners, sponsors, and funders—will respond better if a defined mission is made clear throughout all dealings, visual and verbal. Business and financial people look for unfilled needs. A distinct image is especially important if these same stakeholders assume the parent is paying all your bills.

With a brand, academic museums grow up. It's what any parent wants, and it's an asset to your college or university. You validate them.

Chapter 19

Database of Supporters

Figure 19.1 The Eastman House garden and greenhouse welcomes visitors and other stakeholders with exhibits focusing on horticulture, movie history, science, technology, and medical research, as well as photography and cameras. A marketing database could include almost as many market segments as George Eastman had interests. *Source*: © 2015 Margot Wallace.

What do you know about the people who support your success? How meaningfully are you acquainted with visitors, members, donors, sponsors, volunteers, community partners, and all your supporters? How ready are you to leverage your brand and prosper in a competitive economy? Just for fun, take a guess and

- Name twenty people who are members at the highest level
- Estimate how many e-mail messages you send each week, or month
- Tell how many volunteers you have
- Count how many schools groups are booked so far this year
- Rank your best-attended events in the last two years
- Analyze the types of groups that tend to rent your facilities
- State your busiest day of the week

If you can't answer point number one, you don't have a database, according to Wes Trochlil, nonprofit marketing consultant. Databases don't just keep track of your supporters, but they grow support. And that's a big reason why you work so hard to develop a brand. To maximize good branding, build a good database of supporters. You could have excellent brand reinforcement throughout your organization—brand-relevant programs, website content, fundraising messages, store merchandise, events, print materials, and social media messaging—and it will be squandered if the people who are interested in you aren't contacted meaningfully. This ongoing constituent relationship management, or customer relationship management (CRM), as it's used by for-profit marketers, is made possible with technology. It can be the sophisticated systems used by museums for collections and events databases, or something as simple as Excel. What makes CRM so valuable is that it builds on your brand. It helps you maintain brand awareness, loyalty, and engagement by the people who support you.

This chapter will cover the kinds of information, or data, you collect to keep your various supporters engaged with your brand; some of the means of gathering that data in a brand-enhancing way; and the value of databases for long-term thinking.

KINDS OF DATA TO COLLECT

Branding helps you solidify long-term relationships by identifying your supporters' level of involvement and analyzing how to reach them with relevant information.

Visitors—Get to Know

- Ages of all the people who visit your museum
- Length of stay at your exhibits
- Their favorite place in your museum
- Decision makers
- The people who accompany them

Members

The goal is to enfold each visitor into the museum family, so that he or she becomes a member. Members join organizations whose brand they know well, feel an affinity for, and have pride in. Museums with strong brands speak specifically and meaningfully to members, with messages that remind them of why they joined. Databases let you target members specifically. Find out

- Membership levels with the most participants
- Year of first membership
- Number of events/programs members attend each year
- Year of membership that's most vulnerable to quitting

Donors

The goal is for every donor to keep giving year after year, and then to give more. Donors give because your brand mission resonates with their philanthropic mission. Databases help you identify and communicate with them at appropriate times. Memorize

- Names of the biggest donors
- State where the biggest donors spend most months of the year
- Other not-for-profits the biggest donors support
- Number of years the smallest donors have been contributing

Volunteers

Volunteers work for you, without pay, because your brand's values, personality, and identity give them a workplace affirmation. Databases help you keep in touch with workers who want to be treated professionally. Volunteers are usually members and visitors, as well as workers. Identify

- Their reason for wanting to volunteer
- Other not-for-profits they support
- Average number of years of participation
- Year in which a volunteer tends to lose interest and/or resign

Sponsors

Sponsors link up with museums whose collections, goals, and audiences enhance their brand's goals and target markets. Before your brand can sign an agreement with a sponsor's brand, the sponsor will want to know some facts. Databases show them the numbers.

Get to know businesses or individuals who

- Have been solicited by your museum for donations
- Have rented your facilities
- Are nonlocal but have a satellite presence (research and distribution) in your community
- Have sponsored other organizations or events in your community

Grantors

Grantors listen to museums whose proposals mesh with their stated mission; and more than just aligning your brand with theirs, they need facts that demonstrate how your museum approaches its projects differently from other institutions. Databases collect the facts, and analyzing the sets of facts helps you demonstrate your museum's competitive advantage. You'll have not only numbers but also analytical insights. Data-driven analysis also impresses grantors. Identify

- Which of your programs align with which granting institutions' goals
- Which audience segments match populations served by grantors
- Which niche segments might appeal to grantor objectives
- Which other organizations grantors fund

Community Leaders

Communities are complex places; every community leader—governmental or civic—has different goals to achieve. Although your brand earns respect within the community, community leaders change regularly, as do their challenges, and databases help you keep track of all the names, as well as your projects whose aims coincide with theirs. Find out

- Number of times the mayor has been asked to attend an event
- Pet projects of legislators on your e-mail list that correspond with your collection policy
- Business initiatives in the community
- Names of directors/managers of local library, Rotary, Chamber of Commerce, bookstore, restaurant, travel agency, community house, senior center, and lifelong learning program

Educators

Your brand reputation, as well as specific exhibits and programs, will get you in the school door. Then comes the follow-up, with the aim of your museum becoming a trusted resource for each grade. Educate yourself on

- Names of five school principals and/or superintendants
- Names of school board members
- Names of teachers who have brought groups
- Your museum's most popular (by numbers) student activities (e.g., museum trip, in-class visit, and homeschool module)
- Specific grade levels and classes you've hosted
- Times of year favored by each school and/or teacher

Scholars and Researchers

These influential people are arguably the most engaged of all your constituents. They already trust you enough to call or e-mail for information and resources. They frequently visit in person, perhaps for extended periods of time. They spread your good name all over the world as they cite you in their papers, books, and talks. Of course, you not only spend a lot of time helping them, but you also learn from them. Keep these ambassadors informed and involved; get their names in a database, along with

- Their topic of research
- Institutions and organizations to which they belong
- Coauthors, if any, of their publications

New Market Segments

Now, it's time to revisit your visitorship. This is where marketing, with its niche segmentation, helps extend your brand.

This is a big group, comprising a lot of people who aren't very familiar with your brand. They may know about museums in general, but not about you. Thanks to databases, marketing can identify new, niche segments, and target them with appropriate messages. Good brands understand their potential visitors. This short list suggests the many niche segments you might target. Get to know

- New residents
- Teachers at their homes, not schools
- Bloggers and their specific interests that jibe with your mission
- Other social media commenters attuned to your areas of expertise
- Attendees of programs about medieval art, or Latin American cultures, or conservation
- Attendees who attend more than one program, and what those are
- Store purchasers of books—or jewelry or toys

- Companies that rent facilities
- Residents of specific ZIP codes

ZIP codes truly are codes: five numbers that unlock reams of information about people who live within them: home ownership, education level, ethnicity, occupation category, age, and household size. This data can be analyzed to reveal many more characteristics of the people in your market. Strong brands can expand to new ZIP codes, even ones that haven't yielded many visitors in the past.

Facilitators

They accompany the person who received the e-mail announcement, bought the admission, or purchased the store item. They usually are ignored by survey-takers. But these tag-along companions have entered your museum, seen your exhibits, and learned a lot about you. Don't let partners of the decision-maker slip from your grasp. Get to know names and e-mail addresses of

- Friend—who came along to be supportive
- Child—who is too young to visit alone, but not for long
- Chaperone—mother whose turn came up for school volunteering
- Colleague—stuck around while his or her friend shopped in the store
- Caregiver—who is just following mother's instructions
- Tourist on a tour—who is just following tour manager's agenda
- Assistant to the tour manager—that all-powerful person who does all the ground work and knows your museum and staff very well

Ask Why

Now that you know the people to track, add a field to your database that identifies their reason for contact with the museum. Always ask why! Brand relationships are a two-way street: between your museum's brand and an individual who also has a brand name. **Rachel Smith**, whose fourth grade class visited this year, belongs in a different data set than State Senator **Tom Smith**; President **Eleanor Smith** of the Smith Family Foundation; **Juan Smith**, the bank manager who books your facility for monthly meetings; **Pat Smith**, the 2-year volunteer; **Danielle Smith** who retweets regularly; **Henry Smith**, your fifteenth biggest donor; **Terry Smith**, a long-time member; and **Matt Smith**, who came with his mother and younger siblings. Their names have been changed to protect their privacy, but be assured they are very distinct individuals who value your brand's relevance to them.

BRAND-ENHANCING WAYS TO COLLECT DATA

You don't have to purchase additional functions from your existing collection or event management system, but if you can afford it, there are some methods that will help you better communicate your data needs. Excel is also excellent for collecting data and mining it.

Here are sixteen ways to collect data—methods that will also reinforce your brand identity:

1. Social media comments

   Follow up on comments and collect e-mail addresses. Or simply organize the information learned in a distinct area of your database.
2. Store receipts

   Purchasers are engaged enough to put their money where their mouths are.
3. Restaurant comment cards and/or receipts

   As diners relax and refresh at the lunch table, it's a good time to have them reflect in writing and attach their names and e-mail addresses. It's also a good place to offer a coupon for their next meal—e-mail necessary to redeem.
4. Website signup for your newsletter with e-mail address

   This is a quick and almost-automatic way to collect the names of those who are familiar with your brand through your well-branded (see chapter 12) website.
5. Business cards

   Whether collected in a glass jar or electronically, these represent supporters who are also businesspeople. You get data on both a visitor or program attendee and a potential sponsor.
6. Guest book—manual or electronic—at exit

   You capture memories that are fresh, and other visitors get to see how appropriate your brand is through the eyes of peers—very reinforcing!
7. Gallery laptop for comments

   It engages visitors at the point where they're most immersed in your brand.
8. Candidates for internships and volunteer posts

   You may not be able to hire these interested people, but you've captured their names for future communication.
9. People who took a museum tour

   These visitors are highly engaged, information hungry, and likely to associate their experience with the brand that provided it.

10. Community/business presentation

    Businesses that trust your museum to enhance their employees' knowledge are wonderful prospects at every level. Employees who take advantage of a lunchtime program are ripe for follow-through. Gather their names with discount tickets for their whole family.
11. Response card

    These cards target people who want answers. Lucky you—you now have the e-mail of a person who wants to interact with you.
12. People who contacted you with a question

    Often these are students, scholars, and researchers. Don't click Reply before entering their e-mail address, so that you can continue to send them information again. Thus, begins a long-term relationship.
13. Organization that booked a facility

    They appreciate the prestige that your facility will give their event. Get the names of the decision-maker, of course, and also the assistants who handled the details.
14. Book borrowers

    If your library loans books, you'll have the borrowers' contact information. Add fields on the book, subject matter, purpose, and comments.
15. Speaker request

    Here's a person or group that knows and respects your brand sufficiently to ask for an expert to speak at their important event. Consider making free tickets to the museum available—along with the requisite names and e-mail information.
16. Event attendees

    Although events have been discussed amply elsewhere, consider hosting an event for the sole purpose of gathering new data. Consider a low-cost networking night. Not-for-profit organizations of all types like them because of their popularity. Attendees won't necessarily be museum prospects, but there will be lots of them, inside your door and learning about your brand.

DATA COLLECTION AND LONG-TERM THINKING

Databases exist to help you manage and maintain information. They're essential for targeted follow-up, reminders, and news announcements. Databases force you to think long term. With that sustainability goal in mind, there are several imperatives for collecting, organizing, and analyzing your trove of information.

Put all your data in one big integrated database. Don't keep separate databases for visitors, members, volunteers, shoppers, and scholars. You always want to expand your brand identity in new ways to the same people.

View events and programs as membership builders (see chapter 4, "Events"); now you'll understand their value in sponsorship nurturing. The difference is long-term versus short-term thinking. Events raise awareness now. Databases are for always. They allow you to follow through with supporters as they progress through their own life stages, and as you evolve through yours.

Add as many fields, or datasets, as your staff can handle. The more sets of information you have on current and potential supporters, the more you can maintain and grow those relationships.

When planning traditional events such as fundraisers, annual meetings, and conferences, choose topics that will attract niche market segments.

The Winnetka Historical Society presented a good example with their July 2015 Annual Meeting. The speaker at the event was a local historian speaking on conservation. This topic switches the target audience—subtly, but distinctly—from local residents who always support their museum, to people who are intellectually intrigued by museums. Sure, these could be the same people: Ben and Joan Smith who support their community and Ben and Joan Smith who like an intellectual evening. Here's the big difference: the former attend your events now; the latter become members for good.

Don't Be Afraid to Cast Your Net Wide to Target Totally New Audiences

Anchorage Museum has found an unexpected event that both raises money for now and expands its audience for the future. It's an arts-road show-type of event, featuring appraisers from the British auction house Bonhams. Its May 2015 event allowed anyone (members at a lower ticket price) to bring three items of Asian and Native American art, books and manuscripts, and decorative art for appraisal. It's a brand-expanding event that encourages current and potential publics to perceive the museum in a different way, one that might be more relevant to them.

Think Ahead to Grant Proposals

Job creation is a data set that funders ask for. When you collect data on jobs created, take a closer look at the people filling those jobs. You might not think to target electrical repairmen, or catering waitresses, but you should. They're already inside your door! That's the best target there is.

Read the Numbers—Analyze and Evaluate

This is where you analyze why people choose your brand and evaluate what to make of the numbers. Analyze the program itself, not just the receipts. And always ask: "So What?"

To glean insights along with facts, say to yourself, "Hmm . . .

- "Eighty percent of our visitors heard about us from an e-mail [friend, mailing, poster]? So what?"
- "4 p.m. is the busiest time in the store? So what?"
- "Most volunteers drop out after their sixth year? Why?"
- "Half of our donors have second homes in different cities. How does this affect their philanthropy? Should we message them more frequently or in different ways?"
- "Fifteen percent of our visitors come with a group of three or more people. What does this mean for return visits? So what?"

Update the Data

You can't keep up to date with your supporters if you don't know where they are, literally and figuratively. Review fields every couple of months. Drop useless ones. Always add one.

Analyze ZIP Codes

They provide tons of information. Some prominent insights: education level, distance they traveled to visit your museum. The website www.census.gov/ opens up a lot of information just by entering a ZIP code.

Think Life Stage Instead of Age

Databases frequently include ages, but that's not as effective as ascertaining a person's life state. Life stage avoids stereotype, at all points in the age spectrum. Life stages let you follow supporters as their interests, habits, and addresses change. That's long-term brand thinking.

Income level is another cliché that should be reconsidered. Many low-income people will dig deep into their pockets for learning they can identify with; it is a source of pride and satisfaction. People of vast resources, on the other hand, have legions of cultural institutions vying for their patronage; they may prove a very difficult target to solicit if the brand isn't relevant.

DIFFERENTIATE BETWEEN PROGRAM ATTENDEES AND SUBSCRIPTION HOLDERS

One is short term, the other long term.

Follow Up

E-mail program attendees after the event, while the memory is fresh and interest is high, Start the relationship now if you hope to sustain it for the future. With data management systems, a lot of future planning occurs at the point of sale—collecting the name at the time of ticket purchase.

Trends versus Trending

Data is useful in examining and refining your brand. As you gather names, you also see what's working—and what's not. You understand what constitutes a year-after-year trend and what is just trending. Numbers shine a harsh light on deficiencies, and frequently reveal situations that are better than supposed. A 2014 survey by the Association of Art Museum Directors (AAMD) showed corporate giving to be more positive than previously estimated. When you get that kind of revelation, it's time to reconsider how your brand can distinguish itself in the new long-term environment.

Expect Everyone to Enter Data

Write data entry guidelines, so that everyone on your staff can enter data. It will go into one master database. Branding is everybody's responsibility because each member of your staff is part of the museum's ongoing brand identity. By the way, many people should be involved in mining and analyzing the data, because each department of the museum has a different vision of what the future might promise.

Prepare for Social Media Demands

If there's an overriding reason to jump full body into data collection, it's social media, which requires information that goes far beyond basic demographics and builds long-term communities of interest. Social media audiences are targeted by interests and behaviors, and some of these can last a lifetime. For example, people who want to save the environment, dog lovers, fans of a sports star, and grandparents are types who don't change with the calendar. Tweets, posts, photos, and pins are sent to groups of peers who are meant to endure, much like brands. Your brand must align with their brand. And you can't understand their distinctive identity if you don't do the numbers.

Information is a wonderful thing and—as you surely tell others every day—you must get as much of it as you can. Then put it in a database.

References

CHAPTER 1

"About," Crystal Bridges Museum of American Art, http://crystalbridges.org/about/, http://us6.campaign-archive2.com/?u=f3c74e7836&id=9a89266e5e&e=fbd9846bd4 [accessed August 23, 2015].

"The Art of Diplomacy: Winston Churchill and the Pursuit of Painting," Exhibitions, Telfair Museums, http://us2.campaign-archive1.com/?u=b0f1fb5c32cb1e1a8b583e1a1&id=e670f0fbfd&e=2668e5031f [accessed August 29, 2015].

"Audio guide stop for George Bellows, *Dempsey and Firpo*, 1924," Watch, "Whitney Museum of American Art," http://whitney.org/WatchAndListen/Artists?context=Artist&play_id=1143 [accessed September 2, 2015].

Linda DeBerry, "*Five Reasons Why: Chamberlain and Gottlieb*," Five Reasons Why: A look at how and why curators arrange works the way they do, Part 1, Crystal Bridges Museum of American Art, July 10, 2015, http://crystalbridges.org/blog/five-reasons-why-chamberlain-and-gottlieb/?utm_content=buffer71370&utm_medium=social&utm_source=twitter.com&utm_campaign=buffer [accessed September 2, 2015].

Civil War Museum Kenosha, https://www.google.com/?gws_rd=ssl#q=civil+war+museum+kenosha+wi [accessed August 23, 2015].

Mario S. De Pillis and Christian Goodwillie, "*Gather Up the Fragments: The Andrews Shaker Collection*," Museum Shop, Loyola University Museum of Art, http://www.luc.edu/shaker/shop/thumbnailphoto,299456,en.shtml [accessed August 22, 2015].

"Final weeks!" Yoko Ono: One Woman Show, 1960–1971 closes September 7. #YokoOnoMoMA http://bit.ly/1MK5GIO," Twitter, https://twitter.com/search?q=%23YokoOnoMoMA%20%20%20&src=typd [accessed August 23, 2015].

"From Underwear to Everywhere: Norwegian Sweaters," August 22, 2015 to April 24, 2016, Special Exhibitions, Vesterheim National Norwegian-American Museum and Heritage Center, http://vesterheim.org/exhibitions/special/from-underwear-to-everywhere-norwegian-sweaters/ [accessed August 18, 2015].

Gord Hotchkiss, "The Virtuous Cycle And the End of Arm's-Length Marketing, *mediapost.com*, October 30, 2014, http://www.mediapost.com/publications/article/237255/the-virtuous-cycle-and-the-end-of-arms-length-mar.html [accessed September 20, 2015].

"Homeschool Programs," Learn, The Mariners' Museum and Park, http://www.marinersmuseum.org/homeschool/ [accessed June 27, 2015].

"Homeschool Programs," web page of The Mariners' Museum, http://www.marinersmuseum.org/homeschool/ [accessed June 27, 2015].

"In the Garden," May 9–September 6, 2015, Current Exhibitions, George Eastman House, http://www.eastmanhouse.org/exhibitions/current.php [accessed August 18, 2015].

Lenhardt Library Rare Book Collection, Chicago Botanic Garden, http://www.chicagobotanic.org/library/rarebooks [accessed August 29, 2015].

"Polar Night: Life and Light in the Dead of Night," Current Exhibits, Anchorage Museum, https://polarlab.anchoragemuseum.org/ [accessed August 22, 2015].

Kenneth W. Rendell, "1999 Vision Statement," Museum of World War II, 1999, http://www.museumofworldwarii.com/ [accessed June 13, 2015].

The Ringling, http://www.ringling.org/ [accessed August 29, 2015].

"#MetVanGogh closes tomorrow. Don't miss your chance to see Van Gogh's floral quartet. http://met.org/1PnAWeF," Twitter, https://twitter.com/metmuseum/status/632553665514086400 [accessed August 23, 2015].

"Till We Meet Again: The Greatest Generation In War And Peace," Museum April 4, 2015–January 3, 2016, Museum, Harry S. Truman Library and Museum, http://www.trumanlibrary.org/wwii/WWIIExhibit.pdf [accessed August 4, 2015].

Margot Wallace, *Writing for Museums*, New York: Rowman & Littlefield, 2014.

"Welcome to the Civil War Museum," Civil War Museum, http://www.kenosha.org/wp-civilwar/ [accessed August 23, 2015].

"Why the Chicago Botanic Garden's 'Corpse Flower' Didn't Bloom," News, *5NBC Chicago*, August 31, 2015, http://www.nbcchicago.com/news/local/Why-Chicago-Botanic-Gardens-Corpse-Flower-Didnt-Bloom-323375051.html#ixzz3kbvG4zfC [accessed September 2, 2015].

http://www.nytimes.com/2015/06/21/arts/design/curators-straddle-the-museum-gallery-divide.html?ref=design&_r=0.

Zoo Miami, iTunes Preview, iTunes store, https://itunes.apple.com/us/app/zoo-miami/id491794992?mt=8 [accessed August 28, 2015].

CHAPTER 2

"Anniversary of Caravaggio death in 1610," Met Museum, @metmuseum, Twitter, https://twitter.com/metmuseum/status/622473435101335553 [accessed July 18, 2015].

Arnsdorf, I., "The Museum Is Watching You," *The Wall Street Journal*, August 18, 2010, http://www.wsj.com/articles/SB10001424052748704554104575435463594652730 [accessed July 18, 2015].

Audio Guided Tour, Lucille Ball Museum, Jamestown, NY, July 2015.

"Bees," Museum of Modern Art @MuseumModernArt, Twitter, https://twitter.com/museummodernart/status/622050602521075712 [accessed July 18, 2015].

Burns, K., "Civil War Episode 1 The Cause (Part 1), YouTube, 1989, https://www.youtube.com/watch?v=OtcZvOAcoew [accessed July 15, 2015].

"Cat Photos," Time.com @TIME, Retweeted by metmuseum, Twitter https://twitter.com/time/status/622181007018561536 [accessed July 18, 2015].

"Chicago Botanic Garden: Annual Report Video," Chicago Botanic Garden, http://strategicplan.chicagobotanic.org/annual/video?utm_source=Chicago+Botanic+Garden&utm_campaign=0b02fda907-Strategic_Plan_Eblast_2015&utm_medium=email&utm_term=0_f8c61d87c3-0b02fda907-41947661 [accessed July 17, 2015].

"Collection Highlights," Guided tour anecdote, Museum of Contemporary Art Chicago, 2007–2008.

Crystal Bridges Museum of American Art, Home, http://crystalbridges.org/ [accessed July 24, 2015].

"Cuba reopening embassy in US," Brookings @BrookingsInst, Twitter, https://twitter.com/brookingsinst/status/622420059185479680 [accessed July 18, 2015].

"Happy #World Emoji Day," Vine, @vine. Twitter, https://twitter.com/vine/status/622110221507395584 [accessed July 18, 2015].

Hostetter, K., "Scripting the Exhibition On-line Course," Northern States Conservation Center, 2015, http://www.collectioncare.org/scripting-exhibition-line-course.

"In the Garden," exhibition visit, George Eastman House, July 11, 2015.

Lucy Craft Laney Museum of Black History, Augusta Historic Tours, "Community Walk," http://www.lucycraftlaneymuseum.com/about_laney.htm [accessed June 13, 2015], http://www.communitywalk.com/map/index/1715781 [accessed July 18, 2015].

"Nightscape," Longwood Gardens, July 1–October 31, 2015, http://longwoodgardens.org/nightscape [accessed July 16, 2015].

Rosenbloom, S., "The Art of Slowing Down," *The New York Times*, October 9, 2014, http://www.nytimes.com/2014/10/12/travel/the-art-of-slowing-down-in-a-museum.html?_r=0 [accessed July 20, 2015].

"Transforming SFMOMA: Building Our Future," Future SFMOMA, San Francisco Museum of Modern Art, 2013, http://future.sfmoma.org/#home [accessed July 15, 2015].

Veverka, J. A., "Planning Interpretive Walking Tours for Communities and Related Historic Districts," *Weekly: June 10*, American Alliance of Museums, e-mailed newsletter, June 10, 2014, http://www.magnetmail.net/actions/email_web_version.cfm?recipient_id=14992292&message_id=4432535&user_id=Museum&group_id=443828&jobid=19334924 [accessed July 13, 2014].

Wallace, M., "Audio Tours," *Writing for Museums*, New York: Rowman & Littlefield, 2014.

CHAPTER 3

Blake Crist & Eric Pakurar, "3 Tips for Marketing to Millennials in 2015," Marketing: CPG, *MediaPost*, January 26, 2015, http://www.mediapost.com/publications/article/242421/3-tips-for-marketing-to-millennials-in-2015.html.

General Lew Wallace Study & Museum website, http://www.ben-hur.com/about-us/.

"Louis Kahn—The Power of Architecture Exhibition at Vitra Design Museum," *Design Boom*, February 28, 2013, http://www.designboom.com/architecture/the-power-of-architecture-kahn-exhibition-at-vitra/ [accessed May 19, 2015].

Louis Kahn quoted on wall panels, *Louis Kahn: The Power of Architecture*, Vitra Design Museum, Basel, Switzerland, February 23, 2013 to August 11, 2013, http://www.designboom.com/architecture/the-power-of-architecture-kahn-exhibition-at-vitra/.

http://www.nytimes.com/2014/11/16/arts/design/on-elite-campuses-an-arts-race.html?smprod=nytcore-ipad&smid=nytcore-ipad-share.

http://www.ringling.org/evening-weddings-and-receptions.

Elizabeth Kolbert, "Civic Duty," *The New Yorker*, January 12, 2015, http://www.newyorker.com/magazine/2015/01/12/civic-duty.

New Bedford Whaling Museum, Website facilities rental page, http://www.whalingmuseum.org/visit/rentals/weddings-receptions [accessed May 10, 2015].

Robin Pogrebin, "The Redesign of a Design Museum: Renovating the Cooper-Hewitt," National Design Museum, *The New York Times*, June 16, 2014, http://www.nytimes.com/2014/06/17/arts/design/renovating-the-cooper-hewitt-national-design-museum.html?ref=arts&_r=0.

The Art of Richard Tuttle, November 11, 2006–February 4, 2007, the Museum of Contemporary Art Chicago.

Van Gogh and Gauguin: The Studio of the South, The Art Institute of Chicago, September 22, 2001 through January 13, 2002.

Twitter.com, https://twitter.com/hashtag/artpicks?src=hash [accessed June 2, 2015].

Twitter.com, https://twitter.com/hashtag/TaxonomyTuesday?src=hash [accessed June 2, 2015].

Twitter.com, https://twitter.com/hashtag/WildlifeGarden?src=hash.

Web page for SFMoMA On the Go, http://www.sfmoma.org/exhib_events/exhibitions/585#ixzz3b79XqwAR, San Francisco Museum of Modern Art.

Web page for *Portraits and Other Likenesses from SFMOMA*, Museum of the African Diaspora, San Francisco, May 8–October 11, 2015.

Web page for: http://www.sfmoma.org/exhib_events/exhibitions/585#ixzz3b7ABGeDF, San Francisco Museum of Modern Art.

CHAPTER 4

"About The Foundation & Mission," Ten Chimneys Foundation, http://www.tenchimneys.org/about/about-the-foundation-mission.

"2015 Heritage Harvest Festival at Monticello," September 12, 2015, http://heritageharvestfestival.com/.

Albright, M., "2015 Churchill Leadership Award Dinner," The Churchill Centre and The National Churchill Museum, http://www.winstonchurchill.org/publications/chartwell-bulletin/bulletin-80-feb-2015/albright-dinner [accessed June 12, 2015].

"American Indian Arts Marketplace 2014 Artist List," web page The Autry, http://theautry.org/american-indian-arts-marketplace/artist-list.

"The American Plate: a Historic Dinner with Libby O'Connell," event announcement from Plimoth Plantation, Spring 2015, http://us6.campaign-archive2.com/?u=f3c74e7836&id=2c6c4c6569&e=fbd9846bd4.

"ANCH 2115: A Community Visioning Event." e-mailed Request for Proposals, Anchorage Museum, https://www.anchoragemuseum.org/media/5782/anchorage-museum-fall-event-rfp.pdf.

"Avant Garden 2015," The Walker Art Center's Annual Gala, http://www.walkerart.org/calendar/2015/avant-garden-2015 [accessed June 11, 2015].

"Buck Day," Harry S. Truman Library & Museum promotion, May 8, 2015, http://www.trumanlibrary.org/whistlestop/events/index.php?action=cal&disp=month&currMonth=5&currYear=2015&currDay=1 [accessed June 12, 2015].

"*The Buffalo News*, Summer Jazz Series," program listing, Albright-Knox Art Gallery, http://www.albrightknox.org/education/summer-jazz-series/ [accessed June 16, 2015].

"Chant Macabre: Songs from the Crypt," Merchant's House Museum event, October 17, 2014, http://merchantshouse.org/spirited-october-events/ [accessed June 12, 2015].

Citizen Science project, Museum of Natural History, http://www.nhm.ac.uk/take-part/citizen-science.html#sthash.Z5Z48QE8.dpuf [accessed June 9, 2015].

"Citizen Science Blog," Museum of Natural History, http://www.nhm.ac.uk/nature-plus/community/citizen_science?view=overview&fromGateway=true [accessed June 9, 2015].

"Coffee Talks With Nan Colton," Calendar, Events, St. Petersburg Museum of Fine Arts, http://www.fine-arts.org/event/coffee-talks-with-nan-colton-3/2015-08-12/ [accessed September 28, 2015].

"Events," listing of the Poe Museum, https://www.poemuseum.org/events.php?selected_event=197 [accessed June 16, 2015].

"Folk Art Pilgrimage: The Kinship between Rosemaling and Woodworking Summer 2016," Vesterheim National Norwegian-American Museum & Heritage Center http://vesterheim.org/norway-tours/upcoming/folk-art/.

"Food for Thought," Wild Apricot Idea Exchange, webinar January 14, 2015, 2–3 pm EST.

https://global.gotowebinar.com/join/5130551416643274241/568395842.

http://www.wildapricot.com/community/expert-webinar-series.

https://mail.colum.edu/owa/?ae=Item&t=IPM.Note&id=RgAAAAD2HKkfueTTEZb2AIBfn%2fxfBwBtcRfyNH7SEZbFAIBfn%2fxfAAAAdMiKAAArY%2f8T1cVIQpyECwONnNlQAADZH7xMAAAJ&ph=0&cb=0.

The Henry Ford, e-mail newsletter, April 2, 2015 http://www.thehenryford.org/events/thiSaturdays.aspx [accessed June 14, 2015].

Geller, L., "2015 Churchill Leadership Award Dinner," The Churchill Centre and The National Churchill Museum http://www.winstonchurchill.org/publications/chartwell-bulletin/bulletin-80-feb-2015/albright-dinner [accessed June 12, 2015].

"Getting People to Your Event," Wild Apricot Idea Exchange Webinar, January 14, 2015, https://global.gotowebinar.com/join/5130551416643274241/568395842.

"Historic Lifeways Conference with Stuart Peachey," Plimoth Plantation, April 17–19, 2015, http://www.eventbrite.com/e/historic-lifeways-conference-with-stuart-peachey-tickets-15657204119?aff=eac2.

Christina Lister, LinkedIn post, December 7, 2014, https://www.linkedin.com/groupItem?gid=1952717&type=member&fromEmail=fromEmail&view=&midToken=AQG2XoVGIc-5DA&ut=301TwD1HX8V6E1&item=594734075161137971 6&trk=eml-b2_anet_digest-hero-1-hero-disc-disc-0C:\Users\mwallace\AppData\Local\Microsoft\Windows\Temporary Internet Files\Content.Outlook\7UJP9ISZ\email.mht [accessed March 21, 2015].

Lucy Craft Laney Museum, website http://www.lucycraftlaneymuseum.com/about_laney.htm [accessed June 13, 2015].

Lucy Craft Laney Museum, sponsors http://www.lucycraftlaneymuseum.com/gala_sponsors.htm [accessed June 13, 2015].

"Luminary Night," St. Augustine Lighthouse & Museum members only program, http://www.staugustinelighthouse.com/events/eventsmain#Special.

"The Lunt-Fontanne Fellowship Program with Master Teacher Phylicia Rashad," e-mail announcement, June 4, 2015, http://campaign.r20.constantcontact.com/render?ca=fab144e9-f15f-426b-ba8d-ea1f7ce8f2d2&c=84868a50-ddac-11e3-9357-d4ae52844279&ch=85384e20-ddac-11e3-93b0-d4ae52844279 [accessed June 14, 2015].

"Nightlife Safari -- London's Wild Side," Natural History Museum London/What's On, http://www.nhm.ac.uk/visit/whats-on/programs/nhm/night_safari_-_london%27s_wild_side.html?utm_source=fb-calendar-20150522&utm_medium=social&utm_campaign=public-program-night-safari [accessed June 11, 2015].

"Off the Wall," 2015 Blanton Museum of Art Gala, website/gala http://blantonmuseum.org/get_involved/support_the_blanton/gala [accessed June 11, 2015].

Jeremiah Owyang, "The Collaborative Sharing Economy Has Created 17 Billion-dollar Companies (and 10 Unicorns)," Collaborative *Economy*, June 4, 2015, http://www.web-strategist.com/blog/category/collaborative-economy/ [accessed June 9, 2015].

Park, *K.*, "So Your Season has Just Started? *5 Actionable Tips to Keep Your Contact Base Growing," Arts Reach E-Nuggets, e-mailed October 30, 2014,* www.arts-reach.com *(password protected).*

"Plan a Visit," Figge Art Museum, http://figgeartmuseum.org/Plan-a-Visit.aspx [accessed June 15, 2015].

Shirley, "Getting People to Your Event," Wild Apricot Idea Exchange Webinar, January 14, 2015 https://global.gotowebinar.com/join/5130551416643274241/5683958 42 [accessed June 13, 2015].

"Spring Conferences at Plimoth Plantation," April–June 2015, http://us6.campaign-archive2.com/?u=f3c74e7836&id=28b7f4df62&e=fbd9846bd4 [accessed June 17, 2015].

"Summer Vacation Tips at the Burke's New Festival," Burke Museum announcement, June 28, 2014, https://www.burkemuseum.org/events/browse/know_before_you_go [accessed July 10, 2014].

"Trimmings Conference: Adorning the Fashionable Figure in the 17th Century," Plimoth Plantation, June 5–7, 2015, https://www.eventbrite.com/e/trimmings-conference-adorning-the-fashionable-figure-in-the-17th-century-tickets-16160243724?utm_source=Plimoth+Plantation&utm_campaign=8ad1509ce2-

Spring_Events_at_Plimoth_Plantation5_5_2015&utm_medium=email&utm_term=0_0dca0f2280-8ad1509ce2-59458337&mc_cid=8ad1509ce2&mc_eid=fbd9846bd4 [accessed June 17, 2015].

"Take a deep breath . . . and take a break." Spring 2015 http://www.chicagobotanic.org/orchid [accessed June 16, 2015].

"Tenement Tastings," Tenement Museum events http://www.tenement.org/tours.php [accessed June 11, 2015].

"Travel Program," Crystal Bridges Museum of American Art, 2015, http://crystalbridges.org/get-involved/membership/travel-program/.

"Travel with the Truman Library," web page announcement, Harry S. Truman Library and Museum http://www.trumanlibrary.org/ [accessed June 14, 2015].

"Vernissage 2015: Thursday, September 17, 2015," The Museum of Contemporary Art e-mail newsletter, http://www2.mcachicago.org/events/vernissage-2015 [accessed June 14, 2015].

Wallace, M., "Writing for Museums," Chapter Public Relations, Rowman & Littlefield, 2014.

Waters, J. "Raise More Money with Win-Win Sponsorships," Wild Apricot Expert Webinar Series, May 21st, 2015 3:00 PM (ET) http://www.wildapricot.com/community/expert-webinar-series/raise-more-money-with-win-win-sponsorships.

Susan Whitall, S. "First in flight: David McCullough's 'Wright Brothers," The Detroit News, May 27, 2015 http://www.detroitnews.com/story/entertainment/books/2015/05/22/pulitzer-winner-david-mccullough-discuss-book-wright-brothers-henry-ford/27821419/ [accessed June 10, 2015].

"White Glove Wednesday," Harry S. Truman Library & Museum http://www.trumanlibrary.org/whistlestop/events/index.php?action=cal&disp=month&currMonth=5&currYear=2015&currDay=1 [accessed June 12, 2015].

"Wild About Harry," e-mail announcement of Harry S. Truman Library and Museum celebration http://trumanlibraryinstitute.org/events/wild-about-harry/ [accessed June 14, 2015].

"The Winnetka Historical Society proudly presents a Southern Belle's Birthday," Winnetka Historical e-mail announcement, Spring 2015, http://us7.campaign-archive2.com/?u=72e300f0f509487fd09449f8b&id=34e0e3735a&e=87ae04322d.

CHAPTER 5

"Advocacy and Lobbying: Speaking Up For The Arts," The NASAA Advocate, National Assembly of State Arts Agencies, http://www.nasaa-arts.org/Advocacy/Advocacy-Tools/Advocacy-and-Lobbying-FINAL.pdf [accessed July 4, 2015].

"Are You A Museum Advocate?" Local Network, State Historical Society of North Dakota, Spring, 2014, http://history.nd.gov/book/shsnd/localNetworkSpring2014/pdf/LocalNetwork-Spring2014.pdf.

"Bring the Seahawk Mask to Seattle," Kickstarter, November 10, 2014, https://www.kickstarter.com/projects/burkemuseum/bring-the-seahawk-mask-to-seattle [accessed July 4, 2015].

"Donate Now," Give and Join, The Mariners' Museum and Park, http://www.marinersmuseum.org/donate/.
"Events," Poe Museum, April-October 2015, http://www.poemuseum.org/blog/new-poems-premieres-at-poe-museum/ [accessed July 4, 2015].
"Friends of the Baker Museum?" Donors, Artis-Naples, http://artisnaples.org/baker-museum/membership.
Hall, H., "New Tack Helps Gifts to Popular Museum Jump 90%," *The Chronicle of Philanthropy*. August 11, 2014 http://philanthropy.com/article/Tenement-Museum-Nearly-Doubles/148355/.
"Invite Congress to Visit Your Museum August 8–15, 2015," Advocacy Resources, American Alliance for Museums, http://www.aam-us.org/advocacy/resources/invite-congress [accessed July 4, 2015].
Owyang, J., "The collaborative sharing economy has created 17 billion-dollar companies (and 10 unicorns)," Collaborative Economy, June 4, 2015 http://www.web-strategist.com/blog/category/collaborative-economy/ [accessed June 9, 2015].
Radick, A. K., "How to Join," *Membership*, Art institute of Chicago, 2015.
Rexhausen, J., "Tell Your Story: Demonstrating a museum's economic and cultural worth," *Museum*, Vol. 94, No. 1, pp. 16–23, January 2015.
Shaw, S., "Keep Growing," Chicago Botanic Garden, Summer 2015.
"The Speed Art Museum isn't going away. It's simply changing," Speed Art Museum, http://changingspeed.org [accessed July 4, 2015].
"Support a New Exhibition at the Tenement Museum," email announcement, Tenement Museum, June 30, 2015, http://us2.campaign-archive1.com/?u=0d8160c63fefce8ee1dc43e9b&id=703fcceda8&e=0521cfbea5 [accessed July 3, 2015].
"Support SFMoMA," Get Involved, San Francisco Museum of Modern Art, http://www.sfmoma.org/get_involved/support [accessed July 4, 2015].
"Travel with the Truman Library," Harry S. Truman Library and Museum, July 2, 2015, http://www.trumanlibrary.org/index.php [accessed July 4, 2015].
"Vesterheim Events in Minneapolis and Chicago in April," Vesterheim Current, Vesterheim Norwegian-American Museum, March 17, 2015, http://us4.campaign-archive1.com/?u=6ad9c0cef0af2e3a0fda81f4c&id=0698d955ad&e=fe54520d43.

CHAPTER 6

"2015 Berkshire Region MITS Summer Institute*: Going with the Flow: Using Inquiry Methods to Teach Watershed Science," Professional Development, Berkshire Museum,* http://berkshiremuseum.org/education/professional-development/.
"About ATHM," National Textile History Museum, http://www.athm.org/about-athm/#sthash.pmc51TLr.dpuf.
"American Fact Finder," U.S. Census Bureau, http://factfinder.census.gov/faces/tableservices/jsf/pages/productview.xhtml?src=CF [accessed June 20, 2015].
"The Art of Richard Tuttle," November 11, 2006–February 4, 2007, the Museum of Contemporary Art Chicago.

"Artist Opportunities," About Us, Anchorage Museum, June 2015, https://www.anchoragemuseum.org/about-us/artist-opportunities/ [accessed July 2, 2015].

Ritesh Batra, Vasan Bala,"The Lunchbox," Sikhya Entertainment, DAR Motion Pictures, National Film Development Corporation of India (NFDC), 2013, http://www.imdb.com/title/tt2350496/.

"Beyond Our Walls: State Profiles on Holocaust Education," Resources for Educators, United States National Holocaust Museum, http://www.ushmm.org/educators/beyond-our-walls-state-profiles-on-holocaust-education/new-jersey.

"Building the Future of Education: Museums and the learning ecosystem," American Alliance of Museums, 2014, http://www.aam-us.org/docs/default-source/center-for-the-future-of-museums/building-the-future-of-education-museums-and-the-learning-ecosystem.pdf?sfvrsn=2.

"Conservation Lab," The Ringling, https://www.ringling.org/conservation-lab [accessed June 30, 2015].

Cain, Susan, *Quiet: The Power of Introverts in a World That Can't Stop Talking*, New York: Crown, 2012.

"Conservation," Collections, Indianapolis Museum of Art, http://www.imamuseum.org/collections/conservation [accessed June 30, 2015].

"Educational Materials," Mississippi Children's Museum http://www.mississippichildrensmuseum.com/manage/wp-content/uploads/2014/11/FieldTrip-Guide-2014-SMALL.pdf.

"Engineer Your Future," Visit Us, Science Museum, http://www.sciencemuseum.org.uk/visitmuseum/Plan_your_visit/exhibitions/engineer_your_future.aspx?utm_campaign=Marketing%3A+December+2014+family+newsletter&utm_medium=email&utm_source=SCM+Group [accessed January 10, 2015].

"Extreme Deep: A Journey to the Bottom," Professional Development Course, The Mariners' Museum and Park, June 22–26, 2015, http://www.marinersmuseum.org/teacher-workshops/ [accessed June 27, 2015].

Ellen Gamerman, "Docents Gone Wild," The Wall Street Journal, June 24, 2015, http://www.wsj.com/articles/museums-seek-greater-control-of-docents-1435166404 [accessed June 26, 2015].

Saralyn Reece Hardy, "Director's remarks," *Spencer Museum of Art Newsletter*, University of Kansas, Fall 2014.

"Health and Nutrition," Mississippi Children's Museum, http://www.mississippichildrensmuseum.com/about/mission-vision/mission-possible/health-nutrition-initiative/.

Rex Heer, "A Model of Learning Objectives based on A Taxonomy for Learning, Teaching, and Assessing: A Revision of Bloom's Taxonomy of Educational Objectives, "Center for Excellence in Learning and Teaching, Iowa State University, http://www.celt.iastate.edu/teaching-resources/effective-practice/revised-blooms-taxonomy/ [accessed July 2, 2015].

Neal Hirschfeld, "Teaching Cops to See: At New York City's Metropolitan Museum of Art, Amy Herman schools police in the fine art of deductive observation," Smithsonian Magazine, October 2009, http://www.smithsonianmag.com/arts-culture/teaching-cops-to-see-138500635/?no-ist [accessed June 22, 2015].

"Ice Balloons," Science Museum Learning, Science Museum, http://www.sciencemuseum.org.uk/~/media//Educators/Educators_downloads/ice_balloons.ashx [accessed July 2, 2015].

Brian Kennedy, "Do You Speak Visual?" *Museum*, May–November 2015.

Brian Kennedy, "TEDxDartmouth - Brian Kennedy - Visual Literacy: Why We Need It," YouTube, May 26, 2010 https://www.youtube.com/watch?v=E91fk6D0nwM [accessed June 29, 2015].

"Learn," Anchorage Museum, https://www.anchoragemuseum.org/learn/ [accessed June 27, 2015].

Shantrelle P. Lewis, Corinne Rose, Amy M. Mooney, "Introductory Questions for Looking and Discussion, '*Dandy Lion: (Re) Articulating Black Masculine Identity, April 6-July 12, 2015*,'" http://www.mocp.org/exhibitions/2015/04/DandyLionEdPacket.pdf.

Amy Dockser Marcus, "Doctors Enlist Paintings to Hone Skills," *The Wall Street Journal,* December 31, 2014, http://www.wsj.com/articles/doctors-enlist-paintings-to-hone-skills-1420052107?autologin=y [accessed June 22, 2015].

"Out-of-home experiences: The chance for homeschoolers to branch out," web page of Carnegie Museums of Pittsburgh, http://www.carnegiemuseums.org/interior.php?pageID=60 [accessed June 28, 2015].

"Programs for Homeshools," Plimoth Plantation, http://www.plimoth.org/learn/programs-homeschools [accessed July 1, 2015].

"Questions of Conscience: Teaching about the Holocaust and Genocide," School of Professional and Continuing Studies, University of Richmond, July 13–17, 2015, http://spcs.richmond.edu/degrees/education/teacher-institute/holocaust-museum.html [accessed June 27, 2015].

"Registration Open!" Home School, Burpee Museum of Natural History, June 2015, http://www.burpee.org/page.asp?PageID=13 [accessed June 28, 2015}.

Sir Ken Robinson, "Changing Paradigms," Ted Talks, October 14, 2010, http://www.youtube.com/watch?v=zDZFcDGpL4U&feature=share.

Aaron Smith, "Older Adults and Technology Use," Pew Charitable Trusts, April 3, 2014, http://www.pewinternet.org/2014/04/03/older-adults-and-technology-use/ [accessed July 1, 2015].

"Summer of Make," Fort Worth Museum of Science and History, http://www.fwmsh.org/make [accessed June 22, 2015].

"Teacher Zone at Science Museum Lates," Science Museum, http://www.sciencemuseum.org.uk/educators/teacher_cpd_and_events/teacher_zone_at_lates.aspx?utm_campaign=Learning%3A+newsletter+October+2014&utm_medium=email&utm_source=SCM+Group [accessed September 4, 2014].

`"Tenement Inspectors," Visit, Tenement Museum, http://www.tenement.org/tours.php?tour=meet-residents [accessed June 24, 2015].

"Through the Looking Glass: Preservation from Mount Vernon to Crow Island," Annual meeting announcement, Winnetka Historical Society, July 9, 2015, http://us7.campaign-archive1.com/?u=72e300f0f509487fd09449f8b&id=e7ce84d914&e=87ae04322d [accessed June 30, 2015].

"Training," In *The Museum* web page, Toledo Museum of Art, http://www.vislit.org/in-the-museum/.

"The VARK Modalities," *VARK A Guide to Learning Styles*, VARK Learn Limited, 2015, http://vark-learn.com/introduction-to-vark/the-vark-modalities/.

"Visual Literacy," web page of Toledo Museum of Art, http://www.toledomuseum.org/learn/visual-literacy/ [accessed June 29, 2015].

Morris J. Vogel., "Please help the Tenement Museum bring history to life for thousands of schoolchildren," e-mail announcement of Lower East Side Tenement Museum, June 18, 2015, http://us2.campaign-archive2.com/?u=0d8160c63fefce8ee1dc43e9b&id=c79ac1c104&e=0521cfbea5 [accessed June 19, 2015].

CHAPTER 7

Board of Trustees, About, Contemporary Art Center, http://www.contemporary-artscenter.org/about/board-of-trustees [accessed September 27, 2015].

Chicago Botanic Garden Volunteer Application, April 2015.

Chicago Botanic Garden: Volunteer Handbook, April 2015.

Grant Application Samples, Institute of Museum and Library Services, http://www.imls.gov/applicants/sample_applications.aspx [accessed June 5, 2015].

http://museumtwo.blogspot.com/2015/05/familiarity-breeds-loveand-desire-for.html [accessed June 5, 2015].

Roles and Responsibilities of the Nonprofit Board, Minnesota Council of Nonprofits, http://www.minnesotanonprofits.org/nonprofit-resources/leadership-governance/board-basics/roles-and-responsibilities-of-the-nonprofit-board [accessed September 27, 2015].

Nina Simon, "Familiarity breeds love . . . and a desire for things to stay the same: guest post by Karen Wise," posted in *Museum 2.0,* May 13, 2015.

Strategic Planning Survey, Delaware Art Museum https://www.surveymonkey.com/r/?sm=6QzgoBTWrQ4KNfBIiPtn8Q%3d%3d [accessed September 27, 2015].

Volunteer Survey used by Hammonds House Museum, http://www.hammondshouse.org/volunteer-survey.html [accessed June 5, 2015].

https://www.eventbrite.com/e/living-proof-celebrating-the-makers-spirits-tasting-tickets-15929838576?utm_campaign=0f2953d089-Living+Proof&utm_medium=email&utm_source=Plimoth+Plantation&utm_term=0_0dca0f2280-0f2953d089-59458337.

Weintraub, S., "Woody Allen Interview—VICKY CRISTINA BARCELONA," *Collider*, August 15, 2008, http://collider.com/woody-allen-interview-vicky-cristina-barcelona/ [accessed September 27, 2015].

CHAPTER 8

"About Us," St. Augustine Lighthouse and Maritime Museum, http://www.staugustinelighthouse.org/ourstories/os_main.

"About Vesterheim," Vesterheim National Norwegian-American Museum & Heritage Museum, http://vesterheim.org/about/.

Board of Trustees, About, Contemporary Art Center, http://www.contemporary-artscenter.org/about/board-of-trustees [accessed September 27, 2015].

Brochure, Musee EDF Electropolis, www.electropolis.edf.com.

Chicago Botanic Garden Volunteer Application, April 2015.

Chicago Botanic Garden: Volunteer Handbook, April 2015.

"Community Tool Box," University of Kansas, http://ctb.ku.edu/en/table-of-contents/participation/promoting-interest/public-service-announcements/main.

Egan, N., "Annual Report 2013, Museum of Contemporary Photography," Chicago: Columbia College Chicago, May 2014.

Grant Application Samples, Institute of Museum and Library Services, http://www.imls.gov/applicants/sample_applications.aspx [accessed June 5, 2015].

http://museumtwo.blogspot.com/2015/05/familiarity-breeds-loveand-desire-for.html [accessed June 5, 2015].

Historic Charleston Foundation, https://www.historiccharleston.org/Home.aspx.

"Identity and Editorial Style Guide," University of Georgia, http://styleguide.uga.edu/index.php?/entries/georgia_museum_of_art/.

Hales, C., "Historic Civil Rights Milestone in July 2015," *Gazette*, Vol. 21, No. 2, Winnetka Historical Society, Fall/Winter 2014, http://winnetkahistory.org/?s=historic+civil+rights+milestone&submit.x=8&submit.y=8.

Hardy, S. R., "Director's remarks," *Spencer Museum of Art Newsletter*, University of Kansas, Fall 2014, Siera Heavner, S., Ed., "Researching Your Winnetka Property," *Winnetka Historical Society*, May 2014, http://winnetkahistory.org/wp-content/uploads/2014/05/researching_your_winnetka_property.pdf.

Lawrence, L., "Rethinking 'Islamic Art,'" The Wall Street Journal, January 13, 2015.

Rack card, Museum of Glass, Tacoma, WA, www.museumofglass.org/membership.

"Media Release," Spencer Museum of Art, The University of Kansas http://www.spencerart.ku.edu/exhibitions/gard-blue.shtml.

Roles and Responsibilities of the Nonprofit Board, Minnesota Council of Nonprofits, http://www.minnesotanonprofits.org/nonprofit-resources/leadership-governance/board-basics/roles-and-responsibilities-of-the-nonprofit-board [accessed September 27, 2015].

Schneiders, S., "When Art Was Threatening," Gazette, Vol. 21, No. 2, Winnetka Historical Society, Fall/Winter 2014, http://winnetkahistory.org/?s=art+was+threatening&submit.x=0&submit.y=0.

Simon, N., "Familiarity breeds love . . . and a desire for things to stay the same: guest post by Karen Wise," posted in *Museum 2.0,* May 13, 2015.

Strategic Planning Survey, Delaware Art Museum https://www.surveymonkey.com/r/?sm=6QzgoBTWrQ4KNfBIiPtn8Q%3d%3d [accessed September 27, 2015].

"Teacher Resources," Steelworks Centers of the West, http://steelworks.us/newsite/index.php/education/teacher-resources.

Volunteer Survey used by Delaware Art Museum.

Volunteer Survey used by Hammonds House Museum, http://www.hammondshouse.org/volunteer-survey.html [accessed June 5, 2015].

https://www.eventbrite.com/e/living-proof-celebrating-the-makers-spirits-tasting-tickets-15929838576?utm_campaign=0f2953d089-Living+Proof&utm_

medium=email&utm_source=Plimoth+Plantation&utm_term=0_0dca0f2280-0f2953d089-59458337.

Weintraub, S., "Woody Allen Interview—VICKY CRISTINA BARCELONA," *Collider*, August 15, 2008, http://collider.com/woody-allen-interview-vicky-cristina-barcelona/ [accessed September 27, 2015].

CHAPTER 9

"American Indian Arts Marketplace 2014 at the Autry," *At the Autry What's Next*, e-mail of November 7, 2014.

"By the Numbers," *Museum*, Vol. 94, No. 1, p. 9, January 2015.

"Conyers in the House," John Conyers, Jr. blog, http://conyersinthehouse.blogspot.com/2011/11/wright-museum-confers-lifetime.html [accessed September 27, 2015].

County of San Bernardino, "Reserve now for Santa's pajama parties at Redlands, Apple Valley museums," County Wire, November 13, 2014, http://wp.sbcounty.gov/cao/countywire/?p=1863 [accessed September 27, 2015].

Curriculum Guide, Wells Fargo History Museum, http://www.wellsfargohistory.com/resources/1226036-sf-museum-teacher-curriculum-fin.pdf [accessed September 28, 2015].

Connecticut Art Trail, http://ctarttrail.org/ [accessed September 27, 2015].

"The Fondation," Fondation Louis Vuitton, http://www.fondationlouisvuitton.fr/en/LaFondation.html [accessed September 28, 2015].

Four Centuries of Massachusetts Furniture, http://www.fourcenturies.org/ [accessed September 28, 2015].

Garfield Farm Home Page, Garfield Farm and Inn Museum, http://www.garfieldfarm.org/calendar.html [accessed September 28, 2015].

"Gilbertson Presents Gjerset Lecture at Luther," Vesterheim Current, Vesterheim Museum, http://us4.campaign-archive1.com/?u=6ad9c0cef0af2e3a0fda81f4c&id=0698d955ad&e=fe54520d43 [accessed September 27, 2015].

Ilnytzky, U., "New Americans Learn English At New York City's Tenement Museum," Portland Press Herald, December 1, 2014,
http://www.pressherald.com/2014/12/01/new-americans-learn-english-at-new-york-citys-tenement-museum/ [accessed September 28, 2015].

Litvak, E., "Tenement Museum's Building at 103 Orchard St. Now Affiliated with National Park Service," *The Lo-Down: News from the Lower East Side*, December 30, 2014, http://www.thelodownny.com/leslog/2014/12/tenement-museums-building-at-103-orchard-st-now-affiliated-with-national-park-service.html?utm_source=The+Tenement+Museum+Newsletter+List&utm_campaign=90f2afa8c9-Weekly_Update_1_13_151_5_2015&utm_medium=email&utm_term=0_42667ed4e8-90f2afa8c9-225141813.

"Nordic Celebration and Marketplace - Twin Cities," Vesterheim National Norwegian-American Museum & Heritage Center, http://vesterheim.org/events/away/twin-cities.

Partners, Zoo Miami, http://www.zoomiami.org/Corporate-partners [accessed September 28, 2015].

"Polar Express Pajama Party, December 6, 2015. Antique Auto Club of American Museum, http://www.aacamuseum.org/polar-express-pajama-party-600-900-pm/ [accessed September 27, 2015].

Povoledo, E., "Capitoline Museums in Rome to Join With University of Missouri to Catalog Artifacts," *The New York Times*, September 15, 2014, http://www.nytimes.com/2014/09/16/arts/design/capitoline-museums-in-rome-to-join-with-university-of-missouri-to-catalog-artifacts.html?smid=nytcore-ipad-share&smprod=nytcore-ipad [accessed September 28, 2015].

Seligson, J., "Corporate, Culture? One Part Education, One Part Sales, This is the Corporate Museum," *Museum* October–December 2010, http://www.wiu.edu/cas/history/pdf/Corporate-Museums.pdf [accessed September 28, 2015].

Vogel, C., "Bold Addition to Paris skyline Gets Art to Match," *The New York Times*, February 2, 2015, http://www.nytimes.com/2015/02/02/arts/design/the-louis-vuitton-foundation-in-paris-will-display-modern-masterpieces.html.

"What's Next," Autry Museum, http://us4.campaign-archive1.com/?u=dee130c52671d690ce268dfef&id=706ac914f6&e=54125b2ee0 [accessed September 27, 2015].

"Woodworking Forum," Old Sturbridge Village, March 29, 2014, https://www.osv.org/event/woodworking-forum [accessed September 28, 2015].

CHAPTER 10

"About Our Collection," Our Collection, NEQM Home, New England Quilt Museum, http://www.nequiltmuseum.org/our-collection.html [accessed August 1, 2015].

"About Us," Learn, Wing Luke Museum of the Asian Pacific American Experience, http://www.wingluke.org/about/ [accessed August 1, 2015].

"Ask 'why' five times about every matter," Toyota Traditions, Company 2006, http://www.toyota-global.com/company/toyota_traditions/quality/mar_apr_2006.html.

Badalamenti, A., "The ubiquitous 'founding myth' in American branding . . . and how to create yours," *Gray Matter*, CI-Group, December 10, 2014, http://www.ci-group.com/founding-myth/ [accessed August 1, 2015].

"History," About Us, Mystic Aquarium, http://www.mysticaquarium.org/about/history [accessed August 1, 2015].

"Make a Donation to AANM," Support the Museum, Arab American National Museum, https://www.accesscommunity.org/national-initiatives/arab-american-national-museum/aanm-donation [accessed July 16, 2015].

"Mission," Join & Support, Aga Khan Museum, https://www.agakhanmuseum.org/about/his-highness-aga-khan [accessed July 16, 2015].

Ries, E., "The Lean Startup: How Today's Entrepreneurs Use Continuous Innovation to Create Radically Successful Businesses," Crown Business, 2011, reprinted in, "To Get To The Root Of A Hard Problem, Just Ask "Why" Five Times," Design, *Fast Company*, May 21, 2012, http://www.fastcodesign.com/1669738/to-get-to-the-root-of-a-hard-problem-just-ask-why-five-times [accessed July 31, 2015].

"Strategic Planning: Discovery + Defining the Issues," News, PMA Consulting, http://pattonmcdowell.com/strategic-planning-discovery-defining-the-issues/ [accessed July 30, 2015].

Wallace, M., "Branding for What's Next," American Alliance of Museums, Annual Meeting Houston, April 2011.

Wallace, M., "Smart Children of Famous Parents," Association of Academic Museums and Galleries Annual Meeting Atlanta, April 2015.

Williams, D., "Find the Heart of Your Brand: Storytelling with These 6 Questions," Content Marketing Institute, Content Strategy, June 19, 2013, http://contentmarketinginstitute.com/2013/06/heart-of-brand-storytelling-6-questions/.

CHAPTER 11

"About the Museum," National Cowboy * Western Heritage Museum, http://nationalcowboymuseum.org/ [accessed September 27, 2015].

"About the Museum," Snyder County Historical Society, http://snydercountyhistoricalsociety.org/museum [accessed September 27, 2015].

"About," Steelworks Center of the West, http://steelworks.us/newsite/ [accessed September 27, 2015].

"The Adventurers Exhibit Grand Opening. Winnetka Historical Society, http://winnetkahistory.org/news/the-adventurers-exhibit-grand-opening/ [accessed September 27, 2015].

"Antiques, Garden & Design Show: Lecture Series," Chicago Botanic Garden, September 27, 2015, http://www.chicagobotanic.org/antiques/lecture?utm_source=Chicago+Botanic+Garden&utm_campaign=6ca7389d14-AGDS_Preview_Eblast_03__12_2015&utm_medium=email&utm_term=0_f8c61d87c3-6ca7389d14-41947661 [accessed September 27, 2015].

"Are You a Grandparent," The Putnam Museum & Science Center, http://putnam.org/Visit/Who-are-you/Grandparent [accessed September 27, 2015].

"Are You a Member?" The Putnam Museum & Science Center, http://putnam.org/Visit/Who-are-you/Member [accessed September 27, 2015].

"Are You a Kid? The Putnam Museum & Science Center, http://putnam.org/Visit/Who-are-you/Kids [accessed September 27, 2015].

Bell, Dr. F. W., "Testimony by Dr. Ford W. Bell, President of the American Association of Museums, to the House Appropriations Subcommittee on Commerce, Justice, Science, and Related Agencies, March 22, 2012, http://aam-us.org/docs/advocacy/fy13-ford-bell-cjs-comments-testimony-3-22-12.pdf?sfvrsn=0 [accessed August 27, 2015].

"Center of the West Blogs," Buffalo Bill Center of the West, http://centerofthewest.org/center-west-blogs/ [accessed September 27, 2015].

"The Combat Air Museum Story," Combat Air Museum, http://www.combatairmuseum.org/history.html [accessed September 27, 2015].

"Community Process," Wing Luke Museum of the Asian Pacific American Experience, http://www.wingluke.org/community-process/ [accessed September 27, 2015].

"Community," Mint Museum, http://www.mintmuseum.org/community [accessed September 27, 2015].

Combat Air Museum, *Facebook*, June 9, 2015, https://m.facebook.com/CombatAirMuseum?refsrc=http%3A%2F%2Fwww.combatairmuseum.org%2F [accessed September 27, 2015].

"Conducting Research," Dwight D. Eisenhower Presidential Library, Museum, and Boyhood Home, http://eisenhower.archives.gov/research/conducting_research.html#8 [accessed September 27, 2015].

"Conference, April 13–16, 2016, Historical Society of New Mexico, http://www.hsnm.org/conference-2/ [accessed September 27, 2015].

"Death Salon: Mütter Museum," http://muttermuseum.org/events/, October 5, 2015 [accessed September 27, 2015].

"*'Eisenhower: The Public Relations President' to be Discussed by Author,*" Dwight D. Eisenhower Presidential Library and Museum, March 24, 2015, Library and Museum, http://archive.constantcontact.com/fs141/1102308225095/archive/1119520739662.html.

"F Street Gallery Exhibition," Art Museum of the Americas, March 11–May 1, 2015, http://www.museum.oas.org/exhibitions/2010s/2015-fordlandia.html [accessed September 27, 2015].

Friends of the Barnes Foundation, *Facebook*, https://www.facebook.com/permalink.php?id=80161246446&story_fbid=10152533010841447 [accessed September 27, 2015].

Historical Society of New Mexico, *Facebook*, https://www.facebook.com/Historical-SocietyofNewMexico [accessed September 27, 2015].

"Living Proof: Celebrating the Makers Spirits Tasting," April 23, 2015, https://www.eventbrite.com/e/living-proof-celebrating-the-makers-spirits-tasting-tickets-15929838576 [accessed September 27, 2015].

"Mission," Arab American National Museum, http://www.arabamericanmuseum.org/About-the-Museum.id.3.htm [accessed September 27, 2015].

"Native Voices at the Autry," Autry National Center of the American West, http://theautry.org/press/native-voices-at-the-autry-presents-its-16th-annual-playwrights-retreat-and-festival-of-new-plays [accessed September 27, 2015].

"Polar Lab," Anchorage Museum, https://polarlab.anchoragemuseum.org/ [accessed September 27, 2015], http://tickets.centerofthewest.org/ [accessed September 27, 2015].

"St. Augustine Lighthouse Archaeological Maritime Program," St. Augustine Lighthouse and Museum, http://www.staugustinelighthouse.org/LAMP/Scientific_Diving/field-school-workshops [accessed September 27, 2015].

"Science on Tap," Columbia River Maritime Museum, April 2, 2015, http://www.crmm.org/maritimemuseum_education_communityevents_science_on_tap.html [accessed September 27, 2015].

"Smithsonian Exhibit Celebrates the Invention of the American Backyard," Dwight D. Eisenhower Presidential Library and Museum, March 4, 2015, http://archive.constantcontact.com/fs141/1102308225095/archive/1119699142669.html.

"Spring Break Day Camp: Stories and Art of the Northwest Coast," Burke Museum April 14, 2015, http://www.burkemuseum.org/mobile/events_browse/springbreakcamp.

"Tenement Talks," Tenement Museum, http://tenement.org/tenement-talks-details.php?id=831&utm_source=The+Tenement+Museum+Newsletter+List&utm_campaign=095f5b85da-https://www.eventbrite.com/e/living-proof-celebrating-the-makers-spirits-tasting-tickets-15929838576 [accessed September 27, 2015].

"Toni Cade Bambara Scholar-Activism Conference Opening Celebration and the Atlanta Premiere of "Women's Work" (2015), Spelman College Museum of Art, http://museum.spelman.edu/programs/toni-cade-bambara-scholar-activism-conference-opening-celebration-and-the-atlanta-premier-of-womens-work-2015/ [accessed September 27, 2015].

"Two Harbors Light Station," Lake County Historical Society, http://www.lakecountyhistoricalsociety.org/museums/view/two-harbors-light-station [accessed September 27, 2015].

Wallace, M., *Writing for Museums*, New York: Rowman & Littlefield, 2014.

"Western Music Association Showcase," Autry National Center of the American West, http://theautry.org/programs/music-festivals/third-sunday-jam-with-the-western-music-association.

"Winter Camp Connect," Glazer Children's Museum, http://glazermuseum.org/camps/winter [accessed September 27, 2015].

CHAPTER 12

"For Kids," Store, San Francisco Museum of Modern Art, http://museumstore.sfmoma.org/art-for-kids.html [accessed September 13, 2015].

Illinois Holocaust Museum, Yelp, http://www.yelp.com/biz/illinois-holocaust-museum-and-education-center-skokie?hrid=t0xno52Ruu-jDDu_IcWQKw&utm_source=ishare [accessed September 7, 2015].

Highfield, R., "From Moscow to the Museum," *Inside the Science Museum,* Science Museum, September 7, 2015. http://blog.sciencemuseum.org.uk/insight/ [accessed September 7, 2015].

Honeycombe, B., "Wonderful Things: Roller Skates, 1880," *Inside the Science Museum*, Science Museum, August 25, 2015, http://blog.sciencemuseum.org.uk/insight/category/inventions/ [accessed September 13, 2015].

Mount Moriah Cemetery, City of Deadwood, http://www.cityofdeadwood.com/index.asp?Type=B_BASIC&SEC=%7BA0DB4AD3-F0E9-4EAC-8E22-995D27A3329B%7D [accessed September 7, 2015].

Nantucket Whaling Museum, *ACK,* Nantucket @ackhistory, https://mobile.twitter.com/ackhistory/status/639128394752524288.

Bob R., Recommended Reviews, Illinois Holocaust Museum & Education Center, January 1, 2015.

Science Museum, September 5, 2015, Science Museum @sciencemuseum, http://bit.ly/1faeIjD.

Science Museum, September 5, 2015, Science Museum @sciencemuseum, #CatStreetView #LunchtimeReading, http://bit.ly/1UrBneo.

Science Museum, September 5, 2015, Science Museum @sciencemuseum, #Lunchtimereading, Science Museum, September 4, 2015, Science Museum @sciencemuseum, http://wrd.cm/1Ur2y93.

Science Museum retweeted, Gina, September 4, 2014, Gina @GinaMCooke.

"Sharing Carrots," National Museum of the Morgan Horse, *American Morgan Horse Association,* Facebook https://www.facebook.com/American-Morgan-Horse-Association-Sharing-Carrots-111766915152/timeline/?ref=hl.

"Staff Picks: Favorite War Movies," First Division Museum, YouTube, https://www.youtube.com/watch?v=UpuDyTNY1rw [accessed September 13, 2015].

"Tell The Strong Museum Where You Are Visiting From This Summer," Press Room, The Strong National Museum of Play, http://www.museumofplay.org/press/releases/2015/06/2132-summer-strong-social-media-campaign [accessed September 14, 2015].

Timeline, Washington Heritage Museums, https://www.facebook.com/Washington-HeritageMuseums [accessed September 13, 2015].

Timeline. National Museum of Mexican Art, Facebook, https://www.facebook.com/NationalMuseumofMexicanArt/timeline/ [accessed September 14, 2015].

Timeline, The High Desert Museumm Facebook, https://www.facebook.com/highdesertmuseum [accessed September 13, 2015].

Timeline. Burke Museum. Facebook, https://www.facebook.com/burkemuseum [accessed September 14, 2015].

"Trimmings Conference: Adorning the Fashionable Figure in the 17th Century," electronic invitation, Plimoth Plantation https://www.eventbrite.com/e/trimmings-conference-adorning-the-fashionable-figure-in-the-17th-century-tickets-16160243724?utm_source=Plimoth+Plantation&utm_campaign=8ad1509ce2-Spring_Events_at_Plimoth_Plantation5_5_2015&utm_medium=email&utm_term=0_0dca0f2280-8ad1509ce2-59458337&mc_cid=8ad1509ce2&mc_eid=fbd9846bd4 [accessed September 13, 2015].

Vesterheim, the National Norwegian-American Museum & Heritage Center http://vesterheim.org/ [accessed September 14, 2015].

The voices of the Walker Art Center: what we're thinking about, who we are, and how you can connect, Walker Art Center, http://blogs.walkerart.org.

"Volunteer Opportunities," Support Us, Chicago Botanic Garden, http://www.chicagobotanic.org/volunteer [accessed September 13, 2015].

Wallace, M., *Writing for Museums*, New York: Rowman & Littlefield, 2014.

"Welcome to The Henry Ford Digital Information Center," Visit, The Henry Ford, http://www.thehenryford.org/visit/digitalInfoCenter.aspx#4 [accessed September 13, 2015].

CHAPTER 13

"'Gallery' to 'Museum' Name Change," Association of Academic Museums and Galleries, AAMG-L@yahoo.com, December 12, 2014.

"Burke Museum Education Department E-News," email from Burke Museum, University of Washington, April 4, 2015.

Burke Museum education email header, http://engage.washington.edu/images/content/pagebuilder/Logo.jpg.

Burke Museum email header, http://engage.washington.edu/images/content/pagebuilder/email-header1.jpg [accessed March 8, 2015].

Email from South Dakota Agricultural Heritage Museum, "Pioneer Girl, Easter Cards, and Land in Her Own Name Exhibit," March 24, 2015, http://us4.campaign-archive2.com/?u=91abe11d7fc0cf22cc93fefd5&id=ec2b92c9d7&e=73187ca9ce [accessed April 12, 2015].

Email from Plimoth Plantation, "Plimoth Plantation," March 18, 2015, http://us6.campaign-archive1.com/?u=f3c74e7836&id=cbcbdce1be&e=fbd9846bd4 [accessed April 10, 2015].

Email from Telfair Museums, April 8, 2015, http://us2.campaign-archive1.com/?u=b0f1fb5c32cb1e1a8b583e1a1&id=7940e8118d&e=2668e5031f.

Email from the Anchorage Museum, "Message from Anchorage Museum Director and CEO Julie Decker - March, 2015," March 18, 2015, https://www.anchoragemuseum.org/about-us/news/news-archive/message-form-anchorage-museum-director-and-ceo-julie-decker-march-2015/ [accessed April 12, 2015].

Email from Telfair Museums, "Check out what's in bloom this April at Telfair Museums," April 8, 2015, http://us2.campaign-archive1.com/?u=b0f1fb5c32cb1e1a8b583e1a1&id=7940e8118d&e=2668e5031f.

Email announcement, "What's Next, April 10–26," *at The Autry*, The Autry Centre of the American West, April 10, 2015, http://theautry.org/exhibitions/floral-journey-native-north-american-beadwork [accessed April 10, 2015].

Email announcement, "An invitation from the Smart Museum of Art," Smart Museum of Art, The University of Chicago, April 2, 2015, http://us2.campaign-archive1.com/?u=aba2086a45b4ee8391b89447b&id=b867f2d816&e=fe28758f59.

Jack Loechner, "More Consumers Reading Email; Still Too Many Offers, Too Little Interesting" mediapost.com, 10/16/14, http://www.mediapost.com/publications/article/235978/more-consumers-reading-email-still-too-many-offer.html.

National Postal Museum email, http://campaign.r20.constantcontact.com/render?ca=6cbbbc03-af9d-4993-81ce-38c85c185d53&c=eb740260-367c-11e3-aeac-d4ae528ecd49&ch=ebe2c9c0-367c-11e3-aeb6-d4ae528ecd49 [accessed May 8, 2015].

"Notes from the Tenement: The Search for General Tso," email from the Tenement Museum, March 31, 2015, http://us2.campaign-archive2.com/?u=0d8160c63fefce8ee1dc43e9b&id=26647dee6d&e=0521cfbea5.

"Notes from the Tenement: Walk This Way," email from the Tenement Museum, March 24, 2015, http://us2.campaign-archive2.com/?u=0d8160c63fefce8ee1dc43e9b&id=fcfc7d4bdb&e=0521cfbea5.

"Notes from the Tenement: Luck of the Irish," email from the Tenement Museum, March 17, 2015, http://us2.campaign-archive1.com/?u=0d8160c63fefce8ee1dc43e9b&id=24b5a9cf6d&e=0521cfbea5.

"Notes from the Tenement: Talk the Talk," email from the Tenement Museum, March 10, 2015, http://us2.campaign-archive2.com/?u=0d8160c63fefce8ee1dc43e9b&id=ced9dd9cd6&e=0521cfbea5.

"Notes from the Tenement: Get Your Goat, email from the Tenement Museum, March 3, 2015, http://us2.campaign-archive1.com/?u=0d8160c63fefce8ee1dc43e9b&id=c47b94599a&e=0521cfbea5.
"Notes from the Tenement: Tenement Inspectors," email from the Tenement Museum, February 24, 2015, http://us2.campaign-archive1.com/?u=0d8160c63fefce8ee1dc43e9b&id=f5ad973353&e=0521cfbea5.
Notes from the Tenement: A Queen of New York," email from the Tenement Museum, January 20, 2015, http://us2.campaign-archive2.com/?u=0d8160c63fefce8ee1dc43e9b&id=6354e83b9b&e=0521cfbea5.
"Social and mobile are top priorities," *Warc*, January 19, 2015, http://www.warc.com/Content/News/N34172_Social_and_mobile_are_top_priorities.content?PUB=Warc%20News&CID=N34172&ID=b47de0ef-09cd-42a3-ae12-448dd105b249&q=email+marketing+social+media&qr= [accessed April 4, 2015].
Versterheim Norwegian American Museum email http://us4.campaign-archive1.com/?u=6ad9c0cef0af2e3a0fda81f4c&id=277468210b&e=fe54520d43 [accessed May 8, 2015].
Margot Wallace, *Writing for Museums*, New York: Rowman & Littlefield, 2014.

CHAPTER 14

http://crystalbridges.org/eleven/.
http://mam.org/ [accessed May 30, 2015].
https://www.google.com/?gws_rd=ssl#q=museum+pajama+party&start=180.
https://www.google.com/?gws_rd=ssl#q=museum+overnight&start=130.
http://www.amazon.com/s/ref=nb_sb_ss_i_2_10?url=search-alias%3Daps&field-keywords=floor+sign+stand&sprefix=floor+sign%2Caps%2C206.
Pogrebin, R., "The Redesign of a Design Museum: Renovating the Cooper-Hewitt, National Design Museum, *The New York Times*, June 16, 2014.
http://www.nytimes.com/2014/06/17/arts/design/renovating-the-cooper-hewitt-national-design-museum.html?ref=arts&_r=0.

CHAPTER 15

About MSA, Museum Store Association http://www.museumstoreassociation.org/about-msa/ [accessed September 27, 2015].
"Celebrating our 10th Anniversary," Arab American National Museum, May 2015-–May 2016, http://store.arabamericanmuseum.org/ [accessed September 27, 2015].
E-mail from Science Museum Shop, January 23, 2015.
Events, Crystal Bridges Museum of American Art September 20, 2014, http://crystalbridges.org/event/museum-store-booksigning-artist-george-dombek/ [accessed September 27, 2015].
"Give us your feedback," British Museum Shop, https://www.kampyle.com/feedback_form//ff-feedback-form.php?site_code=9946655&lang=en&form_

id=40842&push=1&time_on_site=4724&stats=k_button_js_revision%3D13892%26k_push_js_revision%3D13967%26view_percentage%3D100%26display_after%3D0&url=http%3A%2F%2Fwww.britishmuseumshoponline.org%2Fexhibition%2Fitalian-renaissance%2Ficat%2Fitalian_renaissance_draw%23esp_pg%3D2&utmz=65349629.1425149633.1.1.utmcsr%3Dbritishmuseum.org|utmccn%3D%28referral%29|utmcmd%3Dreferral|utmcct%3D%2Fwhats_on%2Fexhibitions%2Fming%2Fshop.aspx&utma=65349629.1325852111.1425149633.1425149633.1425149633.1&utmv=null## [accessed September 27, 2015].

"Legends and Legacies," Anchorage Museum, http://www.anchoragemuseum.org/shop/DisplayDetail.aspx?pid=370 [accessed September 27, 2015].

"Mammoth Floaty Pen," Anchorage Museum, http://www.anchoragemuseum.org/shop/DisplayDetail.aspx?pid=544 [accessed September 27, 2015].

Musee francais du Chemin de Fer, Milhouse, France.

Museum Gift Shop, Steelworks Center, http://steelworks.us/newsite/index.php/buy-photos/museum-gift-shop [accessed September 27, 2015].

Museum Store, Delaware Art Museum, http://www.delart.org/visit/museum-store/ [accessed September 27, 2015].

Museum Store at MIM, Musical Instrument Museum, http://mim.org/museum-store/ [accessed September 27, 2015].

Museum Store, San Francisco Museum of Modern Art, http://museumstore.sfmoma.org/?_ga=1.77394525.971912702.1423957086 [accessed September 27, 2015].

"Paper Roses for Valentine's Day Workshop," South Dakota Agricultural Heritage Museum. February 23, 2015, http://us4.campaign-archive2.com/?u=91abe11d7fc0cf22cc93fefd5&id=9542919025&e=73187ca9ce [accessed September 27, 2015].

"Retail Store Management for Small Museums On-line Course," Northern States Conservation Center, http://www.collectioncare.org/retail-store-management-small-museums-line-course [accessed September 27, 2015].

Shipwreck Coast Museum Store, Great Lakes Shipwreck Museum, https://www.shipwreckmuseum.com/shop.php [accessed September 27, 2015].

"Shop," Plimoth Plantation, http://www.plimoth.org/plan-your-visit/shop-dine [accessed September 27, 2015].

Shop, Science Museum, http://www.sciencemuseumshop.co.uk/customer_favourites?utm_campaign=SM+Online+Shop+-+Customer+Favourites&utm_medium=email&utm_source=SCM+Group [accessed Febraury 1, 2015].

"What's New," Japanese American Nation Museum, http://janmstore.com/collections/whats-new [accessed September 27, 2015].

CHAPTER 16

Heumann Gurian, E., Paper presented at the American Association orf Museum Annual Conference, Dallas, Texas, May 11–15, 2002.

http://chicagohistory.org/planavisit/visitorinformation/#cafe.

http://museumofglass.org/visit/museum-cafe.

http://nationalcowboymuseum.org/plan-your-visit/persimmon-hill/.

http://www.citedelautomobile.com/fr/preparer-sa-visite/restaurants.
http://www.illinois.gov/alplm/museum/Event/Pages/Tea.aspx.
http://www.mysticaquarium.org/visit/penguins-cafe.
http://www.smm.org/visit/dining.
http://www.whalingmuseum.org/visit/rentals/weddings-receptions.

CHAPTER 17

Annual report http://www.clevelandart.org/about/reports/engaging-community.

Burke Museum annual report, 2012–2013, http://www.burkemuseum.org/pub/FY13AnnualReport.pdf [accessed April 19, 2015].

Burke Museum annual report, 2013–2014, http://www.burkemuseum.org/pub/FY14AnnualReport.pdf [accessed April 19, 2015].

Course catalog of Longwood Gardens, http://longwoodgardens.org/sites/default/files/wysiwyg/pg_course_catalog_2014_mc_ISSUU.pdf [accessed May 1, 2015].

Cleveland Museum of Art annual report, http://www.clevelandart.org/sites/default/files/documents/annual-report/2009-10_Collections.pdf.

Course catalogue, Art Institute of Chicago, *Keep Growing*, Chicago Botanic Garden, Spring 2015, http://www.saic.edu/cs/ace/noncreditcourses/courses/.

George Eastman House Museum annual report, http://www.eastmanhouse.org/museum/publications/annual-report/2012/9.php.

George Eastman House Annual Report 2012, *George Eastman House*, 2013, http://www.eastmanhouse.org/museum/publications/annual-report/2012/7.php.

Indian, National Museum of the American Indian, Spring 2015, http://content.yudu.com/web/1q1ji/0A1r2jl/Spring2015/html/index.html.

Isaacson, W., *Benjamin Frankin: An American Life*, New York: Simon & Schuster, 2003.

Keep Growing 2020: The Ten-Year Strategic Plan, Chicago Botanic Garden, e-mail June 24, 2014, http://strategicplan.chicagobotanic.org/video [accessed July 10, 2014].

Lowry, G., Helfenstein, J., Druick, D., "Foreword," *Magritte The Mystery of the Ordinary, 1926-1938*, New York: The Museum of Modern Art, 2013.

Mirrer, L., *The Armory Show at 100: Modernism and Revolution*, New-York Historical Society, New York in association with D Giles Limited, London, 2013, p. 7.

Newsletter of the Steelworks Museum, http://steelworks.us/newsite/.

Robert Motherwell: Early Collages, Guggenheim Museum Publications, New York, 2013. "Symphony Center Presents 2015/16 Anniversary Season," 125th anniversary program catalog, Chicago: Chicago Symphony Orchestra, 2015.

Umland, A., editor, *Magritte The Mystery of the Ordinary, 1926-1938*, New York: The Museum of Modern Art, 2013.

Vogel, C., "A New Art Capital, Finding Its Own Voice," *The New York Times*, Arts & Leisure, p. 1, 21, December 7, 2014.

http://www.nytimes.com/2014/12/07/arts/design/inside-frank-gehrys-guggenheim-abu-dhabi.html?module=Search&mabReward=relbias%3As%2C{%222%22%3A%22RI%3A17%22}&_r=0

Wallace, M., *Research for Museum Marketers*, Lanham, MD: AltaMira Press, 2010.

CHAPTER 18

"7 Types of Logo, an Illustrated Guide," The Online Adventures of Buzz and Joe, March 20, 2014, http://caffeinatedcommunications.com/2014/design/logo-just-logo [accessed July 13, 2015].

"Allen Memorial Art Museum," http://www.oberlin.edu/amam/default.html [accessed July 13, 2015].

Bencks, J., "Chris Burden, 'One of the greatest American artists of his generation.'" Brandeis Now, June 2, 2015, http://www.brandeis.edu/now/2015/may/burden-bedford.html.

Bedford, C., quoted in "Chris Burden, 'One of the greatest American artists of his generation.'" *Brandeis Now*, June 2, 2015, http://www.brandeis.edu/now/2015/may/burden-bedford.html.

"Beyond the Gallery Walls," Penn Museum Blog, http://www.penn.museum/blog/ [accessed September 27, 2015].

Bishop, S., "We Have the Map; They Have the Wheel," Association of Academic Museums and Galleries 2015, Annual Conference Atlanta, April 25, 2015.

"Blanton Museum of Art," website, http://blantonmuseum.org/ [accessed July 13, 2015].

Cain, Susan, *Quiet: The Power of Introverts in a World That Can't Stop Talking*, New York: Crown, 2012.

Clark, L., "National Directory, University Art Museums and Galleries in Virginia, 2011, https://sites.google.com/site/universityartmuseumsinvirginia/ [accessed July 16, 2015].

"Cross-Current," Art + Science Learning Lab, Cantor Arts Center, July 9, 2015, http://cantorscience.org/.

"Explore Westminster," Westminster College, http://www.westminster-mo.edu/explore/default.html [accessed July 13, 2015].

"Hammer," http://hammer.ucla.edu/ [accessed July 13, 2015].

Hirschfeld, N., "Teaching Cops to See: At New York City's Metropolitan Museum of Art, Amy Herman schools police in the fine art of deductive observation," Smithsonian Magazine, October 2009, http://www.smithsonianmag.com/arts-culture/teaching-cops-to-see-138500635/?no-ist [accessed June 22, 2015].

"History," Beloit College, https://www.beloit.edu/logan/about/history/ [accessed July 13, 2015].

"Inside the Science Museum: The Science Museum Blog," Science Museum, http://blog.sciencemuseum.org.uk/insight/category/research/ [accessed September 29, 2015].

Love, J., "Talk With Your Hands? You're Doing It Right," The Crux, Discover Magazine, April 21, 2014, http://blogs.discovermagazine.com/crux/2014/04/21/talk-hands-youre-right/#.VbkuUvmGVVc [accessed July 29, 2015].

"National Churchill Museum," home page, https://www.nationalchurchillmuseum.org/.

"Newcomb Art Gallery," http://www.newcombartgallery.tulane.edu/ [accessed July 13, 2015].
"LoweDown Happy Hour," Calendar, Lowe Art Museum, http://www6.miami.edu/lowe/event_lowedown.html [accessed July 14, 2015].
"On loan," *Spencer Museum of Art Newsletter*, University of Kansas, Fall 2014.
"NEHMA Nora Eccles Harrison Museum of Art," website "http://artmuseum.usu.edu/ [accessed July 13, 2015].
Russell, J. S., "On Elite Campuses, An Arts Race, *The New York Times*, November 13, 2014, http://www.nytimes.com/2014/11/16/arts/design/on-elite-campuses-an-arts-race.html?smprod=nytcore-ipad&smid=nytcore-ipad-share [accessed June 2, 2015].
"Snite Museum of Art," home page, https://sniteartmuseum.nd.edu/ [accessed July 14, 2015].
"Strategic Framework," About, Ringling Museums, http://www.ringling.org/strategic-framework [accessed July 13, 2015].
Segal, E., "Museum Beyond the Museum," Association of Academic Museums and Galleries 2015 Annual Conference Atlanta, April 25, 2015.
"The Study of Science through the Study of the Arts," Resources, Harn Museum of Art, http://harn.ufl.edu/universityeducators#sthash.0C64wmku.dpuf [accessed July 27, 2015].
Williams, B., Henderson, L., & Macrae, S, "Introduction," Descourtilz: Jean Theodore Descourtilz (1796–1855) and the Ornithologie Bresilienne ou Histoire des Oiseaux du Bresil, https://descourtilz.wordpress.com/ [accessed July 27, 2015].
"Teaching Innovation Workshop", Center for Innovation and Teaching Excellence, Columbia College Chicago, August 2013.
Wallace, M., "Smart Brands of Famous Parents: Reinforcing Your Distinct Identity," Association of Academic Museums and Galleries 2015 Annual Conference Atlanta, April 25, 2015.

CHAPTER 19

American Fact Finder, United States Census Bureau, http://factfinder.census.gov/faces/nav/jsf/pages/community_facts.xhtml#none [accessed September 5, 2015].
"Bonhams Auction Appraisal Event," Exhibits & Events, Anchorage Museum, 5/16/2015 – 5/17/2015 https://www.anchoragemuseum.org/exhibits-events/calendar/details/?id=20631 [accessed September 5, 2015].
Cassie Dennis, "What is CRM and What Does It Mean For My Business? Customer Relationship Management Defined," *SBAC News*, March 19, 2015, http://www.smallbusinessadvocacycouncil.org/blogpost/sbac-news/2015/3/what-crm-and-what-does-it-mean-my-business-customer-relationship-managemen [accessed September 5, 2015].
Editors of ARTnews, "AAMD Art Museums Got Over 61 Million Visitors Last Year, and Are Stable, New Survey Shows," ArtNews, 01/07/15, http://

www.artnews.com/2015/01/07/aamd-art-museums-got-over-61-million-visitors-last-year-and-are-stable-new-survey-shows/.

"Knowledge Space," Grant Place, http://grantspace.org/tools/knowledge-base/Funding-Resources/Foundations/finding-grants [accessed August 30, 2015].

Emily Steelaug, "Netflix to Add Films and TV Series for Teenagers," *The New York Times*, August 24, 2015 [accessed August 30, 2015].

"Through the Looking Glass: Preservation from Mount Vernon to Crow Island," email announcement of Winnetka Historical Society, June 27, 2015, http://us7.campaign-archive1.com/?u=72e300f0f509487fd09449f8b&id=e7ce84d914&e=87ae04322d.

"Trimmings Conference: Adorning the Fashionable Figure in the 17th Century," Friday, June 5, 2015 at 7:00 PM–Sunday, June 7, 2015, Plimoth Plantation, *Eventbrite*, https://www.eventbrite.com/e/trimmings-conference-adorning-the-fashionable-figure-in-the-17th-century-tickets-16160243724?utm_source=Plimoth+Plantation&utm_campaign=8ad1509ce2-Spring_Events_at_Plimoth_Plantation5_5_2015&utm_medium=email&utm_term=0_0dca0f2280-8ad1509ce2-59458337&mc_cid=8ad1509ce2&mc_eid=fbd9846bd4 [accessed May 11, 2015].

Trochlil, W., "How to grow your organization by using your membership database more effectively," Wild Apricot, June 24, 2015, 3:30–4:30 PM EDT, http://www.wildapricot.com/community/expert-webinar-series/how-to-use-your-database-to-grow-your-membership?utm_medium=email&utm_campaign=Expert%20Webinar%20Thank%20You%20Email%20-%20June%2026%2C%202015&utm_source=Envoke%20-%20June%2024%2C%202015%20Expert.

Index

About the Author

Margot Wallace is associate professor of marketing at Columbia College Chicago where she teaches courses in branding, marketing, and writing, and has researched museum marketing for twelve years.